UNDERSTANDING WOMEN IN ISLAM

SYAFIQ HASYIM

UNDERSTANDING
WOMEN IN ISLAM

AN INDONESIAN PERSPECTIVE

The Asia Foundation

SOLSTICE
JAKARTA SINGAPORE

ICIP
International Centre
for Islam and Pluralism

Solstice Publishing
Menara Gracia, 6th floor
Jl. H.R. Rasuna Said Kav. C-17
Jakarta 12940
Indonesia

ISBN 979-3780-19-3

Originally published in the Indonesian language by Mizan in 2001 with ISBN 979-433-269-0
under the title *Hal-hal yang tak terpikirkan tentang isu-isu keperempuanan dalam Islam*

Produced with the support of The Asia Foundation, Jakarta
Printed in the United States.

10 9 8 7 6 5 4 3 2 1

TABLE OF CONTENTS

AUTHOR'S NOTE

The study of women and Islam has undergone much development in recent years, as we can see by the flood of literature being published on the topic. In Indonesia, this wealth of new literature, whether it takes a conservative or moderate perspective, suggests that there is a promising future for this topic of study. Interestingly, the authors include not only women, but also men, who are engaging seriously with women's issues in relation to Islam.

It has to be admitted that sometimes men's perspectives on this topic are lacking in objectivity and in-depth understanding, although the same failings are equally dangerous in women's writings. The book you are now holding in your hands is written by a man who strives to be objective in these matters. If some of my female readers consider that it is not, perhaps this is my limitation as a male writer. The important thing is that I wrote it to do something for women – at the very least, for my mother, wife, daughters, and other female relatives.

In 1996, I joined P3M to help develop its program on the discourse of women's *fiqh* (Islamic jurisprudence), which has come a long way since it went public in Indonesia. I would like to thank everyone who helped me, both directly and indirectly, in the creation of this book. I would like to thank Masdar F. Mas'udi, the director of P3M, Lies Marcoes-Natsir, currently of the Asia Foundation, and Farhah Ciciek, the coordinator of the Al-Nisa' Division at P3M, as well as my other friends there, including Ana Mukarnawati, Dani, Eka Subiyanti, Maman Abdurrahman, Imam Siswoko, and Wida.

I would also like to thank Dr Mary Zurbuchen, Dr Rosalia Sciortino, and Dr Meiwita Budiharsana, all of the Ford Foundation, Dr. Douglas Ramage and Dr. Robin L. Bush, all of the Asia Foundation, as well as my teachers and friends K.H. Hussein Muhammad in Cirebon, and K.H. Muhyiddin Abdusshomad in Jember. I would also like to acknowledge the support and advice of the members of the Study of Uqudullijain Group, primarily its coordinator, Mrs Nyai Sinta Nuriyah Abdurrahman Wahid. Thanks also go to my English-language editor, Laura Noszlopy.

I also owe boundless thanks to the people closest to my heart – my beloved wife, Diah Rofika, and children, Ambeg Parama Arta Ganashakti. Without the help and understanding of these two people, I might never have finished this book. I thank my father, Mudazkir, who will always remain in my heart for encouraging me to study at an Islamic boarding school (*pesantren*), my mother, Mirahayu, and my siblings, Zulfah, Umi and Luqman.

Syafiq Hasyim
Jakarta, October 2005

PART ONE

UNCONSIDERED ISSUES ABOUT WOMEN IN HISTORY

CHAPTER ONE

UNDERSTANDING WOMEN IN THE CONTEXT OF HISTORY

Any discussion concerning the history of women in Islam cannot be separated from the discussion of history in general. With this in mind, we must explore the history of women in the other major religions as well – because to understand women in the development of history in a particularistic and monolithic way will give us an incomplete and overly subjective understanding of the topic. If the information we attain originates from only one source – Islamic discourse, in this case – we will only get a limited and exclusive version of the truth.

Basically, the histories of Islamic and non-Islamic women are part of an integrated and inseparable development. Viewed in this way, we hope to obtain a holistic and relatively objective picture of the position of women. This view does not lead us to a homogenous view of history; indeed it values all the nuances included within.

The history of women is indeed a unique and controversial portrait – it is unique because within history there are non-objective elements, and it is controversial because the position of women has been problematized and debated everywhere. This is very different to the position of men in history, which can be seen as the grand narrative or history's center[1]. Almost all the

---

[1] The view that men are the center of history is highly influenced by postmodernist theory. According to this view, the modern world is trapped in a dichotomy between center and periphery. The center is

major historical religious discourses in the world, including Islam, view men homogenously, as beings with a special and respected position. In almost all parts of the world, history views men as high-ranking and without disabilities, caused either by religious teachings or socio-cultural constructions. Thus, the history of men is viewed as a history of universal truth. We cannot deny that men have had a vital and well-established role in creating a male-biased historical discourse.

In Islamic discourse itself, the discussion of women is an important issue that has received much attention, particularly with regard to more recent developments. This can be seen from the number of books that have been written illuminating the position of women in Islam. These books are not only circulated in Islamic nations, but all over the world. The writers come not only from Islamic circles, but also from non-Islamic intellectuals who have an interest in the study of Muslim women. Whether or not they help efforts towards women's empowerment or are actually counter productive, it is clear that they are a positive development in the study of women in Islam.

In the first chapter, the writer intends to explain, in summarized form, the position of women in history from pre-Islamic times to the time of the arrival of Islam.

WOMEN IN PRE-ISLAMIC HISTORY

The majority of intellectuals and historians, primarily those from Islamic circles, view the position and lives of women in pre-Islamic times as being very dark and worrying. Women are viewed as having been of no value, as subordinate to males, and often the cause of problems. They are viewed as not being independent, as having their rights oppressed, and their bodies bought and sold. They were placed in a marginal position.

With this in mind, women were considered to have been undeserving of humane treatment, because those valued as 'human' are those who have

---

assumed to be progressive and enlightened, while the periphery is backwards and unenlightened. This is why modernism has viewed the center as correct. The philosopher J. Lacan introduced *decentering* theory, a movement that aimed to decrease the importance and significance of the positioning of the center.

their own independence, and possess full rights to inheritance. At that time, this only referred to men. Women really had no power.

It appears that the aforementioned view did not start with pre-Islamic history in the Middle East, but had cultural and historical references from even further back. In the early Hindu *Laws of Manu*, for example, it is stated that women, for their whole life-span, never possess the right to carry out all the actions they want to. It also states that women must firstly follow their father, then, once married, follow their husband, and then, if their husband dies, they must follow their male children. If they do not have any children they must follow their closest family members. If there is no close family, power over the woman moves to her uncle, and if there is no uncle, it is taken by the government (*waliy al-amri*). This view clearly reflects women as having a very weak (*dha'if*) position.

The same was true in Greek tradition, what we consider as the center and source for the modern era. Women did not have full rights. At that time, the Greek community was divided into three social classes. The first class consisted of free people, the elite. The second was the class of traders. The third class consisted of slaves, whose lives were subjugated entirely to the first and second classes[2].

Viewed from the aspect of poverty, women at the time of Greek tradition were more associated with the third class (slaves). Women's lives were devoted to the interests of men, without being compensated or given anything in return. They had to do anything that was commanded by their husband or boss. On the other hand, the male position was powerful and strong. For example, at that time men could marry women without any limitations. Once already married, women were considered the absolute property of the male who married her.[3] Women could be treated in accordance with the desires of the male who owned her. The view of women as things or objects in the Greek tradition appears to have influenced the concept of marriage in Islam[4].

Although the Greek philosopher Plato began to establish the same principles for both men and women in the fields of culture and education,

---

[2] Muhammad Anas Qasim Ja'far, *al-Huq al-Siyasah li al-Mar'ah*, Cairo: Dar al-Nahdlah al-'Arabiyyah, p.1.
[3] *Ibid.*, p.14.
[4] *Ibid.*

he did not criticize other philosophers, who generally positioned women in a lower position. Aristotle professed a completely different opinion. According to him, it was a natural fact that a woman's intelligence was not able to think broadly, and, thus, their duties were domestic. Crudely put, Aristotle described the relationship between men and women as like that of a slave to his boss, or of a barbarian nation to Greece. Thus males hold a higher position in comparison to females. As an expert speech-writer from Greece once said: "In truth, we only marry our wives to give birth to our children".

Laela Ahmed in her book, *Women and Gender in Islam: Historical Roots of Modern Debate*, said the following about Aristotle:

> Aristotle's theory conceptualized women not merely as subordinate by social necessity but also as innately and biologically inferior in both mental and physical capacities – and thus intended for their subservient position by "nature." He likened the rule of men over women to the rule of the "soul over the body, and the mind and the rational element over the passionate." The male he said, "is by nature superior, and the female inferior and the one ruler and the other is ruled.[5]

The book *Historia Animalium*, as cited by Laela Ahmed, states that the basic characteristics of the male are completeness and perfection, while females are more emotional and prone to jealousy, that they like to complain, and have a greater tendency to get angry and aggressive, are more afraid to protect themselves, make more mistakes and are more deceiving.[6]

Why is important to give attention to Aristotle's opinion here? We know that Aristotle was a very influential philosopher, who began the teaching of logical and systematic thinking. He also had great influence in shaping systematic community principles and social values.

Aristotles' theories did not only influence Western thought, but also thinking in the Islamic world. Well-known philosophers like Al-Kindi, Al-Farabi, Ibn Rushd, and even Al-Ghazali were greatly influenced by Aristotle.

---

[5] See Laela Ahmed, *Women and Gender in Islam: Historical Roots of Modern Debate*, p.29.
[6] *Ibid.*

Aristotle was an important teacher in the field of Islamic philosophy. So it is only natural that his theories are given attention here.

Epistemologically, the process of women's marginalization was not a coincidental occurrence. Long before Aristotle, there was already a systematic process being developed in scientific discourses. At the time of Aristotle, knowledge was already equated with men, and it continued to spread easily amongst the whole system of knowledge. Patriarchal ideology spread through the transmission of science, and a gender-biased perspective developed.

In the Athenian tradition, only the elite and males had the right to obtain an education. Females, even those from the elite class, were not given the opportunity to obtain an education.

Negative views about women have not only appeared in social and cultural discourses, but have also permeated the teachings and norms of religion. These religious norms are a large factor contributing to the marginalization and segregation of women.

In Judaism, for example, we can find negative views about women that are not too different from those of Greek tradition. It was said that it was better to walk behind a tiger than behind a woman. According to Munawar Ahmad Anees, Greek people's antipathy towards women was such that a daily prayer was uttered: "Praise to You God, for You did not create me as a woman".[7]

In Christian traditions, the position of women is also similar to Greek tradition. Women are represented as bad and slanderous. Thomas Aquinas, a well-known Christian theologian, said that women are bent down in submission to males because they are naturally physically weaker. Men are the beginning and final goal in a women's life. It is because of this that God has made women submit to males.[8]

In a book titled *Malleus Maleficarum*, it states that women are imperfect, contrary animals, who like to deceive, are easily tempted by Satan, and often become witches. This is clearly a dehumanizing description of women.

From the above explanation, the pre-Islamic history of women appears to have been gloomy. However, this does not mean that there were not positive elements. What's more, if we look at the history of women in the ancient

---

[7]   Munawar Ahmad Anees, *Islam dan Masa Depan Biologis Umat Manusia, Mizan*: Bandung, 1991, p.188.

[8]   See Will Durant, pp. 182-7, and *Qamus al-Athar al-Masihiyya*, vol. V, p.1300.

Middle East, in the region of Mesopotamia, we find that women were highly respected. Not all pre-Islamic histories contained the elements as often described by theologians and historians these days. The generalization that the whole history of women in pre-Islamic times was drawn from insult will result in viewing the history of women in Islam as being wholly negative. Not all pre-Islamic traditions and cultures of women were revised by Islam; some were legitimized by Islam and became part of its teachings. However, it must be recognized that the respected position of women ended with the arrival of patriarchal power.

There is a clearer and more concrete description about the good condition of women in the ancient Middle East. Laela Ahmed, in *Women and Gender in Islam*, has made a good description of this with reference to Mesopotamia. Generally speaking, the subordination of women in the ancient Middle East happened and became institutionalized together with the appearance of the urban community and, more specifically, with the appearance of the archaic state. Before this, women lived independently. This opinion altogether rejects the androcentric historical theory that maintains that the inferior social status of women was based on biological facts and the natural disposition of the female. According to archaeologists, women held a primary position before the appearance of the centralized urban society and the city-state model.[9]

James Mellaart, in *Catal Huyuk, A Neolithic Town in Anatolia* (New York, McGraw Hill), reports the discovery of archaeological remains of a Neolithic settlement in Asia (6500 BCE) called Catal Huyuk. The houses there included paintings, as well as wall-decorations in the form of females. Based on these findings, it can be concluded that Catal Huyuk not only represented a culture where the role of women was special and respected, but also evidence that Middle Eastern culture, especially during the Neolithic period, deeply honored the Mother Goddess, especially during the Neolithic period.

Many feminist theorists have considered the pre-urban period a time of progress for women because of their relatively dominant role at this time. Garder Larner suggests that the additional population and the importance of

---

[9]   Leila Ahmed, *Women and Gender in Islam*, p.11.

preparing a strong workforce for society was detrimental to women's status. Women's sexual and reproductive capacities became an object of struggle for ethnic groups, which eventually caused the domination of males over females.[10]

So why take Mesopotamia as a case study? According to Laela Ahmed's notes, Mesopotamia was the first urban area to appear in the Middle East. The geographical location of Mesapotamia was located in the valley of Tigris and Effrat rivers near present-day Iraq between 3500 and 3000 BCE. The population of these regions was Ubadian, but nomadic, Semitic people started to enter and seized political power in later periods.[11]

The growth of a more complex urban community and military competition strengthened male domination during this period. This, in turn, caused a division within society, based on classes. The patriarchal family model – which gave inheritance rights to the fathers' side, and emphasized the view that males had authority and control over women – was institutionalized, codified and implemented by the state. Female sexuality was viewed as male property. According to Laela Ahmed, women belong firstly to their fathers, and then to their husbands. Female virginity was used as a bargaining tool, and was considered to be of great economic value.[12]

It was unavoidable that such a situation increased prostitution and drew a line between 'respectable' women – women whose sexual and reproduction capabilities belonged to a certain man – and women who belong sexually to many men. Women with a legitimate partner were generally viewed with respect, while women who had relations with many men were viewed as insolent.

Increasing complexity and specialization within the lifestyles of the urban community, together with the growing population of technicians, traders, and farmers, contributed to the subordination of women. In a situation where professionalism was the standard, women did not share the same opportunities as men; thus they were marginalized economically and socially.

---

[10] Books drawing on theory of the origins of female domination include Robert Briffault in *The Mother: The Matriarchal Theory of Social Origins*, 1931, Frederick Engels in *The Origin of he Family Private Property and the State*, and Garder Lerner in *The Creation of Patriarchy*, 1986.

[11] Laela Ahmed, *Women and Gender in Islam*, p.12.

[12] *Ibid.*

On the level of ritual and mythos, the degradation of women's status was followed by the degradation in status of the goddess and the emergence of supreme gods.

The patriarchal city-state continued to dominate Mesopotamia. State laws disregarded women's rights. For example, the Hammurabi Code (1752 BC) limited the time that men could 'deposit' their wife and children for a period of three years and quickly prohibited any punishment or oppression because of debt. However, the Asysyiria Constitution clearly allowed the punishment of those who mortgaged women, by cutting a hole in their ear lobe and pulling their hair.[13] Even with the Asysyiria Law (Law 185), a husband was allowed to pull his wife's hair or cut her earlobes, without a binding legal responsibility when punishing his wife.

Karen Armstrong put forth a similar opinion in her book, *The End of Silence: Women and Priesthood* (1993). She states that in the past women were the centers of spiritual findings. The origins of religion are still unclear, but it has generally been agreed that one of the highest symbols of religion was the Great Mother Goddess. In principle, the Mother Goddess related to the deep memory and impression of the mother's body as a microcosm of the universe.

According to Armstrong, this kind of worship emerged at the time when women played an important role in farming and hunting, and when people began living in permanent places. When people invented ploughing equipment and building cities, masculine qualities started to emerge and began to be personified with the image of male gods. The Mother Goddess was called Inanna in Sumeria, Ishtar in Babylonia, Anat or Asherah in Caanan, Isis in Egypt, and Aphrodite in Greece.[14]

It can thus be concluded that women had significant roles in history. This was materialized by the role of the Mother Goddess as a spiritual symbol, and the source of goodness. However, social, political and cultural cleavages caused the status of women to decline.

---

[13] Regarding the Code of Hammurabi was translated by Theopile J. Meek, in *Ancient Near Eastern Relating to the Old Testament*, edited by James B. Pritchard, Princeton: Princeton University Press, 1950, pp..170-1. The Code Asyiria was translated by J. Meek in the same book, p.184.

[14] Karen Armstrong, *The End of Silence, Women and Priesthood*, London: Fourth Estate, 1993, pp.7-9.

THE *JAHILIYYA* TRADITION

When discussing women in the historical context, from the pre-Islamic period to the arrival of Islam, we encounter a historical phase known by Muslim intellectuals as the *Jahiliyya* period. The term *Jahiliyya* is identified with the age of ignorance. But what does *Jahiliyya* really mean?

The term *Jahiliyya* originates from the Arabic word *jahlun*, meaning ignorance. *Jahiliyya* means 'unintelligent nation'. According to the Mu'jam al-Wasîth dictionary, the term *Jahiliyya* has two main meanings: first, the condition of ignorance and the wrongfulness of the Arab nation prior to the coming of Islam (*makana 'alaih al-'Arab qabl al-Islam min al-jahala wa al-dhalâla*), and, secondly, the blank period between the two prophets (*zamanul fathra baina rasûlaini*).[15] The first meaning implies that all stupidity and cruelty prior to Islam belonged to the *Jahiliyya* period, whereas the second meaning is limited more to a transitional period (blank period) between the two prophets, recognizing a time when people had been freed from Jesus' prophecies, but had not yet received Muhammad's prophecies. During this time, there had been a violation of Jesus' teachings by his followers who campaigned to deny the possibility of the coming of a prophet after Jesus. This is the common meaning of *Jahiliyya* put forward by Muslim historians.

In Islamic history, everything related to the *Jahiliyya* period appears to be negative. This negativity colored almost all aspects of life, including people's perceptions of women. Could it be true, however, that those living during *Jahiliyya* were really ignorant? Before answering this question, there should be a very careful and objective analysis to avoid generalizing that everything related to the *Jahiliyya* period was ignorant and without use. However, Islam grew and developed in a territory that was culturally and sociologically close to that of the *Jahiliyya* period, and the Qur'an itself is cautious in explaining this matter.

If we use the perspective of the Moroccan Islamic thinker, Muhammad Abid Al-Jabiri, the *Jahiliyya* period represented a part of the fortmation of a logical Arab nation (*'aql al-'Arab*), where Arabic reasoning was the most important aspect of Islamic reasoning (*'aql al-Islam*).

---

[15] See *Mu'jam al-Wasit*, vol. 1, p.144.

Perhaps what Jabiri meant was that there were aspects of the *Jahiliyya* tradition that were positive. Not all the customs during *Jahiliyya* were totally rejected by Islam, some remained. In general, though, the tradition during the *Jahiliyya* period was inhumane.

For this reason, in examining the position of women in the *Jahiliyya* time period, we need a comprehensive and well-balanced perspective in order to understand the environmental and socio-cultural conditions of the time. However, in many cases, women were treated inhumanely. The tradition of killing female babies was one of the most controversial issues, which was not tolerated by Islam.

Ahmad Khayyarat, in his book *Markaz al-Mar'a fi al-Islam*, described the conditions for women during the *Jahiliyya* period as follows: "Women during the *Jahiliyya* period were trapped in inherited damage, a blind obedience, cruelty, and evil – until Islam arrived with direction and revelations, teachings, advice, guidance, values and the like."[16]

Ahmad Khayyarat's statement probably contains some truth, but we should not generalize that the whole *Jahiliyya* tradition was negative. This assumption can not be accepted, as Islam also accommodates the *Jahiliyya* tradition; at least those traditions that were fitting for the Islamic tradition. Concerning the treatment of women, the *Jahiliyya* period was very negative, while in other matters it was in accordance with Islam. Because of this, in *Usûl Fiqh*, the term *shar'un ma qablana* is used to describe the religious *shari'a* (laws) before Islam.

Apart from the influence of the *Jahiliyya* period on Islam, there were differences between Islam and *Jahiliyya* in regards to the treatment of women. We see that much of the treatment of women during the *Jahiliyya* period was rejected by Islam. The following seven characteristics can be regarded as being characteristics of the *Jahiliyya* period:

1) Women as human beings were not recognized by the law. Women were not considered legally as human beings and, thus, they were not included in constitutional regulations. If a woman was included, she was given a deprived position.

---

[16] See Ahmad Khayyarat, *Markaz al-Mar'a fi al-Islam*, Cairo:Dar al-Ma'arif, p.18.

2) Women during this period were perceived as being objects, as property. If we own it, then we have the right to treat it in whatever way we like. We can sell it or use it. Therefore, at this time, a husband commonly sold his wife to other men.

3) According to the *Jahiliyya* tradition, women did not have the right to divorce. Thus if a woman was treated badly by her husband, she had to bear it. Even in the worse situations, she could not break the marriage bond with her husband. Her position was continually dependent.

4) Women did not have the right to inheritance, but were themselves inherited just like land, animals and other property were. Having no right to receive inheritance shows that this pre-Islamic tradition curtailed the opportunity for women to live independently and progressively.

5) Women did not have the right to take care of their children. Children during this period belonged to the man's family, following the patrilineal pattern.

6) Women did not have the freedom to spend their wealth. At the time of *Jahiliyya*, the woman herself was property.

7) The tradition condoned the burying of living female babies. This was the biggest tragedy in pre-Islamic history for women, and one which is recorded directly in the Qur'an.

If we observe the above seven traditions closely, we find that they are in stark contradiction to Islamic teaching.

AFTER THE ARRIVAL OF ISLAM

The arrival of Islam brought with it a set of humane moral messages unrivaled by any other religion. Islam invites human beings to free themselves not only from human bonds and tyranny, but also from the chains of belief in polytheistic gods, to a belief in only one God. This is stated explicitly in the *shahadat* declaration: "I hereby declare there is no God but Allah and Muhammad is His Messenger."

This mission of *Tawhid* (Unity of God) made Islam an effective basis for movements for religious transformation. If, prior to the arrival of Islam, the world was dominated by imperialism and colonialism between groups, tribes and nations, then the arrival of Islam brought with it the declaration that all human beings are equal before God. As such, there is no horizontal power able to oppress the individual freedom of others, be it the state, capital, or individual power. All are valued and treated equally before God. There is no one more special or more deserving of humiliation than any other. There is only one thing that differentiates people and that is their degree of belief in God. As such, Islam is the right vehicle to unify women and men under its vision and mission of equality before God.

However, this pristine vision and mission of equality within Islam does not exist or work perfectly in practical daily life. This is a frequent criticism from intellectuals and activists struggling for women's rights, both within and outside Islam. Certain Islamic discourses also promote slogans that are against efforts to empower women. This is worsened by the emergence of groups of people asserting Islam's rejection of equality between men and women. Islamic fundamentalist movements are a concrete example here.[17]

This is very different to the situation in the present-day Western world. When the idea of equality among men and women was first raised, the West also faced similar problems, but Western thinkers had the courage to confront religion through the process of secularization. In other words, although the West and Christianity faced relatively serious theological problems regarding equality between men and women, this did not become a practical barrier for the Western world to continue its struggle for the empowerment of women. This is strange: how do we live in accordance with religious concepts that are insensitive to gender, and yet be free from the chains they are attached to?[18]

In the history of Islam, in practical terms, there were phases when women were respected and made equal to men. The world's attitude towards women has followed a conjectural line. Islam arrived with an agenda of complete equality.

---

[17] This was very different from the anti-West protest movements in Saudi Arabia and Turkey after the Gulf War. In Saudi Arabia, the protest emphasized the association of feminism with imperialism.

[18] This can be seen in *Genesis* in the *New Testament*, which implies that Woman is the derivative of the body of Man.

Women were respected within Muslim communities during the time of the Prophet. Women were treated no differently from men. They were not prohibited from playing the same roles as men, whether in politics or in other matters. Even the proximity of women to the Prophet was not limited. For example, when men held discussion groups on the Qur'an with the Prophet, women did not want to be excluded. Initially, the Prophet thought that Qur'anic discussion groups were only for men, and that they would later disseminate the knowledge they had learned to the women of the community. However, this idea received protest from the women of the community as they believed that the men might not deliver the knowledge fairly. The Prophet thus decided to open *ta'lim* gatherings to women as well.[19]

This policy demonstrated that the Prophet was democratic and did not differentiate between men and women. For the Prophet, anything that could be received by His male companions could also appropriately be received by females. The Prophet opened the door to both men and woman seeking knowledge. [20]

If we ask whether there has been a more significant time for female voices than during the time of the Prophet, the answer would likely be 'no.' At the time of the Prophet, women had an equal position in rights and responsibilities with all other human beings before God. The Prophet stated clearly that women were men's sisters, and started a new tradition in this regard:

1) He dramatically changed the Arab worldview, which at that time was dominated by the Pharaoh Ramses' worldview. During the Ramses period, there was little respect for women. The birth of a daughter was not welcomed. This is expressed in the Qur'an, Sura Al-Nahl (16):58-59,

---

[19] I heard about this hadith from Chatib Umar, a respected NU *ulama* from Jember, on the occasion of the *Fiqh Al-Nisa* training, 10-11 February 1998.

[20] This view is in accordance with the hadith: *Talab al-ilmi faridhatun 'ala kulli muslimin wa muslimantin,*or, "Searching for knowledge is an obligatory duty for male and female Muslims." The word *"Muslimatin"* is not frequently mentioned. So, it is generally assumed that the obligatory duty to study is addressed only to Muslims. In addition, according to Ibnu Hajar Al-Haitami in the *al-Fatawa al-Hadithissiyya*, women are not obliged to obtain knowledge, except that relating to obligatory rituals like daily prayers. This view has been followed by Indonesian Muslims, especially NU. This view was abandoned because it was in opposition to the Prophet's teaching and vision of progress. Then NU, on the initiative of Bisri Sansuri, tried to build pesantren for women. This *pesantren* is presently led by Aziz Masyhuri.

where it is stated that on hearing of the birth of a daughter, peoples' faces turned red, because they were upset that their child was female. Such families felt they only had two choices: to keep their daughter and live with the shame of it, or to bury her alive.[21] To counter this inhumane practice, the Prophet was openly proud of his daughters. He carried and held his daughters in public. These actions were part of the Prophet's discourse concerning equality between the sexes.

Furthermore, Muhammad was destined by God not to have sons. Theologically speaking, God designed it thus to prevent the making of a male cult of sons of the Prophet in the patriarchal Arab culture. This also brought with it another lesson (*'ibra*) – the breaking of the taboo against a prophet having only daughters. The Prophet was tormented by infidels for not having sons. Like all other humans, he also felt sadness, although the feeling soon subsided. He stated that there was no greater reward for a Muslim than to have two daughters, treating them well and supporting them, unless God took them into His heaven.[22]

The Prophet was supportive of women on many occasions, and was aware of this was a humanistic commitment. His defense of women took place in many forms and on many levels. On one occasion, the Prophet noted the important position women have in raising the family, stating that 'women are the candle of family life'.[23]

2) The Prophet's actions were revolutionary. Privately, the Prophet also demonstrated by example how to treat women well, particularly through his good treatment of his wives (*mu'ashara bi al-ma'ruf*). There were no stories concerning any injustices made by the Prophet towards his wives. While anger and jealousy did exist among his wives, the Prophet attempted to share what he had equally with all of them.

Another example was that the Prophet was never violent towards his wives. In one story, He stated: "The best among you is the best in treating his wives,

---

[21] *Wa idza bushshira ahaduhum bi al-untha zhalla wajhuhu muswada waahuwa kadzim, yatawara min al-qaumi min su'i ma bushshira bihi ayumsikuhu 'ala haunin am yadussuhu fi al-turab ala sa'a ma yahkumun.*

[22] The hadith states: "*ma min muslimin lahu ibnatani fa yuhsinu ilaihima wa sahibatahu au sahibahuma illa adkhala allahu al-jannata.*"

[23] "*Inna al-mar'ata masabih al-buyut.*"

and I am the best among you all in treating my wives."[24] Another hadith states that "The best among you is your best treatment to your family, and I am the best among you to my family." As we know, the Prophet's family was predominantly female, because all of his children were daughters. Because of this, he treated women very well.

The significance of women during the Prophet's era can be seen through their involvement in re-telling the hadith and in the construction of early Islamic discourses. In the various views of the Prophet's companions, women's role in telling the narratives of hadiths was given much importance. Ibn Ishaq, for example, mentioned that there were no less than fifty women who re-told the hadiths. In Malik's book, *Al-Muwatta'*, for example, there were a number told by women.

Women's significance was not limited to their involvement in the collection of hadiths. They also had significant roles in other sectors of public life, which were often viewed as male domains, such as involvement in war.

The intensity of women's involvement in intellectual, cultural and political spheres shows that their position was valued at that time. In general terms, there are seven interests of women supported by Islam. These seven items are revisions of the *Jahiliyya* treatment of women, as mentioned by Ahmat Khayyarat:

1) Women are citizens protected by Islamic laws, as found in the Qur'an and hadith.
2) Women have the right to choose their marriage partner, thus demonstrating the freedom offered to women. This is shown in the hadith that states that: "A widow has more right over herself than her parents do, and permission must be given by a virgin, and her permission is her silence." Similarly, a hadith narrated by Malik explains: "A widow has more ownership over herself than her parents do, and a virgin is asked her permission and her permission is her silence."[25]

---

[24] The hadith states: "*khairukum khairukum li nisa'ihi wa ana khairukum li al-nisa'i.*"

[25] The hadith states: "*al-thayyibu ahaqqu binafsiha min waliyyiha wa al-bikru tusta'danu wa idznuha sukutha.*" See Muslim, *Sahih* Muslim, 1037. Then, a similar hadith states: "*al-aimu ahaqqu binafsiha min waliyyiha wa al-bikru tusta'dzanu fi nafsiha wa idznuha simatuha.*" See Malik, *Al-Muwatta*, vol. II, p.62.

3) A woman has the right to divorce. This right was completely unavailable to women during the *Jahiliyya* period. When husbands did not love their wives anymore, they could just leave them. Consequently, women were often faced with situations of divorce. When there has been conflict and unfair treatment, women can propose their right to divorce. In this case, the Qur'an gives women the freedom and choice of whether to continue or to break their life bond with their husband. The Qur'an (Al-Ahzab 33: 28-29) states: "Oh Prophet, say to thy wives, if you desire the life of this world and its adornment, then come, and I shall give you goods and let you off gracefully". "But if you desire God and His Messenger and the Final Home, then surely God has prepared for the good-doers among you a big wage".

In the next verse it is written: "Oh wives of the Prophet, if any of you commits a flagrant indecency, the punishment shall be doubled for her; and that is easy for God".

4) A woman has the right to inherit and own property. This was an extraordinary breakthrough for women at that time.

5) Women have the full right to raise their children. During the *Jahiliyya* period, the right to care for children belonged to men. It was the man who buried his daughters alive. Islam gives clear argumentation about the importance of daughters, so the right to take care of children is not borne by men alone. In Islamic jurisprudence (*fiqh*), the right to raise children is called *haqq al-hadhana*.

6) Women have the right to use and spend their own money (*tasarruf*). During the pre-Islamic period, property belonged almost fully to men. Property is a symbol of freedom and dignity for both men and women.

7) Women have the right to life. This is an aspect very different to conditions during the *Jahiliyya* period. One prominent example is that during this time, women were not respected as shown by the burying of live female babies.

The seven points listed above show the pristine respect Islam has for women. In principle, these rights were applied during the period of the Prophet.

Following the period of the Prophet, however, women's life began little by little to deteriorate. In this regard, it was a return to the degradations of the past.

THE DEGRADATION PERIOD

As the period of the Prophet Muhammad grew distant, women's involvement in public discourse became more blurred. During His life, the level of female activity was high, but following His death, female activity in public life began to decline. The death of the Prophet meant that women became more disadvantaged. This had actually been anticipated by the Prophet during *Hajj al-Wada'* (the farewell Hajj). In his last sermon, one of the important issues addressed was that of women's destiny in the future.

The changes following the death of the Prophet can be divided into four periods or generations: 1) The period of the 'companions'; 2) The *tabi'in* generation; 3) The *tabi'it al-tabi'in* generation; and 4) The generation after the *tabi'it al-tabi'in* up to the present day.

The Companions

The label 'companions' is attached to the first Muslim generation to follow the Prophet Muhammad during His early military expeditions. The term later developed to refer to 'companions' as those who believed Muhammad to be the last Prophet. These companions included both men and women. The last such companion was a woman, who passed away in 100 H. This point is based on Ibn Sa'd's story that tells of a two-year girl who joined the Current War (*khandaq*). She not only followed, but also understood the situation she experienced.[26]

The role of the companions in Islam is particularly important within the Sunni tradition. The Prophet stated: "My companions are like stars, then those accompanying them, then those accompanying them, and then those accompanying them." They were the transmitters and living witnesses of Islam for the generations to follow.

This view is not just the monopoly of Sunnite Islam. In Shi'ite Islam, such views were also present in their prayers of adoration toward 'Ali, Fatimah, Abû Dzarr Al-Ghiffari and other famous companions, though this Shi'ite view seems to be more exclusive than the Sunnite view. Those most respected in Shi'ah were only those who became the founding fathers of Shi'ah. However, not all Shi'ahs

---

[26] Ruth Roded, *Kembang Peradaban* (Indonesian edition), Mizan, p.38

shared the same view. Some looked down on companions outside their own environment. This group is known as the Shi'ite extremist groups (*ghullat*).

In spite of this, almost all theological-political factions agreed to place companions in an important position in the formation of Islamic discourse. They were the chosen generation and closest to the Prophet. They were witnesses and interpreters of the Prophet's teachings. From here on, Islam developed as a religious discourse, detached from the authority and supervision of the Prophet. After His death, Islam received its sources not only from sacred texts, but also from dialogue concerning matters of daily life. The original of sacred texts were kept, maintained and prioritized in making legal decisions, but other texts developed according to the demands of era. The texts, although still guarded by the law, have disappeared in the above sense because the revelation stopped after the death of the Prophet. However, this does not mean that we live outside the revelation of spirit. We still live in the spirit of revelation, but also relate to the revelations with the empirical realities that occur in daily life. This dialogue has meant that Islam has developed from a simple discourse to a complex and responsive one. Thus, the Prophet's companions played a very important role because they began and continued this dialogic process.

Although almost all theological factions agree about the special status of the companions, there are different characteristics between Sunni and Shi'ite Islam. Sunnite Islam placed the companions in a sacred position and tended to be uncritical of them. Shi'ite Islam is more critical, although toward particular companions, such as (the nuclear family of Phropet Muhammad) Ahl Al-Bait, they are not critical at all.

However, the followers of Sunnite Islam are not critical of information if it was delivered by companions from their group, particularly from great companions such as Abu Huraira or Abu Bakra, for example. This is rather dangerous, because we are unable to evaluate the validity of information from these companions. In this regard, information, including that regarding women, may be accepted without dispute. This means that eventually all hadith, including those of bad quality, will be accepted as long as they are understood as coming from great companions.

Mohammed Arkoun, a postmodernist Muslim thinker from Algiers now living in France, described the formation process of Islamic teaching in terms of layers of soil. By using an archeological metaphor, he stated that many layers formed Islam and that the layers accumulate daily, just as layers of soil do. The problem is that not all the layers are correct – right is mixed with wrong and *vice-versa*. On the other hand, perhaps criticism of Islamic teachings made by thinkers of the past should not be dwelt upon.

As a solution to this, Arkoun proposed a deconstruction (*tafkik*) of the layers of soil so that we can identify which layers are correct and which are wrong. Sometimes the correct ones are forgotten because they are covered, and the wrong ones accepted because they are on the surface. From Arkoun's theoretical perspective, the companions are the second layer of the formation of Islamic discourse. A deconstruction of layers opens up the possibility of adding, reducing and even violating Islamic teachings. For example, during the Prophet's time women could pray in the mosque; it is only since the 'Umar government that women have not been allowed to pray with men. This is a reduction of women's rights.

In fact, the most significant aspect of using Arkoun's theory relates to the role of the female companions. By using his deconstructionist theory, we can see the extent to which female companions were integral to forming Islamic discourse.

Until now, the role of the female companions has been hidden behind the role of male companions. This can be seen clearly through Ruth Roded's research into the roles of the female companions. In her book, *Women in Islamic Biographical Collections from Ibn Sa'd to Who's Who* (Indonesian edition: *Kembang Peradaban: Citra Wanita di Mata Para Penulis Biografi Muslim*, Bandung:Mizan, 1995), she succeeded in uncovering the significant role women have had in Islamic historical discourses.

When noting the role of women, a number of historians only point to the wives of the Prophet. In fact, according to biographical notes, there were no less than twelve thousand female companions directly involved with the Prophet.

Tabi'in

The *tabi'in* period was the period following the death of the Prophet's companions. Following its generic meaning, *tabi'in* means: a person who follows (*tabi'*: follower). This refers to the generation following the Prophet

and his companions as long as they were justified by religion.
However, there are two things that may have occurred here:

1) Islamic teachings delivered by the companions of the Prophet might have undergone some changes, such as reduction, addition, and deviation; and

2) The teachings delivered by the companions to the *tabi'in* still maintained its originality.

At that time, the existence and role of women was relatively overlooked. According to notes recorded by historians, not many women played an important role during this period. In comparison to the number of female companions, the numbers of women *tabi'in* were fewer.

There have been many arguments among Islamic historians concerning the number of female *tabi'in*. According to Ibn Sa'd, female *tabi'in* only numbered about ninety-four, while Ibn Hibban stated that there were only about ninety women. Ibn Hajar in *Tahdzib al-Tahdzib*, however, noted that there were about 140 women.

Why this decrease in numbers? Laela Ahmed suggested that the decrease in the status of women occurred because of ecological reasons related to the transition from a nomadic community to an agrarian urban community; because of economic reasons related to the importance of land; and because of cultural influences from outside, such as those from Byzantium, Persia and Syria.[27] On the other hand, Juynboll argued that the decrease in the status of women during the *tabi'in* period was due to the emergence of hadiths that downgraded the status of women. According to Ruth Roded, however, it can be explained by the choices made by biographers at that time. Women *tabi'in* chosen to be represented in biographies only included those who retold the hadiths, and at that time there was a tendency for hadiths to be retold by a woman only if there was no man available, or if the woman was exceptionally intellectually capable.[28] According to Crone and Martin Hinds, as cited by Ruth Roded, the role of women after the

---

[27] Laela Ahmed, *Women and Gender in Islam*, pp.66, 70-1, and 88-99.
[28] Ruth Roded, pp. 89-90.

Prophet was deliberately downgraded by experts of classical *fiqh* in the era of 'Abbasia caliphs.[29]

Tabi'it al Tabi'in

The *tab'in* period was followed by the *tabi'it al-tabi'in*. No one knows for sure what the activities and numbers of *tabi'it al-tabi'in* women were. Fewer and fewer people paid theoretical attention to the role of women in Islam during this period. This was when *fiqh* scholars began to develop *fiqh* (Islamic jurisprudence) as a form of specific scientific knowledge, examining issues related to formal law. This period will be discussed in depth in the next chapter.

---

[29] *Ibid.*

CHAPTER TWO

WOMEN'S POSITION IN ISLAM: PERSPECTIVES FROM THE QUR'AN AND HADITH

Every discussion of women's position in Islam will necessarily refer to the Qur'an, especially the chapter (*Sura*) Al-Nisa'.[1] This is because Al-Nisa' means "women" in Arabic, and, according to Sayyid Rashid Rida, the chapter is one of the parts of the Qur'an that most often discusses topics related to women's rights, obligations and the legal regulations pertaining to them.

According to experts in Qur'anic interpretation, this chapter, which has 176 verses, falls in the *Madaniyya* category of the Qur'an.[2] The hadiths issued by Ibn Dharis in *Fadhail*, Al-Nuhas in *Nasikh*, and Ibn Mardawai and Al-Baihaqi in *Dala'il*, which all come from the single source: Ibn Abbas, claim that Al-Nisa' was revealed in Medina after the Hijra (the migration of the Prophet Muhammad from Mecca to Medina). This claim is supported by Bukhari's narrative, from A'isha, which states: "[There was] no revelation of the chapter Al-Baqara and Al-Nisa', except [when] I was by His side."[3]

---

[1] Al-Nisa' in Arabic has a synonym: *Al-Mar'a*, though both words have different connotations and are used differently. Usually, Al-Nisa' is used in a positive context while *Al-Mar'a* is used differently. The Qur'an calls the wife of Abu Lahab *imra'a*, from the root *Al-Mar'a*. But this does not always apply, as an Egyptian writer, Qasim Amin, entitled his two books: *Mar'atun Jadilah* and *Tahir Al-Mar'a*.

[2] Muhammad Rashid Rida, *Tafsir Al-Manar*, Beirut: Dar Al-Ma'rifah. Vol. IV, p.322.

[3] Jalal Al-Din Al-Suyuti, *Al-Dur Al-Ma'thur*, Beirut: Dar Al-Fikr, 1983, Vol. IV, p.422. The *Madaniyya* chapters, according to interpretation experts, are the chapters which were revealed in the Medina period.

The substance of Al-Nisa', in keeping with its etymological meaning, pertains to various topics related to male-female relations, as human beings, spouses in the home, as well as in social, cultural and political life. Not all its contents discuss gender relations; but Al-Nisa' tells us more about women than the Qur'an's other chapters do. This is also the opinion of the *Al-Manar* authors, Rashid Rida and Muhammad Abdu.

The stance of the *Al-Manar* authors is shared by Sayyid Tabataba'i, a noted *ulama* from Iran, who wrote a monumental interpretation of the Qur'an titled *Mizan*. According to Tabataba'i, the revelation of Al-Nisa' aims to explain issues relating directly to women, such as marriage regulations, number of wives, people who it is forbidden (*haram*) to marry, and inheritance laws.

Although women are the focus of attention in Al-Nisa', problems relating to the discrimination, segregation, and subordination of women are believed to be derived from, and legitimated by, it. For example, in Al-Nisa' (4), verse 34, Allah speaks thus: "Men are leaders for women, because God has made some of them (men) excel over others (women), and because they (men) spend from their [own] means."

In several interpretations of the Qur'an, the word *qawwamuna* is translated as 'leader'.[4] No less than seven different interpretations translate the word *qawwamuna* as leader – meaning leader in all aspects of life.

Such an interpretation leads to a general understanding than men are leaders, and that, as superiors, they can not be challenged, even when they are mistaken. This interpretation is then applied to life in more practical terms. Of course, by implication, an interpretation may not always be correct. Although we acknowledge that leadership may be the onus of men, it should be true leadership – just, democratic, and understanding.

The more serious practical implications of male leadership are visible in the contents of books of interpretation, such as *fiqh* (Islamic jurisprudence), hadith, etc. For instance, the Qur'anic interpretation experts, especially

---

[4] These books of *tafsir* are *Tafsir al-Qur'an al-Adzim* by Ibn Katsir, *Al-Manar* by Rashid Rida, *al-Wadhiha* by Dr. Al-Hijazi, *Safwa al-Tafasir* by Ali Al-Sabuni, *al-Mizan* by Imam Al-Tabataba'i, *Al-Furqon fi Tafsir Al-Qur'an* by Dr. Muhammad Sadiqi and *al-Amthal fi Tafsir Aal-Kitab al- Munazzal* by Nasir Makarim Al-Shirazi. See Agus Effendi, *Perempuan dalam Pandangan Tafsir Modern* (in a discussion held by Forum "Rahim", April 19, 1996, P3M, Jakarta.)

those specializing in *fiqh* (*fuqaha*), use this verse to justify and legitimize men having a higher position than women.[5] If we review the verse, however, through an analysis of hermeneutics, syntax and history, possibilities open up for different interpretations. Leadership is limited in certain aspects, and may not apply to all aspects of life. This divergent interpretation is rarely mentioned in the classical books of Islam, especially *fiqh*. In keeping with the character of *fiqh*, the views contained within are highly normative, and take a literalist interpretation of the Qur'an.

If we look again at Al-Nisa', besides verse 34 as discussed above, the other key verse which is used as a basic justification for giving men a superior position to women is verse 1. This verse is about the origins of humankind. It is generally understood to indicate that Woman (Eve) was created from Man (Adam's rib).

The interpretation of verse 1 has had great influence on the whole of Islamic discourse, especially in *fiqh*, on the subject of womankind. At this point, though, it is important to further investigate Al-Nisa' (4), verse 1.[6] I will now explore the various opinions of *tafsir* experts on the topic of human creation.

THE ORIGINS OF WOMANKIND IN THE QUR'AN

Is it true that Islam views humankind as originating from part of the body of Adam?

The issue of human origins has taken up many centuries of debate, and thousands of sheets of paper. The debate became even more interesting when Charles Darwin put forth his biological theory that humans originated from apes. Darwin's statement shocked both the scientific and religious worlds. Various responses were released, both rejecting and supporting Darwin. Religious leaders, both Islamic and non-Islamic, were among those who firmly opposed his theory. Judaism and Christianity also maintain that humanity was borne of Adam's rib.

---

[5] See *Uqud al-Lijain* written by a Javanese *ulama* who was born in Banten, namely Nawawi. This verse is a major justification for the lower position of women in Islam.

[6] The selection of Al-Nisa' is based on the philosophical consideration that all human life is started from the process of creation.

In Islam, the primary source on the origin of humankind is Al-Nisa' (4): 1: "Oh humankind, be dutiful to your Lord, Who created you from a single being (*nafs wahida*), and from him, He created his wife, and from them both, He created many men and women. Fear God from Whom you request and take care of this loving relationship. Surely, God is always guarding and watching over you."

The above verse explains human creation, the development of human beings as social creatures, the praise of God, and the importance of maintaining love among people.

This translation of the account offers no clear explanation of the origin of human beings being Adam (Man). There is no indication at all about Adam himself. It may even be believed that Adam was formulated by God in the feminine form (*mu'annath*); that is *nafs wahida*. How could a feminine form mean men? Certain experts in Arabic grammar (*Nahwu*) defend this phrasing, but they have no really strong argument, especially on the consistency of language.[7]

A question that needs to be raised here is why the verse is given such importance?[8] Among many Qur'anic experts the verse is treated as evidence that the origin of humankind is Adam, and the phrase *nafs wahida* itself is given as the source. The verse has been used as a guideline for maintaining unbalanced patterns of relationship between men and women. Logically, since human beings – including women – were created from Adam, and he is a man, women are substantially subordinate to men. This logic holds true if Woman (Eve) is created from Man (Adam). But Islam has no clear description of such a creation; what is revealed in the Qur'an is that human beings were created from *nafs wahida*.

The logic cited above has been widely criticized by Muslim feminists, many of whom suspect the source of women's subordination depends on the particular interpretation of the verse. Riffat Hassan, for instance, defines three theological assumptions, running throughout the Semitic religions, that cause the subordination and segregation of women. First: that God's

---

[7] Some experts on *Nahwu* (the science of Arabic grammar) said that *mudzakar* (the masculine) could have *mu'annath* (feminine adjective). But the theory is rarely applied as it is categorized as *shadz*.

[8] The point here is not the truth of the Qur'anic verse itself, but the interpretations made of it.

principal creatures are men, not women, because it is believed that women were created from Adam's rib, women are therefore ontologically derivative and are second-class citizens. Second: Woman is the cause of Man's fall from heaven. Third: Woman was not only created from, but also *for*, Man.[9]

Nonetheless, the general interpretation has remained that human beings were created from *nafs wahida*, and that means Adam.[10] There follows a series of examples of the interpretations of leading thinkers, both traditional and contemporary.

IMAM ZAMAKHSHARI (467-536 H)

Imam Zamakhshari's original name was Abu Al-Qasim Mahmud ibn 'Umar Al-Khawarizmi. He was also sometimes called "Jar Allah" (the neighbor of God). He was a follower of the Hanafi in the field of *fiqh*, and the Mu'tazila school of theology. Zamakhshari was born in the Islamic month of Rajab in 476 H in Zamakhshar, part of the Khawarizmi region. In keeping with tradition, his popular name was taken from his birthplace. Al-Zamakhshari passed away on the night of Arafa in 538 H, in Jurjaniya, Khawarizmi region, after his return from Mecca.[11]

Al-Zamakhshari is noted as an expert in *tafsir* among the theology-politics faction of the Mu'tazila school. He was known especially for his expertise in hadith, literature, and Arabic language and grammar. His *tafsir* work, titled *Al-Kashshaf*, is regarded as representative of Mu'tazila's most liberal and rational interpretation of the Qur'an. Al-Zamakhshari's interpretation of Al-Nisa' (4): 1 gets directly to the heart of the matter. Without long or complicated explanations, he claimed that the phrase *nafs wahida* referred to Adam. He therefore believed that Adam was the first human being, and the father of all others.

As an expert on Arabic grammar (*Nahwu*),[12] however, it is strange that Al-Zamakhshari did not give a clearer explanation of how the masculine

---

[9] Riffat Hassan, *Women's Rights and Islam, From the ICPD to Bejing*, Copyright material, p.5. Hassan takes a philosophical approach – all socio-economic factors return to the philosophical assumptions.

[10] This is reflected in the following interpretations.

[11] Imam Bukhari was another famous *ulama* from this region.

[12] There is a theory that the subject (*fail*) in *jama'taksir* can have the predicate of *fi'il muannats*. This is very gender biased.

form (*mudzakkar nafs*) could be a feminine adjective. I think that the answer is clear from his interpretation.

JALALUDDIN AL-SUYUTI (849-911 H)

Jalaluddin Al-Suyuti's full name was Jalaluddin Abu Al-Fadhal Abdurrahman ibn Abu Bakar ibn Muhammad Al-Suyuti. He is noted as one of the most productive *ulama*, writing many books. He was born in Rajab around 846 H. His parents passed away before he was six years old, but he finished his Qur'anic study by the age of eight. He memorized thousands of the *matan* (the main text) of hadith, which were recited by his teachers. Al-Dawadi, one of Al-Suyuti's students, said that Al-Suyuti had fifty-one teachers. Throughout his life, he wrote various books, in areas ranging from hadith, *fiqh*, *tafsir*, history and other fields of Islamic knowledge. According to Al-Dawadi, his teacher authored more than five hundred texts, usually writing three pages each day.

He was known as one of the brightest intellectuals working on hadith and its derivatives, such as *Rijal al-Hadith*, *Gharib al-Hadith*, *Matn al-Hadith* and *Sanad al-Hadith*. He was said to have memorized 200,000 hadiths, and is quoted as having said: "If I find more than that, I will memorize them [too]."

At the age of forty, his life-course changed. He stopped teaching and giving *fatwa* (religious decrees), and decided to concentrate on worship and moving closer to God, which he continued to do until the end of his life. He passed away on Friday night, Jumadi Al-Ula 19, 911 H.

One of his most famous works, besides *Al-Itqan fi 'Ulum Al-Qur'an*, is titled *Al-Durr Al-Ma'thur fi Tafsir Al-Ma'thur*. According to a noted contemporary *tafsir* expert, Muhammad Husain Al-Dzahabi, *Al-Durr Al-Ma'thur* is a shortened edition of his *tafsir* book, *Tarjuman Al-Qur'an*. This book, as mentioned in *Al-Itqan*, is a collection of the Prophet Muhammad's interpretations of various Qur'anic verses. This *tafsir* contains many hadiths, and is a kind of *tafsir al-manqul*. It contains ten thousand hadiths, categorized as *marfu'*, *mauquf* and *dha'if*.

There is no doubt that *Al-Durr Al-Ma'thur* contains the application of the method of *bil Al-Ma'tsur* in its purest sense. Al-Suyuti explained it thus:

I wrote this book, *Tarjuman Al-Qur'an* – based on the Prophet Muhammad's interpretation of the Qur'an – and finished with several volumes. I presented many hadiths, with their literary references, and I saw certain summaries (constructions) that carried misunderstandings within them. Most people wished to [read] summaries of the *matan* (content) of hadith without explanation of the chain of transmission (*sanad*) or extensive versions of the interpretations, so I wrote this short work.[13]

The methodology used by Al-Suyuti can be seen in the interpretation of Al-Nisa', verse 1. Influenced by the hadiths of Ibn Abbas, Mujahid, Al-Dhahhak and so on, Al-Suyuti claimed that the origin of human beings was Adam; that *nafs wahida* was Adam.

The hadiths used by Al-Suyuti included:

1) A hadith issued by Abu Al-Shaykh from Ibn Abbas, which said that *khalaqalakum min nafsin wahida* means 'Adam', while *khalaqa minha zaujaha* refers to Hawa (Eve), who was created from Adam's rib.[14]

2) A hadith issued by 'Abd ibn Humaid, Ibn Abu Shaiba, Ibn Jarir, Ibn Al-Mundzir, Ibn Abi Hatim and Mujahid, which makes similar claims to those of Ibn Abbas. This hadith, however, states explicitly that Hawa was created from Adam's curved rib when he was sleeping.[15] This explanation is similar to the biblical one.

3) A hadith issued by 'Abd ibn Humaid and Ibn Al-Mundzir from Ibn 'Amru, which states that Eve was created from Adam's back, left rib, and a demonic female was also created from his back, left-hand side.[16] This hadith seems to equate the creation of Eve with the creation of the female demon.

---

[13] See *Al-Dur Al-Ma'thur*, Vol. I, p.51-5.

[14] The hadith states: *"Akhraja Abu Al-Shaykh 'an Ibn Abbas fi qaulihi khalaqakum min nafsin wahida qala min Adam, wahalaqa minha zaujaha, qala, huliqa Hawwa min qushairi a'adha'iha."*

[15] The hadith states: *"Akhraja Ibn Humaid wa Ibn Abi Shaykh wa ibn Jarir wa Ibn Al-Mundzir wa ibni Abi Hatim 'an Mujahid fi qaulihi "khalaqalakum min nafsin wahida", qala, Adam wa khalaqa min zaujiha qala, Hawwa min qaishaira'i Adam wa huwa na'imun fa istaiqhazha fa qala, a ana al-nabthiya imara'tun."*

[16] The hadith states: *"Akhraja 'Abd Humaid wa ibn Mundzir 'an Ibn Amru qala khuliqat Hawwa min khalfi Adam al-aisari, wa khuliqat imraa'tu iblis mi khalfihi min al-aisari."*

4) A hadith issued by Ibn Abi-Hatim from Al-Dhahhak, also said Eve was created from Adam's back rib – explicitly stated to be his most crooked bone.

5) A hadith issued by Ibn Al-Mundzir, Ibn Abi Hatim, and Baihaqi di Shi'bi from Ibn Abbas, which states that Woman was created from Man, and are therefore dependent on men. So, according to Ibn Abbas, women must be protected by men, who were created from the earth. This hadith seems to suggest women's dependence on men is far greater than men's dependence on women.[17]

All five hadiths should be reviewed for several reasons:

1) These hadiths contain a similar conception of the Creation to that in the New Testament (Bible). This is in contrast to Al-Nisa' (4), verse 1, which has no clear explanation that Woman (Eve) was created from Man (Adam). They also need to be compared with others verses in the Qur'an, which tell of the creation of human beings from soil, dust, or sperm.

2) These hadiths (especially #3) contain a misogynistic attitude towards women by equating the creation of Woman to the creation of a female demon; a sinful creature who disobeys the will of God. This is contrary to the stance of other, stronger hadiths that state that human beings were originally pure of sin and other bad deeds. These hadiths can be rejected, on a theological basis, for these two reasons.

MUHAMMAD AL-RAZI

Al-Razi's complete name was Abu Abdillah Muhammad ibn 'Amru Al-Husain ibn Hassan ibn Ali Al-Tamimi, Al-Tabiristan, Al-Razi. Born in 544 H, Al-Razi was also called Fakhr Al-Din and was best known by his other name Ibn Khatib Al-Shafi'i. Besides being known as a theologian, he was noted for being a person of great *farid* (beauty).

Al-Razi was an intellectual leader (*imam*) in the fields of Qur'anic exegesis, Islamic theology, rational sciences, and linguistics. He learnt much

---

[17] Jalaluddin Al-Suyuti, *Al-Durr Al-Ma'thur fi' Al-Tafsir Al-Ma'thur*, Dar Al-Fikr, Vol. II, p.422-424.

from his father, Khatib Al-Ra'y, who was a noted *imam* among followers of the Shafi'i School. He also studied with Kamal Al-Sam'ani, Majid Al-Jilli, and other noted *ulamas*. Al-Razi passed away in 606 H, in Ra'y. It is said that his death resulted from a serious theological conflict with the Karamiya sect.

Al-Razi's most important works include:

Mafatih al-Ghayb, in the field of *tafsir*, *al-Muthalaba al-Aliya* in theology, *Kitab al-Bayan wal al-Burhan fir Raddi 'ala Ahli Zaighi wa Tughyan*, *al-Mausul* in legal maxim (*Usul Fiqh*), and *al-Mukhlish, Sharh al-Isharat li Ibn Sina, Sharh 'Uyun al-Hikma* in Islamic philosophy and wisdom.

Al-Razi's interpretation of Al-Nisa' (4), verse 1, like most others, suggests that *nafs wahida* means 'Adam'. Part of his reasoning was that this interpretation had been generally accepted by the Muslim community, likely meaning an *ijma'*. *Ijma'* depend on an agreement between *ulamas*, made at a certain point in time and space, and therefore making the interpretation contingent and open to change.

But again, how could the phrase *mu'annath* (feminine) was understood as *mudzakkar* (Adam)? Al-Razi defended his argument, stating that the phrase *mu'annath* contains *maushuf mudzakar* or its opposite as it is mentioned in the phrase *nafs wahida*, can also be found in other verses of the Qur'an, for instance, a*qatalta nafsan zakiyatan bighairi nafsin*. According to Al-Razi, there are also similar phrases in Arabic poetry; for instance, *abuka khalifa waladathu ukhra fa anta khalifa dzaka al-kamal*. The word *khalifa* is considered to be feminine. At the same time, a masculine word could carry a feminine adjective, although it is an exception in Arabic tradition.[18]

On the part of a verse *wa khalaqa minha zaujaha*, Al-Razi argues that the term *zauj* (spouse) refers to Hawa (Eve). There are two opinions on the creation of Eve from Adam:

1) As believed by the majority, said that God created Adam, and then Adam slept. While he was sleeping, God created Eve from his back, curved rib

---

[18] Al-Razi, *Tafsir Kabir* (*Mafatih al-Ghaib*), Dar Al-Fikr, vol. IX, p.166.

on the left-hand side. When Adam awoke, he saw Eve and loved her because she was created from part of himself. The opinion was based on the hadith of Prophet Muhammad: *"anna al-mar'atu khuliqat min dhila'i a'waj fa in dzahabta tuqimaha kasarta, wa in taraktaha wa fiha 'iwajun istam'ta bih."*

2) Abu Muslim Al-Asfihani, as quoted by Rashid Rida in *Al-Manar*, states that Adam's wife was created from the same material as Adam. But, according to Al-Qadhi, during Al-Razi's time, the first opinion was stronger. This is because if Eve is considered as one of the first creature, it follows that human beings were created in two kinds, not one. However, the Arabic letters *'min'* in the verse *min nafs wahida* includes the phrase *li al-ibtidha'i al-ghaya*, meaning "the start of the destination". If the first creation was Adam, it is true to say that all of us were created from Adam. But, according to Al-Qadhi, if God had the power to create Adam from soil, God also had the power to create Eve from soil. So what would be the purpose of creating Eve from Adam's crooked rib?[19] Quoting Ibn Abbas, Al-Razi answers this rhetorical question, supporting the argument for the creation of Eve from Adam.

Ibn Abbas stated that Adam was called Adam because he was created from a mess of red and black soil, a mixture of good and bad (*udaim*). And this is why Adam's children were red and black, good and bad. Eve, however, was created from Adam's rib, a living part of Adam.

MUHAMMAD ABDU AND MUHAMMAD RASHID RIDA

Before discussing the interpretations of these two *ulamas* on the Al-Nisa' verse 1 in full, there are two issues that need to be clarified:

1) We often think that a teacher and his student share similar views. This was not always the case with Muhammad Abdu (the teacher), and Muhammad Rashid Rida (his student). One issue they disagreed on was the interpretation on *nafs wahida* in Al-Nisa'.

---

[19] *Ibid.* p. 167.

2) For those unfamiliar with reading *Al-Manar*, it may be difficult to differentiate between Rashid Rida's and Muhammad Abdu's opinions. As such, *Al-Manar* needs to be read with care.[20]

Muhammad Abdu Hasan Hairullah was a pioneer of the reformist movement in Islam, appealing to the jargon of a "return to the spirit of early Islam". He was very influential in the Middle East, especially Egypt. Muhammad Abdu was born into a highly respected and educated family in Mahalla Nashr village in 1265 H.

Abdu started his religious studies in the Ahmadi complex in Tanta. After experiencing a spiritual crisis later in life, Abdu turned to mysticism. He was taught Sufism by his uncle, Shaykh Darwis, a leader of Sufi order of Shadziliyya. Abdu became an enthusiastic sufi until he met Jalal Al-Din Al-Afghani. This meeting became a friendship and a forum for dialogue, with Abdu strongly influenced by Al-Afghani's stance on models of political agitation.

Muhammad Hushain Al-Dzahabi considered Abdu to be the pioneer of modern Qur'anic interpretation, using various influential modes of thinking typical of the times. He used modern approaches such as sociology, anthropology and other sciences and was characteristically far removed from fanatic Islamic schools, both in terms of *fiqh* and theology.

According to J.J.G. Jansen, Abdu's interpretation ended the implementation of purely academic interpretation (writings before Abdu were for other *ulamas*). Abdu's style of interpretation was conducted in simple language and was in keeping with the context of the times.[21]

Muhammad Rashid Rida, Abdu's student, was also a *tafsir* expert who became a pioneer in the emergence of modern interpretation, with scientific methods. He was born in Sham in 1282 H, and passed away in 1354 H. His admiration to Abdu was inspired by *Al-'Urwa Al-Wuthqa* magazine which was managed by Abdu and Jamal Al-Din Al-Afghani. He first met Abdu in Rajab, 1315 H. Later, Rashid Rida became one of Abdu's students at Al-

---

[20] To differentiate between Abdu's statements and Rashid Rida's statements, it could be seen from the use *"qala al imam"* means Abdu and *"qultu"* means Rashid Rida's opinion.

[21] J.J.G. Jansen, *Diskursus Tafsir Al-Qur'an Modern*, Tiara Wacana, 1997, p.27.

Azhar University, where he wrote up his teacher's ideas, which were later published in *Al-Manar* magazine, after being checked and edited by Abdu. This is the beginning of their collaboration.

According to Abdu and Rashid Rida, Al-Nisa', verse 1, was aimed not only at Mecca residents as earlier suspected by other *tafsir* experts. They suggest that the chapter be included in the *Madaniyya* category (revealed in Medina), except one verse which remains unclear and may have been *Makkiyya* (revealed in Mecca). They argued their case on the basis of the term, *al-Nas*, which becomes the *mukhatab* (reciever of speech) of this chapter. It becomes *ism jism* (the noun) for all human beings, thus showing the generality of this chapter.[22]

Rashid Rida, quoting Al-Razi's opinion based on Ibn Abbas, stated that the chapter was a call (*khithab*) for the experts of Mecca. On the other hand, theological experts in the foundations of Islam (*usulliyun*) agreed that the verse was aimed at all human beings who carry the obligation (*mukallaf*). According to Rashid Rida, the latter opinion was the strongest, supported by the following arguments:

1) The Arabic letter, *lam*, in the word *al-Nas* means *li al-isthighraq* (general/ whole).[23] All human beings are created and ordered to fear and obey God.

2) The discipline of *tafsir* has developed an understanding that God always called Mecca residents with the term *Ya Ayyuha al-Nas*, while Medina residents used *Ya Ayyuha al-ladzina*. *Ya Ayyuha al-Nas* is often used in *Makkiyya* chapters, such as Al-A'raf, Yunus, Al-Hajj, Al-Naml, Al-Mala'ika. But the phrase is also used for Al-Baqara, Al-Nisa' and Al-Hujurat, which are categorized as *Madaniyya*. According to Rashid Rida, the use of *Ya Ayyuha al-Nas* is common (*ghalib*) and, if the phrase is found in a chapter, it is aimed as a call for all human beings (*mukallaf*). Rashid Rida doubted that Ibn Abbas believed that the beginning of Al-Nisa' was only for experts in Mecca.[24]

---

[22] Muhammad Rashid Rida, *op. cit*, p.322.
[23] In Arabic grammar, *Al-lil isthiraq* is used for general meanings.
[24] *Ibid*, p.323.

As such, Rashid Rida's interpretation of Al-Nisa', verse 1, is as follows:

1) In interpreting sequence of the verse, *alladzi khalaqa lakum min nafsin wahida* (He created you from a single being), he states that the verse is actually meant to show the *qudrah* (power) of God, as it was mentioned by some other interpretations. But according to Al-Imam, it is actually a sort of *tamhid* (introduction) for the sentences that follow, which explain peoples' responsibilities towards orphans.

2) Abdu claimed that the meaning of *nafs wahida*, both textually and in its original sense, was not Adam. According to him, if the *tafsir* experts agreed that the term *ya ayyuha al-Nas* was for Mecca residents or Quraish tribe, the *nafs wahida* could be for Quraish tribe or Adna tribe. If the verse for Arabic, so the *nafs wahida* is for Arabic or Qathan. But, if we agreed that the *khitab* (call) is for all human beings, all human being believed that they come from a single person. They believe that they originated from Adam, the "single person" (*nafs wahida*) is Adam.

But, based on the verse's indications (*qarina*), Muhammad Abdu believed that *nafs wahida* did not mean Adam in this particular case, because the words *rijalan wa nisa'an in ba'atha minhuma rijalan kathira wa nisa'an* are used in the form of *nakira* (a general noun form). How can it be said that the verse calls to all human beings, when not everybody recognizes the verse's meaning? There are people who have never heard of Adam and Eve. For instance, the descendents of Noah may have believed that they originated from Adam, because of their relative historical proximity. But Chinese people, for example, would relate their origin to a different 'father', closer to their own historical background.[25]

Abdu did not only use rational and empirical conventions in his understanding of the verse, but was also relied heavily on God's revelations to the Prophet Muhammad. Abdu maintained that he would not add or subtract from what was written in the Qur'an. According to Abdu, the wording on creation was intentionally ambiguous so as to challenge pre-Islamic books

---

[25] Al-Ustadz Al-Imam Muhammad 'Abdu and Muhammad Rashid Rida, Al-Manar Vol. IV, p.324.

(before Islam), which are likely to have been influenced by the leanings of their authors.[26]

Rashid Rida, however, acknowledged the length of debates among *tafsir* experts regarding the status of Adam. The majority indeed interpreted *nafs wahida* as Adam, an interpretation based not only on textual factors and original context, but also based on established general opinion. They also had a different stance on Sura Al-A'raf (7):189: "He created you from a single being, and He created from him his wife, in order that they might enjoy living together."

In this context, Rashid Rida quoted Al-Razi who interpreted the verse as having three allegorical meanings (*ta'wil*):

1) Based on Al-Qaffal's opinion, God revealed the verse to offer an example.
2) The verse, and *nafs wahida*, is aimed at the Qurais tribe in the Prophet's era, and the descendents of Qusayyi's family.
3) That *nafs wahida* is Adam.

Rashid Rida also discusses the opinions of the Shi'ite Imamiyya and various Sufi sects about the plurality of Adam. According to these, before 'Adam' was known as the father of human beings, there were many Adams. It was said in *Ruh Al-Ma'ani* that the author of *Jami Al-Akhbar*, in the fifteenth article, revealed that God created many Adams before Adam, the father of human beings, was created. There were a thousand years of time between Adam the Father, and the other Adams. The earth was quiet and uninhabited for fifty thousand years, and then became busy again, and only then Adam, our Father, was created.[27]

Ibn Babawai revealed a hadith in the book titled Tauhid issued by Imam Sidiq: "Do you think that God did not create other human beings besides you? Yes, for God's sake, He created thousands of other Adams, while you are the last Adam." (*Sharh Kabir li Nahja*), quoted by Muhammad Ibn 'Ali Al-Aqr, also states that there were thousands of Adams before Adam (our

---

[26] *Ibid.*
[27] *Ibid.* p.324.

Father). Shaykh Al-Akbar, the popular name of Ibn Arabi, in *Futuhat Al-Makkiya,* stated that forty years before Adam, the Father, there were other Adams.[28]

Despite this, Rashid Rida claimed that Abdu had two opinions on the Adam discourse.

1) Based on the visible meaning, *nafs wahida* is not Adam since this claim is in contradiction with scientific knowledge and history.
2) There is no definite text (*qat'iy*) in the Qur'an which states that all human beings originated from Adam, and Abdu stated that human beings are logical animals. (*hayawan natiq*).

This is not to suggest, though, that Abdu denied people's belief in Adam as the Father, because the Qur'an itself was not clear on this matter. Rashid Rida said that Abdu's view was often misunderstood, and that his stance was only that the textual basis was unclear and scientific views suggested that humanity had various origins.

To mediate his teacher's opinion, and take care that his teacher's views were not viewed as a deviation of Qur'anic teaching, Rashid Rida presented a moderate view. He maintained that the most accurate meaning of *nafs* is 'essence' (*mahiya*) or substance, and that the existence of humans is different to that of other creatures. God created human beings from one substance, whether or not that substance was started from Adam, as believed by the majority.[29]

He concluded that human beings were created from a single being: humanity (*insaniyya*), the tendency to strive for goodness and reject bad. This was his understanding of the meaning of *nafs wahida.*

SAYYID TABATABA'I

Sayyid Tabataba'i was a pioneer in the development of modern Shi'ite thinking. His great work was the book, *Mizan,* written in twenty volumes.

---

[28] *Ibid.* p.326.
[29] *Ibid.*

Among modern Shi'ite intellectuals, Tabataba'i is noted as an expert in Qur'anic exegesis. He is also highly respected by Sunni thinkers. His books are used for references among Sunnite Muslims, especially in Indonesia.

According to Tabataba'i, linguistically speaking, *nafs wahida* refers to Adam, and humanity was created from Adam's single being. Eve was then created from Adam. Adam and Eve are the father and mother of all human beings. This kind of interpretation, according to Tabataba'i, was in line with the literal interpretation of the Qur'an as noted in the chapter Al-Nisa' (4) verse 1, Al-Zumar (39) verse 6, Al-A'raf (7) verse 27 and Al-Isra' (17) verse 62.

Tabataba'i criticized many *tafsir* experts, and argued instead that the phrase *nafs wahida* and the word *wa zaujaha* mean that all human existence derives from Man and Woman, both of whom have important functions, neither of which is higher than the other. This is in line with the God's word: "Oh mankind! I created you from male and female, and made you into nations and tribes, that you may know one another." (QS. Al-Hujurat (49):13).

According to Tabataba'i, these opinions were not acceptable since both verses have differences. The chapter Al-Hujurat, verse 13 explains the unity of humanity, based on its essential humanity (*haqiqa al-insaniya*), and thus negates the differences among them by stating that all originated from the same Father and Mother. So, there is no honor, except in their obedience to God. Meanwhile, the chapter Al-Nisa', verse 1, according to Tabataba'i, claims that humanity is made from substance. Humankind, spread throughout the world, both men and women, originated from the One. They formed groups and nations from *mansha* (their place of origin), which is also singular. Then, they grew larger, and became many, as stated in the verse: "...and from them both He created many men and women..." (Al-Nisa' 4:1). An understanding that analogizes the chapter Al-Nisa', verse 1, with Al-Hujurat, verse 13, is not in accordance with the aim of the gardu Al-Sura text.

According to Tabataba'i, Eve was created from part of Adam's body, which he claims is supported by the chapter Al-Rum (30), verse 21; Al-Nahl (16), verse 72; Al-Surah Al-Shura (42), verse 11; and Al-Dzariat (51), verse 49.

Such is Tabataba'i's position on Al-Nisa' and on the creation of woman. Although Tabataba'i is a contemporary expert among Shi'ite *ulamas*, his interpretation was not so different from those of more conservative Shi'ite *ulamas*.[30] He still used grammatical and historical methods that carry deep patriarchal nuances.

Nonetheless, all the interpretations discussed above are open to criticism as they are a product of their times, and are not the word of the Qur'an, which should not itslef become a closed text. Al-Qur'an is a 'traveling text', aimed towards the improvement of humanity.

INTERPRETIVE CRITICISM

In this work of interpretive criticism, I will review the conclusions of the *ulamas* mentioned above. It is important to be clarify that the criticism is not aimed to challenge the 'truth' of the Qur'an as a religious text, revealed to the Prophet, but on the interpretations made afterwards and the methodologies used to make them.

I will split this exercise into two themes:

1) Criticism of the long-standing methodologies used by *tafsir* experts.
2) Criticism of the content of their interpretations, particularly relating to the phrase *nafs wahida* (as 'single being') and the assumption that "Eve is created from Adam." This criticism is not only addressed to the five *tafsir* experts discussed above, but also to the general Qur'anic interpretations that carry the same nuances. Each of the five *tafsir* is just one example, and each interpretation has its own *raison d'etre.*

CRITICISM OF INTERPRETATIVE METHODOLOGIES

The methodology of interpretation (*manhaj*) is one means used by *tafsir* experts in interpreting Qur'anic verse. The methodology developed and changed from time to time. During the life of the Prophet Muhammad, the interpretation of the Qur'an was the authority of the Prophet or close friends legitimized by him. After the Prophet Muhammad's death, his close friends innovatively used Arabic poems and pre-Islamic books as the basis of their

---

[30] *Ibid.* p.134-9.

interpretations. Methodologically, this kind of interpretation is called *tafsir bi al-ma'thur*. (tafsir which based on hadiths)

The *bi al-ma'thur* approach is no longer considered to be sufficient to face the challenges of the changing times. An alternative method emerged along side it; interpretation based on *naql* (texts) and reasoning (*bi al-ra'yi*). *Tafsir* experts called this method *tafsir bi al-ra'yi*. (tafsir which is based on hadiths & reason)

The methodology of *tafsir* is now developing rapidly. There are the thematic method (*maudhu'i*), analytical method (*tahlili*), Sufi method (*Al-Ishari*), scientific method (*'ilmi*), and so on. These are all developments from the two earlier methods.[31]

In my view, on the interpretation of the chapter Al-Nisa', verse 1, only one method of the five experts discussed above shows signs of liberal thought. This is the method used by Muhammad Abdu and Rashid Rida in *Al-Manar*, which is more scientific and logically acceptable when compared with the other four.

I will now borrow a methodology developed by Riffat Hassan, in order to view the interpretations from a female perspective. So far, the *tafsir* we have discussed have shared a patriarchal bias, but we have nonetheless still used a methodology developed by that same patriarchy. Methodology can not be neutral.

Riffat Hassan is a Pakistani-born feminist whose interpretive methodology will reveal the weaknesses of the five interpretations above. The methodology has three stages:

1) Linguistic accuracy: to check that the terms or concepts used in the *tafsir* are based on the original contextual meanings of the language, culturally, politically as well as theologically.

2) Philosophical consistency: to assess the consistency between different verses.

3) Ethical criteria: to assess whether the interpretation considered ethical criteria.[32]

---

[31] A history of interpretation was written by Muhammad Hushain Al-Dzahabi in two thick volumes entitled *Al-Tafsir wa Al-Muffasirun*. These books are the first to completely discuss the history of the development of interpretation since the era of the Prophet until the modern day. Besides this, the book also categorized forms of interpretation.

[32] Riffat Hassan, *Women's Interpretation of Islam, Women and Islam in Muslim Societies*, The Hague: Poverty and Development, 1994, p.116.

In terms of linguistic accuracy, interpretations by the experts of *tafsir* of Al-Nisa', verse 1, except Abdu and Rashid Rida (in *Al-Manar*), showed inaccuracy in language application. The phrase *nafs wahida*, based on Arabic terms, should be treated as a feminine form (*mu'annath*), both the spirit and the material. But for the *ulamas* it was viewed as a masculine form (*mudzakkar*), which means Adam. Although Muslim feminists generally do not hold the pretension that the first creation of God was feminine (*mu'annath*), they question the transformation of *nafs wahida* as (*marja'*) in reference to a personal pronoun (*dlamir*) ha, which has the ability to transform the feminine into masculine. How is it possible that the application of Arabic grammatical order can occur like this?

These issues should have been considered by the *ulamas*, such as Imam Zamakhshari who was known as an expert in Arabic linguistic and grammar. But Zamakhshari himself seemed not to have been interested in clarifying the matter. Although many *ulamas* tried to explain it on a linguistic basis, they all seem to have shared a patriarchal bias.

One such expert was Al-Razi. According to Al-Razi, it was applicable in pre-Islamic tradition, such as poetry, that masculine forms become an adjective of feminine form. Some *ulamas* said that the masculine could also become a feminine word (*dhamir*), but this applied only in abnormal situations or *shadz*, meaning 'applicable but not common'. This reasoning, although rational, shouldn't just be accepted. Perhaps God offered this grammatical dilemma for it to be solved. God intentionally created the phrase consisting of *mu'annath* and *mudzakkar* to show that human beings originated from both male and female. In Rashid Rida's terms, this was called *insaniya*, an opinion similar to Abdu's statement that the verse is intentionally addressed in a *ibham* (blurred/undercover) form by God.

Ibham is used to correct older scriptures, including the Old and New Testaments, which both state that human beings were created from Man (Adam). The Qur'an, however, offers an ambiguous phrase, suggesting that humankind was created from two substances, male and female.

Secondly, there are several philosophical inconsistencies in the reasoning of these *tafsir* experts. We should not look to only one verse of the Qur'an, but seek other discussions of Adam in other verses. Consistency in interpretation is useful because the style of the Qur'an is not chronologically structured like the Bible. The Creation story in the Qur'an is found not only in Al-Nisa', verse 1, but also in thirty other verses. According to Riffat Hassan's study, there are three terms which are used to refer to humanity (*al-Nas, basyar* and *al-insan*), all of which do not go back to a male being. So we have no reason to say that Adam was a male being, rather than just a *human* being.

Thirdly, there is an ethical problem, as these *ulamas* did not fulfill Islamic ethical criteria for justice and equality, as reflected in the Qur'an itself. Their interpretations of *nafs wahida* as Adam implies an unjust gender perspective. And more worryingly, the suggestion in Al-Nisa' that Woman was created from Man is used as the main basis for the interpretation of other verses, and women's practical subordination to men.

WOMEN'S POSITION IN HADITH

Hadith is a major source for Islamic teaching, although it is one level lower than the Qur'an. Hadith are reports of the Prophet Muhammad's activities. Due to its high status, hadith can influence Muslim conduct in full obedience without questioning its validity. Not all the hadith, however, are direct reports on the sayings and doings of the Prophet, which there are several names for types of hadith, such as *dhai'if* (weak), *maudhu* (made/fake), or *sahih* (legitimate). Many hadith that were unquestionable in the past may now be challenged by current standards and criteria. Many of the hadith regarding women are now being so questioned by certain parties.

HADITH ON THE DIVINE CREATION OF WOMEN

In our reading of the Qur'an, we found no strong indication that Adam was the first male person, and that Eve was created from him. Although many *ulamas* interpret the phrase *nafs wahida* as Adam, a male being, current studies show that the origin of the word Adam was borrowed by the Arabic language from a Hebrew root, *'adama*, which means earth. The word Adam appears in the Qur'an twenty-five times, although twenty-one of these instances uses the word as a reference to conscious humanity.[33]

---

[33] Riffat Hassan, *Women's Rights and Islam: From the ICPD to Beijing*.p.5

As suggested by Muhammad Iqbal, in the Qur'an, 'Adam' does not refer to a particular human being. Iqbal claimed that the verses describing the origin of human creation used the words *al-insan* or *bashar*, instead of Adam. The use of Adam is more suitable as a concept, instead of a name of a concrete person.[34]

The problem remains, though, why Muslims believe that Eve was created from Adam's rib?

There are three myths among Muslims relating to Adam and Eve.

1) Adam was the first man, created by God, and Eve was created from Adam's rib.
2) Although Eve was the first woman created by God, she was the first who made the error that caused the fall from Heaven.
3) Woman is not only created from Man, but also for Man, meaning that she is subordinate and inessential.

These three myths are still deeply rooted in the mind of the Muslim community. The Qur'an never clearly states these matters. Their source is hadith, not the Qur'an.

I will now explain the contents of two important hadith: *Sahih Bukhari* and *Sahih Muslim*.

1. Both Abu Khuraib and Abu Hizam said, after being told by Husain ibn Ali from Za'idah and Maisara Al-Ashja'i from Abi Hazim from Abu Huraira, that the Prophet Muhammad said: "Speak nicely to women since a woman is created from a rib and the rib, which is the most curved, is the upper part. If you straighten it, you will break it up. But if you leave it, it will still be curved. So, speaks nicely to her." (Bukhari).
2. Narrated by 'Abd Al-Aziz ibn 'Abdilla from Malik from Abi Zinad from A'raj from Abu Huraira: the Prophet said: "Woman is like a rib, if you try to straighten it, it would break it up. So, if you want to take advantage of her, just take it but leave her curved." (Bukhari)

---

[34] M. Iqbal, *The Reconstruction of Religious Thought in Islam*, Lahore, 1962, p.83.

3. Narrated by Ishak Ibn Nasar from what Hasan ibn Ja'fi has told us from Za'ida from Maisara from Abu Hazim from Abu Huraira, the Prophet said: "Those who believe in God and the Hereafter, do not hurt neighbors and speak to women goodly. Actually, they are created from a rib, a most curved bone. If you want to straighten it, you will break it up and if you leave it, it will still be curved. So speak goodly to women." (Bukhari).

4. Narrated by Harmala ibn Yahya from Ibn Wahhab, I had been told by Yunus from Sihab, I have been told by Ibn Mussyab from Abu Huraira, the Prophet said: "The woman is like a rib, if you tried to straighten it, you would break it up, and if you wanted to take advantage (pleasure) from her, she would still be curved." (Muslim).

5. Narrated by Amru Naqid and Ibn Abi Umar from Sufyan from Abi Zinad from A'raj from Abu Huraira, the Prophet said: "Really, woman is created from a rib and you would be able to straighten it in just one way. If you want to take advantage from her, take it and she will still be curved. If you want to straighten it, you would break it up, breaking up mean divorce her." (HN Muslim).

6. Narrated from by Abu Bakar ibn Abi Shaiba, from Hussain ibn Ali from Zaida from Maisara from Abu Hazim from Abu Huraira, the Prophet said: "Those who believe in God and the Final day, if they face problems, they should speak in good terms and carefully. If you tried to straighten it, you will break it up. If you leave it, it will still be curved, so speak goodly to women." (Muslim).

The six hadiths above are still used by *ulamas* to this day as the basis for tracing the origin of the creation of women. Based on theological history, the inferior status of women in Islamic tradition – as happened in Jewish and Christian traditions – started from hadiths (about the creation of Eve). The issue of the creation of women, theologically, is more fundamental that others. If we hold this view that Man and Woman were created equally by God – as is stated in the Qur'an – inequality between Man and Woman could not be seen as God's gift, but as a subversion of God's plan for human beings.

According to several studies, the hadiths were influenced by earlier religions, such as Judaism and Christianity, which have a gender-bias. These biases were mixed up with pre-Islamic Arab traditions and the heritage of ancient Greek dualism, which maintains that men are rational and women are emotional in their conduct.

MORE INTERPRETIVE CRITICISM

Doing interpretive criticism on hadiths, we must consider the whole body of hadith which consists of *matn*: the content of the hadith; and *Isnad*: which consists of the names those who issued the hadith, which, theoretically, should reach the Prophet.

According to Riffat Hassan, the sixth *matn* of the hadiths mentioned above were influenced by a story about the rib noted in the Bible, Book of Genesis 1: 26-27 and 2: 18-24. As quoted by Riffat Hassan:

> God said, let us see Adam in our image, in likeness of ourselves and let them be master of fish and sea. God created Adam in an image of God, he created it male and female.

The Book of Genesis 2: 18-24 contains the story that God created Adam, but since Adam felt alone, God tried to find him a companion. God made Adam sleep and took his rib to create Eve from it. When Adam saw Eve, he felt happy and claimed that Eve came from his own flesh and bone.

Although it is said that the five books (articles) of the Bible were written by Moses, many experts do not believe that it was written by Moses or any single person. Its different parts are attributed to different authors, and the two Creation stories in Genesis, Chapters 1 and 2 are attributed to two separate authors, although their true identities are unknown as they used code names. The first writer is thought to have been a priest, writing five centuries before Christ. The second story is attributed to a Hebrew writer.

The stories have had a huge impact on Christian tradition since they had been used by the founders of the tradition to reduce women's status in relation to men. St Paul, for example, who played a very important role in establishing Christian tradition, said that the God is the source of Christ, and God is the leader of Christ; Christ is a leader for all men, and men are the leaders for women. For a man, worshipping with a covered head is disrespectful of God, while for a woman, worshiping without a veil is disrespectful.

> Men, of course, do not cover their heads since they are created in God's image and show God's greatness while a woman is a shadow of man's greatness. A man does not come from a woman while a woman comes from a man; and a man is not created for woman's pleasure but a woman is created for man's pleasure.
>
> Kor 11: 8-9

Thus is the hierarchy in Christian tradition: God, Christ, Man, and last of all – Woman.

What is happened in Christian tradition also happened in Islamic tradition. What Prof. Leonard Zwidler meant in his article, 'Jesus was a Feminist' was that Jesus respected and viewed men and women equally, but that St Paul and other early Church leaders were deeply gender biased.

In Islam, the hadiths are used as a lens through which to read the Qur'an, but the hadiths themselves contain many distortions of the meaning of the Qur'an. Despite this fact, Islamic culture is very derivative and depends more heavily on the hadiths than the Qur'an, even though many were not the actual sayings of the Prophet.

The implementation of allegorical interpretive method (*majazi*) was not easily conducted to these matters. It is clear that the rib story developed in pre-Islamic as well as Islamic traditions. It is not possible that it entered Islam through the revelation of the Qur'an, but rather through the codification of the hadiths, which were compiled long after the death of the Prophet. According to Riffat Hassan, the rib story entered Islamic thinking at the beginning of the Hijriah century. It is very difficult to say whether it was taken directly from the Book of Genesis, but it is very possible that its reading was influential. So, it is not impossible that the hadiths mentioned above are weak in their *matn*, if not actually invalid.

There is a system by which to resolve contradictions between the hadith and the Qur'an. This is called *ta'arudh*. If no compromise can be reached, then the Qur'an succeeds the hadith. Since there is no suggestion in the Qur'an that Eve was created from Adam's rib, the Qur'anic version should be upheld. There is an even more extreme view that any hadith that contradict the Qur'an should be considered false or *maudhu*.

Isnad, the chain of individuals through which hadiths are transmitted, can also be criticized. It should only be the first individuals who had contact with the Prophet who should have responsibility for the content of the hadith. Criticism of *Isnad* is very sensitive and can lead to controversy since it relates to people who were believed to be close the Prophet and who were some of the most respected people in the sect of *Ahl al-Sunna wal Jama'a*. This issue seems to be related to Abu Huraira. With the six most misogynistic hadiths, besides *Sunan Ibnu Maja*, the chain of narration ends with Abu Huraira, particularly in *Sahihain*, the two books of *Sahih* by Imam Bukhari and Muslim. Both these books are highly respected by Muslims and can be said to be one level lower than the Qur'an itself.

Bukhari's full name was Abu Abdilla Muhammad ibn Ismail ibn Ibrahim ibn Al-Mughira ibn Bazdiyah Al-Ja'fi Al-Bukhari. He was born on a Friday (*sayyidul ayyam:the leader of days*), 13 Shawal, 194 H in Bukhara. He started his studies at an early age (205 H), and went on the pilgrimage to Mecca with his parents. He enthusiastically collected hadiths from regions that had some connection with the Prophet, such as Baghdad, Basrah, Kufa, Mecca, Medina, Shams, Khums, Asqolan and Egypt. He is said to have written hadiths from more than a thousand teachers. Bukhari memorized more than one hundred thousand *sahih* hadiths, and two hundred thousand non-*sahih* hadiths, which is why he was called a leader among believers (*amir al-mukminin:leader of believers*) in the field of hadiths.

Imam Muslim's full name was Hujjatul Islam Abul Husain Muslim ibn Al-Hujaj Al-Qushairi Al-Naisaburi. He was born in 204 H. Imam Muslim started studying with several noted hadith experts when he was a child. He visited several major Islamic cities including Baghdad, Hijaz, Shams and countries, such as Iraq and Egypt. Among hadith experts, his work, *Sahih Muslim*, is considered to be one level below *Sahih Bukhari*.

Despite their seriousness and accomplishment as hadith narrators, they were not immune to human weaknesses and error.

So what was it with Abu Huraira? It is no accident that all six misogynistic hadiths were narrated by Abu Huraira, whose background we will now explore.

Abu Huraira was a member of the Yaman tribe in the area of Daws. Once called the "The Slave of the Sun", he converted to Islam at the age of thirty. The Prophet Muhammad called him 'Abdullah and Abu Huraira due to his habit of walking around with small female cats. He did not like the feminine implications of his name. Someday, he said, "Do not call me Abu Huraira since the Prophet called me with Abu Hirr because male is better than female." According to Fatima Mernissi, Abu Huraira was over-sensitive about femininity because he had no traditionally masculine employment.

In Medina's relatively prosperous economy, it seemed Abu Huraira was more interested in helping household of the Prophet, along with the women. Abu Huraira once narrated a hadith which stated that the Prophet had once said that a female cat is worthier than a woman. It is said that A'isya heard this and made a direct response.

> Abu Huraira," she asked, "was it you who reported that you once heard the Prophet saying that a woman will go to hell if she neglects a female cat in hunger and gives it nothing to drink?"
> "I heard the prophet say that," Abu Huraira replied.
> "A Muslim believer is worthy in the eyes of God" said A'isya. "How could He give punishment because of a cat? Abu Huraira, if you want to quote the Prophet's words, you should be more careful with your own words.

This was just one of the hadiths issued by Abu Huraira that resulted in conflict with A'isya, the Prophet's bright young wife. According to Mernissi, A'isya claimed that Huraira was not a keen listener and was often mistaken in his accounts. This is, of course, highly relevant since he was responsible for transmitting some of the most misogynistic hadiths, and became a key figure in the dominant school of Islamic orthodoxy, *Ahl al-Sunna wal Al-Jama'a*.

But given the critiques offered above, Abu Huraira's credibility seems to be limited. While the Prophet was alive, He closely supervised his aides, but by the time the hadiths were being written down, they were open to human error. The various Shi'ah sects considered his hadiths to be weak and unreliable, whereas the Sunni sects, that put far greater importance on the close followers of the Prophet, did not start to criticize his writings until later.

The hadiths by Abu Huraira were considered to be gharib, the lowest level of hadith, because of their sole narrator. They were also considered weak (*dhaif*) because the chain of narrators were people who could not be trusted, such as Maisara Al-Ashja'i, Harmala ibn Yahya and Za'ida also Abu Zinad. In general A'isya's powers of memory and recital are considered to be more reliable than Abu Huraira's, and therefore her criticism of his hadith and personality has been influential.

CHAPTER THREE

THE HISTORICAL DEVELOPMENT OF FIQH AND ITS PATRIARCHAL TENDENCIES

PATRIARCHAL *FIQH*: A STUDY

The term 'patriarchal *fiqh*' may sound unfamiliar to us as it is not found in the classical Islamic references. 'Patriarchy', meaning the rule of the 'father', has negative connations for many, as it suggests a system of rule by and for men only.

Hibbah Ra'uf 'Izzat, in his book *al-Mar'a wa al-Amal al-Siyasi, Ru'yatun Islamiyatun*, said that patriarchy (*hukm al-abi*) was a Roman concept, by which the male head of the household had absolute power over all its other members.[1] This power included legal matters, expenditure and the arrangement of childrens' marriages.[2]

The concept was used by a British intellectual, Robert Vilmer, in the seventeenth century to analyze the legal system. He stated that the legal system at that time was applied by judges acting in the same manner as a father acting in his household.[3]

---

[1] Hibbah Ra'uf Izzat, *al-Mar'a wa al-Amal al-Siyasi, Rukyatun Islamiyatun*, al-Ma'had al-Alami li al-Fikr al-Islam, 1990, 1st ed. p.203.

[2] *Ibid.*

[3] *Ibid.* See also Aelen Tiermey (ed.) *Women Studies Encyclopedia, View from the Sciences*, New York, Greenwood Press, 1989, Vol, I pp.265-6, Seldon, *op. cit.*, pp.131-4.

The term is now also used beyond sociology, in fields including theology and, in the context of Islam, in *fiqh*. In Islamic discourse the term applies to theological and socio-religious attitudes that are male-focused. Riffat Hassan, for example, used the term 'patriarchal theology' in her writings.

My own study uses the concept to analyze *fiqh*, which is a male discourse. But to challenge *fiqh* is to challenge a great tradition upheld by Muslims over the centuries. *Fiqh* is rarely questioned as other branches of theology are, for instance. And therefore it has evolved more slowly.

There are also technical problems to consider since theoretically (*usuliya*), the term was not established in classical Islamic literature. The term *fiqh al-abawi*, the Arabic translation of 'patriarchal *fiqh*', is unknown in the literature.

Historically speaking, *fiqh* was not established not only to implement the messages of the Qur'an and the hadiths in practice, but there were also many subjective and ideological factors involved. Although *fiqh* began as a religious call, there were also many interventions in terms of cultural and political values.

Al-Mawardi's construction of his political *fiqh* (*fiqh al-siyasa*) in the popular book, *al-Ahkam al-Sultaniyya*, for example, was different from that of Ibn Taymiyya, who implemented the hard-line *fiqh* of the Hambalite school. Although their motivations were the same – they were trying to actualize the values of *siyasa al-Islamiya* (political Islam) in a realistic and empirical formulation – they were both also different from al-Ghazali. All three were not only influenced *li l-Lahi-ta'ala* (only for God), but also had secular motivations.

It may seem disturbing to consider that such great *ulamas* had vested interests, but many were attached to the leanings of particular parties and sects. For example, Nasr Hamid Abu Zayd, an Egyptian intellectual who wrote *Imam Shafi'i wa Idiulujiya al-Wasatiya*, was severely challenged by many *ulamas*, because they thought that he had not paid enough respect to the great innovators, of shafi'i as well as some problems with his formulation of law. Another area where such vested interests, along the lines of race, ethnicity and other subjective matters, was when the *fiqh* experts decided which foods would be legal for eating, and which would be unlawful. Local Arab traditions were taken into account in the formulation of a religious law. Similar patterns occured in the formulation of *fiqh* regarding women.

My argument will be based on the notion of 'social engineering'. This situation was admitted by the *ulamas* of *Usul al-Fiqh* as the principle of "*al-hukmu yadurru maʿa illatihi*": that a law is based on its particular reasons (*illat*). Reasons are varied, and can be based on racial, ethnic, sociological, cultural, as well as religious reasons. It is still considered deviant to criticize the great *ulamas* of the past, perhaps we may even be criticized for being unIslamic. Many would say: "The cleverest people of today are not as smart as Imam Shafi'i."

Reluctance to criticize creates stasis in thought. Islamic culture differs from Western culture in that criticism and liberalism is not encouraged. Although orthodox dogmatism considers criticism to be unethical, it often helps to reveal truth.

Let us return to the complex problem of how far the patriarchal perspective has penetrated the configuration of *fiqh* discourse.

For a simple illustration, we can take a statement from an important *fiqh* book that quotes Abu Laith on the benefits and problems of gatherings of eight people.

1) Those who gather with rich people, God makes them love the world – a view disliked by Sufis.
2) Those who gather with poor people, God gives thankfulness and blessings. This stance was considered to be a backward step by modern people as it has no creativity (*ikhtiyar*).
3) Those who gather with kings, God makes arrogant and angry.
4) Those who gather with women, God makes stupid and lustful.
5) Those who gather with children, God gives a childish attitude.
6) Those who sit together with sinful people, God gives courage to commit sinful things.
7) Those who sit together with good people (*salihin*), God gives obedience.
8) Those who gather with *ulamas*, God offers knowledge and good conduct.[4]

---

[4] Quoted from *Bujairimi ʿala al-Iqna* by Shaykh Abdurrahim ibn Muhammad ibn Hussain ibn Umar, a *mufthi* of Hadramauth, in *Bughyat al-Mustarshidin*, p.5.

Abu Laiths' formula is interesting on two counts. Firstly, people who sit together with women are made stupid and lustful. Secondly, on the category of pious or *saleh* people, he uses the *jama mudzakar* (masculine plural) form *salim salihin* without mentioning the term *salihat* (good female).

These examples are a common reality of the image of women in *fiqh* and other classical texts. Why do women inherit stupidity (*al-jahla*)?

There is a common assumption that the intellectual grade of women is lower than men's. This assumption is based on a hadith of the Prophet: "*al-nisa'u naqisatun dinun wa aqlun*, women lack of reason and religiosity." Without careful checking of the hadith, it might be concluded that women are naturally stupid and that it is normal that she inherits stupidity. Second, to sit together with a woman could create lust and it could disturb man's clear reasoning since he would only think about making love with her.

Then, why good people are formed in the masculine form, *salihin*? Surely 'piety' has no gender? This assumption shows a narrowing of the meaning of piety as written in the Qur'an. Although there were thousands of pious women in Abu Laits' time, he used the patriarchal structures of his era. Similarly, in the introduction of *fiqh* books, for instance, there are always prayers for conservative classical *ulemas*, *salihin* and *mu'minin*. It is rare or almost impossible to read *mu'annath* (feminine forms) such as *salihat* and *mu'minat* as a subject of admiration in these books. This is influenced by Arabic grammatical rules. In Arabic grammar, this phenomenon is called *li taghlib*, meaning that if a form is both masculine and feminine, it is enough to represent it with the masculine form.

FIQH AS A MALE DISCOURSE: A HISTORICAL STUDY

The development of Islamic law and *fiqh* is still debated by Muslim intellectuals up to this day. Although it is still uncertain, Joseph Schacht developed a thesis – based on the work of two previous Western scholars, Snouck Hurgronje and Ignaz Goldziher – that claimed Islamic law was born in the second century H. According to Schacht, it was not the Prophet Muhammad who developed Islamic law, but jurists who appointed during the reign of the Ummayad dynasty. These jurists transformed the popular administration into Islamic laws.[5]

According to Schacht, the Prophet Muhammad was not interested in developing law, since throughout his lifetime, the Prophet played more political and military roles. His position as the messenger also gave him a role in creating laws.[6] Schacht said the Prophet's mission was not formulating a system of law, but teaching people how to conduct themselves in order to saved on the Final Day.

The most shocking aspect of Schacht's thesis was his claim that Islamic law was first developed at the end of the Umayyad dynasty and the beginning of the Abbasid dynasty. Responses to Schacht came not only from Muslim intellectuals, but also from other orientalists. According to Layish, for example, Schacht's study related not to jurisprudence and theology, but to pure history and sociology. Islamic laws were not treated by Schacht as a unity of legal norms, but as a historical phenomenon rooted in its social reality.[7] M.M. al-Azami criticized Schacht because he neglected evidence of Islamic laws in the Qur'an, which is an already established source.[8] Sharp criticism also came from Islamists, such as Gotein, Ostorog, David S. Power, J. Coulson and others. Most of them criticized Schacht for underestimating the Qur'an, especially verses related to *al-ahkam* (laws). However, Schacht's study opened new horizons on Islamic law studies, because he was the first Western scholar to discuss Islamic law based on history and sociology. There is a contrary view, however, that claims that *fiqh* developed long before the Abbasid period, during the time of the Prophet.

The meaning of *fiqh*, based on the Arabic lexicology, means 'understanding' or 'knowledge'. According to al-Zuhaili, *fiqh* means all understanding, either narrow or deep. In Arabic tradition, the term *fiqh* was used to refer to special expertise, such as camel breeding. It was used in this context by Al-Tha'labi (died 429 H) to name his book, *Fiqh al-Lughah*, which had no relation to Islamic law, but which dealt with Arabic grammar (Nahwu). During pre-Islamic era, *Fiqh al-arab* (Figh of Arab) was a name given to al-Harit ibn *Kalada*.[9]

---

[5]   Faisar Ananda Arfa "Debate on the Birth of Islamic Law," *Ulumul Qur'an*, No. 1 Vol. IV, 1995 p.52.
[6]   Joseph Schacht, *Introduction to Islamic Law*, (Indonesiann edition), Jakarta:Departement of Religion, 1985, p.15.
[7]   Faisar Ananda Arfa, *op.cit.*, p.5.
[8]   *Ibid*.
[9]   Ahmad Hasan, *Pintu Ijtihad Belum Tertutup*, Bandung Pustaka, 1984, First Edition, p.1.

In the Qur'an, the term *fiqh*, meaning 'to understand', is used more than once. In the verse: *li yatafaqqahu fi al-din* indicates that it is not only legal term, but has a more general meaning in Islam. It was often used by *ulamas* in the sense of: *targib wa tarhib* (suggestion to do good) in the search for knowledge. Al-Ghazali, in *Ihya Ulum al-Din*, also quoted this verse when discussing the excellence of sciences.

The Prophet Muhammad once used the term *fiqh* when he prayed for Ibn Abbas (died 68 H), saying: *"O' Allah, give him understanding in religion."*

In its wider use, the term *fiqh* also carried an ascetic meaning. An early Sufi, Farqad (died 131 H), held a debate with Hasan al-Basri (died 110 H) on a topic of whether *fiqh ulamas* should live ascetically or concentrate on the Hereafter, and their prayers for the community.

Based on Islamic historical notes, until the era of al-Ma'mun (died 218 H), *kalam* and *fiqh* sciences could not be separated. Even, the writing of Hanafi, *Fiqh Al-Akhbar*, is not only a treaty on Islamic jurisprudence, but also discusses theology (*kalam*). Hanafi defined *fiqh* as the knowledge for people to know their rights and obligations.[10]

According to Al-Zuhaili, Hanafi's definition is a *shar'iyya* definition. Al-Zuhaili said that knowledge (*ma'rifa*), in Hanafi's definition, is a partial understanding (*juz'iyat*), but could be applied to many aspects of religious law.[11]

The term *'ilm* also carries the meaning of 'knowledge', in a comprehensive sense. After the Prophet's era, the meanings of the terms *'ilm* and *fiqh* changed. *Fiqh* was often used to describe intelligence, while *'ilm* was used to refer to knowledge about tradition, the Sunna and hadiths.[12]

Eventually, *fiqh* and *'ilm* got specific meanings. There is another term, *shari'a*, which is difficult to differentiate from *fiqh*, in that it means 'Islamic law'. The Qur'an uses the terms *shir'a* and *shari'a* as a form of religion (*din*), while *shara'* was used during the Prophet's era to define principles of Islamic teachings, such as *salat*, *zakat*, and *hajj*.[13]

---

[10] In Arabic: *"ma'rifatu al-nafs ma laha wama alaiha."* See Al-Zuhaili, *Al-Fiqh Al-Islam wa Adillatuhu*, Damascus: Dar al-Fikr, 1983, Second Edition, p.15.

[11] Al-Zuhaili, *al-Fiqh al-Islam wa Adillatuhu*, p.5.

[12] Ahmad Hassan, *op. cit.*, p.4.

[13] *Ibid.*, p.7.

On this basis, it can be said that *fiqh* has been known since the time of the Prophet and His companions. The need for *fiqh* was the need to arrange social life, and to know rights and obligations in religion.[14] Al-Zuhaili stated that *fiqh* was the practical aspect of *shari'a*, which was itself determined by God through the Qur'an and Sunna.

Following Abu Hanifa, *fiqh* was used as a distinct discipline of knowledge relating to religious practice.

IMAM ABU HANIFA

Montgomery Watt claimed that the first and most important contribution to Islamic jurisprudence happened in the areas of Kufa and Medina. There was a dynamic period of intellectual activity at the end of the Umayyad period until the early Abbasid period. Abu Hanifa was an important figure in this development. Throughout his life, Abu Hanifa lived in Kufa as a farmer and silk merchant.[15] He grew up in a family that had a silk business.[16]

To begin with, Abu Hanifa concentrated his studies on memorizing the Qur'an, in the usual study cycle of a formulator and codifier of Islamic laws of that time. His teacher, Imam 'Ashim, taught him the seven ways of reading the Qur'an (*qira'ah sab'ah*). But Abu Hanifa's career started when he started to study *kalam* (theology). His famous work, *Fiqh al-Akhbar*, was not a *fiqh* book in terms of legal knowledge, but dealt with laws in theology. The debating aspect of studying *fiqh* interested Abu Hanifa, and he approved of the way it was used in practice as well as theory, unlike theology. He employed scientific methods in his studies of *fiqh*, so he could assess the agreements and differences of the attitudes of the old *ulamas*.

Hanifa said: "I was once in the mine of knowledge and *fiqh* (Kufa). I sat down with the experts and I chose one of them to be my teacher." In Kufa, Abu Hanifa learned from Ali Ibn Abi Talib, Abdullah Ibn Mas'ud, and among the close companions of the Prophet. Among the *tabi'in* (most learned *ulamas*), he learned *fiqh* from Ibrahim Al-Nakha'i.

---

[14] Al-Zuhaili, *op. cit.*, p.18.
[15] Montgomery Watt, *The Majesty That was Islam*, U.K.: Edinburg University Press, 1961, pp.121-2.
[16] Muhammad ibn Abu Zahra, *Tarikh Madzahib al-Islamiyya*, p.346.

He concluded that there are at least three things that are important for people seeking knowledge. 1) They should live in a scholarly situation, conducive to learning. 2) They should gather with *ulamas*. If you want to be an *ulama*, you gather with *ulamas*; if want to be a thief, gather with thieves. 3) They should have teachers with the ability to supervise them.

Abu Hanifa found these three things in Kufa. As a city, Kufa was a breeding ground for theology and philosophy. Kufa could challenge Medina in studies of *fiqh*. In the city, noted *ulama* Ibrahim al-Nakha'i and his students developed the system of *qiyas* (analogy) methodology.

Abu Hanifa learnt *fiqh* from many teachers with various backgrounds. Some had a rational approach, while others used the *naql* (textual) approach, whether from the schools of Sunnite, Mu'tazilte and Shi'ite Islam. Ideologically, he favored four kinds of *fiqh*:

1) Fiqh Umar, which was developed on the basis of a principle of public welfare (*maslaha*).
2) Fiqh 'Ali, which was developed on the basis of *shari'a*.
3) Fiqh Abdullah Ibn Mas'ud, which was developed on the basis of the *takhrij* principle of researching a particular hadith.
4) Fiqh Ibn Abbas, on the basis of the Qur'an. Ja'far al-Mansur once asked Nu'man (another name of Abu Hanifa): "Nu'man, where did you get your *fiqh* knowledge?" He answered: "From Umar, through his friend, from Ali, through his friend, from Abdulla Ibn Mas'ud, through his friend, nobody on this earth is smarter than Ibn Abbas."

Nonetheless, the only teacher he was really close to was Hammad Ibn Abi Sulaiman. Hamad studied *fiqh* with Ibrahim al-Nakha'i and al-Shi'bi. From these two, Hammad studied with Suraih al-Qadi, Alqamah Ibn Qais and Masruq Ibn al-Ajda, who studied *fiqh* from the close aides of the Prophet, Abdulla Ibn Mas'ud and Ali. Then, through Hammad, Abu Hanifa studied *fiqh* from his close friends and *ulamas*.

Before the founding of the four schools of *fiqh* (*mudzahib al-arba'a*), Islamic discourse recognized only two schools. The first, rationalism, tended to use logic in solving legal problems and was often called *ahl al-ra'yi*. The second, traditionalism, tended to use tradition (hadith texts), and was often called *ahl al-naql.*

Genealogically, Abu Hanifa's intellectual development was influenced by the emphasis on high rationalism in Kufa, which had a reputation almost equal to that of Medina, despite the scarcity of hadiths. Due to the limited number of hadiths, *ulamas* in Kufa often used logical processes (*ra'yu*) in their studies.

The companion of the Prophet's who first supported rationalism was Abdulla Ibn Mas'ud. He had close friends, such as Alqama ibn Qais al-Nakha'i (d. 62 H), al-Aswad Ibn Yazid al-Nakha'i (d. 75 H), Masruq (d. 63 H), Shuraih (d. 82 H), al-Harith Al-Anwar (d. 81 H) who were all experts in *fiqh.* The school of rationalism was led by Ibrahim Al-Nakha'i before it was taken over by Abu Hanifa.[17]

Abu Hanifa's intellectual success was not replicated in his political life. He lived through two major dynasties and witnessed the succession of the Abbasid dynasty over the Umayyad. He was sympathetic to the Zaidiyya Shi'ite group, although he did not join it. When Zaid Ibn Ali fought Hisham Ibn Abdul Malik in Kufa, he analogized Zaid as the Prophet. It is said that Abu Hanifa donated ten thousand dinnar for Zaid's troops. He felt during Abassid dynasty, there was no figure who understood how to manage an administration. He considered Zaid to be a leader.

Zaid's rebellion ended with his death in 122 H. Zaid was replaced by his son Yahya in 125 H in Khurasan, and he went on to conduct a rebellion against the Umayyad dynasty. Like his father, Yahya was killed. Alawid dynasty was then led by Abdulla Ibn Yahya who conducted a rebel against Umayyad dynasty in Yemen. But Marwan ibn Muhammad sent someone to kill him in 130 H. Along with many other *ulamas,* he disliked the cruelty of the Umayyad dynasty. He was offered a position handling state funds by the administration, but refused it. He was then arrested, imprisoned and tortured.

Abu Hanifa's suffering continued until the Abassid dynasty. In the beginning, he cooperated Abassid, but when there was a conflict between the authority and the Shi'ah, he grew angry. According to Abu Zahra, two rebels,

---

[17] Hasbi Al-Shiddieqi, *Pengantar Ilmu Fiqh,* p.100.

Al-Mansur Muhammad Al-Nafs Al-Zakkiya Ibn Abdilla Ibn Hasan and his brother Ibrahim, became Abu Hanifa's teachers. So, it is understandable that Abu Hanifa defended them.[18] Due to Abu Hanifa's association with them, Al-Mansur assigned people to spy on Abu Hanifa.

The conflict between Abu Hanifa and Al-Mansur continued until he was arrested. He was jailed and lashed ten times a day. On his release, the authorities still banned him from issuing religious decrees or teaching. Shortly after his release, Abu Hanifa passed away in 150 H. Before he died, he asked to be buried in *ghasab* land (land which was used without permit from its owner). He passed away as a *salihin* and *shuhada* (a pious person and a martyr).

Abu Hanifa's political life did not decrease the *ulama*'s respect for him. Some even called him a *wadi* (basic founder) of *fiqh*. Shafi'i once suggested that people who wanted to learn *fiqh* should study with Abu Hanifa. Abdulla Ibn Mubarak called him *"mukh al-ilmi"* due to his ability to penetrate the borders of sciences without distortion. Malik also appreciated his expertise in *fiqh*.

His *istinbat* (legal decision making) methodology can be viewed in his words: "First, I use God's book (the Qur'an). If I do not find the answer, I follow the deeds of the Prophet, and if I do not find it in the Qur'an and hadiths, I use his companion's explanations."
Abu Hanifa's methodology was based on seven principles:

1) The Qur'an is the pillar for all God's laws.
2) The Sunna of the Prophet which explains and details of the God's book.
3) The words of the close companions. The Prophet's close companions explained the Prophet's mission, and understood the relationship between the Qur'an and hadiths. Abu Hanifa did not include opinions of *tabi'in* (*ulamas* after the companions) in his legal decision-making.[19]
4) The legal principle of *qiyas* (analogy), a process of legal decision-making without a textual basis and working from analogy to similar problems.
5) The basic principle of *istihsan* (a juristic methode considering equity in applying the law). Among followers of Hanifite school, the *istihsan* method was used to solve new problems.

---

[18] Muhammad Abu Zahra, p.268.
[19] Muhammad Abu Zahra, p.372.

6) *Ijma"*, an agreement among *ulamas* of a certain period about specific problems. Almost all *fiqh* experts used *ijma"* as a legal basis, but some doubted that *ijma"* could be reached after the era of the Prophet's companions. Ahmad Ibn Hanbal insisted that it was impossible to reach an agreement after the era of the Prophet's companions.

7) The principle of *'urf* (customary laws). In daily language, *'urf* means 'tradition', and refers in the context of *fiqh* to the non-textual traditions of Muslims. There are two types of *'urf*: *urf sahih* (good customary law), not in contradiction to the Qur'an; and *'urf fasiq* (bad customary law), those that contradict the Qur'an.[20]

Alongside the above principles, Hanifa's thought on *fiqh* was greatly influenced by his daily life making transactions in the market as a trader. Hanafi used *'urf* and ihtihsan in his paradigm of how *fiqh* applied to the world of trade.

It is good to see how Abu Hanifa considered human rights in formulating his *fiqh*. 1) Making *ibada* (worship) and *mu'amala* (social obligation) easier. 2) Looking after the poor and *dhaif* (marginal). 3) Giving freedom of conduct, according to capability. 4) Maintaining human freedom and humanity. 5) Making sure leadership was dignified and obedient.[21]

Abu Hanifa was respected in intellectual circles as a serious thinker who got to the deeper meanings of a text. He was also known for his unwillingness to legitimize authority without thinking it through first. This was experienced by Hammad, who was often involved in debates with Abu Hanifa. Another characteristic of Abu Hanifa was his sincerity in seeking goodness, and his lack of personal ambition.

The use of rationalism in Hanifa's school caused its *fiqh* to be considered as liberal (*al-fiqh al-hurriya*). The liberal tendency enabled the legal processes to be more flexible. In his marriage *fiqh*, for example, Hanifa made a completely different legal decrees in opposition with the other three schools. He stated that women should not be forced to marry against their will, whereas the Shafi'i who allowed fathers to force their daughters to marry. Imam Malik and Ibn Hanbal shared a similar view with the Shafi'i.

---

[20] *Ibid*, p.372
[21] Harun Nasution et al, *Ensiklopedi Islam*, vol. I, p.397

In his *fiqh* on *mu'amala* (social obligations), Hanifa made a controversial decision. He disagreed with the ban that stated that mentally impaired people (*safi*) and forgetful people could not conduct trade. He maintained that all mature people had the right to spend their wealth and that any such prohibition was against human freedom.

Besides Dawud al-Dzahiri, Abu Hanifa was one of the *imams* who did not write large books, but concentrated on smaller works such as *Fiqh al-Akhbar*, *al-Alim wa al-Muta'allim*, letters to Uthman al-Buti and a paper rejecting the thinking of *Qadiriya* (Islamic sect that believe in the supremacy of human's capability). These papers, assuming they were really Abu Hanifa's works, were not *fiqh*, but *kalam* (theology). In *fiqh*, it was Abu Hanifa's students that codified his thoughts, in keeping with the oral tradition of the times.

The two students who did most in this regard were Ya'qub Ibn Ibrahim Ibn Habib al-Ansari, who was called Abu Yusuf, and Muhammad Ibn Hassan al-Shaibani, who have both come to be known as *fiqh* experts or *sahibani* (two companions) for their consistency in developing their teacher's thoughts.

Abu Yusuf wrote several books, including *Al-Athar*, a collection of Abu Hanifa's religious decrees (*fatwa*) which were narrated by Abu Yusuf from his father. The book has links leading back to the Prophet, his companions and *tabi'in*, including the *tabi'in* of Iraq. His other book, *Ikhtilaf Ibn Abi al-Laili*, described the differences between Abu Hanifa and another *qadi* (legal expert), Ibn Abi al-Laili, who passed away in 148 H. He also wrote *al-Radd ala Sirri al-Auza'i* and *al-Kharaj*, a reference book for Islamic states on how to manage wealth.

Abu Hanifa's second main student was Muhammad ibn Hassan al-Shaibani (132-189 H). Although he did not study with Abu Hanifa for a long time, he is considered to have completed the work done by Abu Yusuf.

Al-Shaibani wrote six books which were used to study in the Hanafi school: *al-Asl, al-Mabsut, al-Ziyada, al-Jami al-Saghir, al-Jami' al-Khair,* and *al-Sirr al-Kabir*. All six books were called *Zhahir al-Riwayat*. He also wrote two other books, *Al-Radd al-Ahl Madina* and *al-Athar,* and several other works, such as *al-Kaisaniya, al-Haruniya, al-Jurjaniya, al-Ruqaiya, al-Ziyadut Ziyada,* are also sometimes attributed to him, although the reference to Al-Shaybani is not strong.[22]

---

[22]   Abu Zahra, p.380.

The three men established the Hanafite school of *fiqh*. After Abu Hanifa's death, the school grew rapidly. Starting in a small area in Iraq, it developed in almost all areas of the first Abbassid dynasty, and eventually spread to Khurasan, Transaxonia, Afghanistan, India, Central Asia, China and Indonesia.

In the fifth century H, under the Moghul authority, the Banu Maza dynasty held an important political position in Bukhara as *rais* (leader) of the Hanafi school or *shadr* (original source).[23]

The Hanafite school is now followed by Muslims in Egypt, Afghanistan, China, and the former Soviet Union. Its teachings are upheld by one third of the [Muslim] population of the world. One of its noted followers in the past was Al-Kashsyaf (267 H.), a legal expert under the caliph Al-Muhtadi. Al-Kashshaf wrote a book on *waqf*, a guidance book on duties for *qadi* (jurists) as well as other legal works. Other important followers of Abu Hanifa included al-Hakim al-Shahid (d. 334 H.), Tahawi (d. 321 H.) who later changed to the Shafi'ite school, Abu Laith al-Samarqandi (d. 375 H.) and many others. Abu Hanifa passed away in a prison in Baghdad in 767 H.

MALIK IBN ANAS

The second major school of *fiqh* was established by Imam Malik ibn Anas ibn Abi Amir Al-Ushbukhi (93-179 H), who was known as an expert in hadith and *fiqh*. He was born during the era of *Walid* ibn Abdul Al-Mulk, and died during the era of Harun al-Rashid. During his life, he never left Medina. Malik lived during the Umayyad dynasty and the Abbasid dynasty, during which time the authority of Islam reached China and Europe, especially Spain. Malik's teachers were Abdurrahman ibn Hurmuz, Nafi' Maula ibn Umar and Abi Shihab Al-Zuhri, and his *fiqh* teacher, Rabi'a ibn Abdurrahman.

In admiration of his achievements, Shafi'i once said, "Malik is my teacher, from him I learned knowledge, he is the argument (*hujja*) between me and God, and there is no teacher who gives me more knowledge than Malik. Among *ulamas*, Malik is the bright star."

---

[23] Ali Ihram, *Encyclopedia of Islam*, Leiden, p.163.

Malik's students spread throughout various regions in Egypt, Africa and Andalusia. In Egypt, they included Abu Abdilla ibn Rahman al-Qasim (d. 191 H), who studied with Malik for twenty years as well as Al-Laith ibn Sa'ad. His other students included Abu Muhammad Abdulla ibn Wahab ibn Muslim (120-197H), Ashab ibn Abd al-Aziz Al-Qaisi (150-203 H), Abu Muhammad Abdulla ibn Abdul Hakim (d. 214 H), Ashbagh ibn Faraj and Muhammad ibn Ibrahim Al-Iskandari ibn Ziyad (d. 269 H).

Malik's students in Africa and Andalusia were Abu al-Hasan Ali ibn Ziyad Al-Tunisi (d. 183 H), Abu Abdilla Ziyad ibn Abdurrahman Al-Kurtubi (d. 193 H), who was the first to enter the Andalusia area, Isa ibn Dinar (d. 212 H), Asad ibn Farat ibn Sanan Al-Tunisi (d. 213 H), Yahya ibn Yahya ibn Kasir al-Laith (d. 234 H), Abd Mulk ibn Hubaib ibn Sulaiman Al-Sulami (d. 238 H), and Sahnun Abd. Al-Salam ibn Sa'id al-Tanukhi (d. 240 H).

His students in Hijaz and Iraq included Abu Marwan Abu Al-Mulk ibn Abi Salama al-Majusiyyun (d. 212 H), who became a *mufti* in Medina, Ahmad ibn al-Mua'dzal ibn Ghailan Al-Abdi, and Abu Ishaq Isma'il ibn Ishaq (d. 282 H).

Malik's full name was Abu Abdilla Malik ibn Anas ibn Malik ibn Abi Amr ibn Al-Harith ibn Ghaman ibn Khutayn ibn Amr ibn Harith Al-Ashbahi. It is thought that he was born between 90 H and 97 H, although Abu Zahra claimed that Malik was born in 93 H in Medina, of Arab descent in the Yemen tribe. His mother was Aliyah bint Al-Asadiya and his grandfather was Ibn Amar, a leader among *tabi'in*.

Malik grew up in a family that laid great importance on hadith and other sciences. His studies started with memorizing the Qur'an, an activity which was also conducted by Hanafi and Shafi'i. His mother supported his study, dressed her son with his best clothes when he went to study, and also chose teachers for him: "Go to Rabi'a to learn his knowledge and also his ethics," his mother advised Malik.

Like a bird, Malik jumped from one teacher to another. But Malik needed a specific teacher to supervise him; he chose Ibn Hurmuz. The young Malik admired his teacher. He said, "I have learned from Ibn Hurmuz for thirteen years about things that I never learnt from anybody else." Ibn Hurmuz was known for being able to refuse *ahl al-hawa* and whatever became human controversies. Malik was heavily influenced by his teacher. He imitated his teacher, especially his caution in issuing *fatwa* (religious decrees). Besides learning Rabi'a ibn Abdurrahman, Malik also studied with Ibn Hurmuz, Nafi Maula ibn Umar and Shihab Al-Zuhri.

Malik was involved in various fields of knowledge, including the Qur'an, hadiths and *fatwa* (religious decrees) from the Prophet's companions, and as well as the stories from the companions (*athar*) and other tales (*riwaya*). During his life, theology had become a hot topic of discussion. The Khawarij and Shi'ah, aas well as sub-sects such as the Kisaniya, Zaidiya and Imamiya had their own understandings of theology, while the Mu'tazila had their own methodology for interpreting texts.

Malik was exemplary of a great *imam*. He once memorized thirty-one hadiths from his teacher without writing them down. During his time, oral tradition was still strong and books were rarely written. Shafi'i acknowledged his ability as a memorizer, saying: "In hadith, Malik is the star." Ibn Shihab, one of Malik's students, similarly said that: "Malik is science's robe." Malik was also known to be a patient man, with a pure heart. He once said that the sciences could only be maintained in a heart full of obedience to God.

He issued his *fatwa* (religious advices) slowly and cautiously. When asked about a legal problem, he never answered it directly. Ibn Abdul Hakim said that Imam Malik often suggested that people go and wait for a while, since they should think through their answer first. Malik considered that all problems seriously, especially those related to the legality of things. This characteristic differentiated him from other *fiqh* experts in Iraq. He always avoided pointless debates about religion, saying that they caused hard hearts.

Muhammad Amin, in his book *Duha al-Islam*, claimed that Malik had several teachers among the Prophet's aides and *tabi'in*. Of the aides, Malik learnt the *fiqh* of Umar, Uthman, Abdulla ibn Umar, Aisha, Ibn Abbas and Zaid ibn Thabit. Among *tabi'in*, he followed the thinking of seven experts: Ubaidilla ibn Abdulla ibn 'Ataba ibn Mas'ud (d. 94 H), Zurwa ibn Zubair (d. 94 H), Qasim ibn Muhammad ibn Abu Bakar (d. 106 H), Sa'id ibn al-Mushawab (d. 93 H), Sulaiman ibn Yasir (d. 100 H), Kharija ibn Zaid ibn Thabit (d. 100 H) and Salim ibn Umar ibn Al-Khattab (d. 124 H). Among the *tabi'it al-tabi'in*, Malik studied with Ibn Shihab Al-Zuhri (d. 124 H), Nafi' Maula Abdulla ibn

Umar (d. 117 H), Abu Zinad (d. 121 H), Rabi'a al-Ra'yi (d. 136 H) and Yahya ibn Said (w. 143 H).[24]

Those people developed the Medina School (*madrasah al-madina*). Said ibn Al-Mushayyab was an especially important figure in the Medina school, and he studied with Umar ibn al-Khatab. He knew all legal decisions made by the Prophet, Abu Bakar, Umar, Uthman and Ali. Of the people who came after him, Nafi' and Al-Zuhri were known to have a deep knowledge of *fiqh* and hadith. They both memorized many hadiths of the Prophet, thus supporting the reputation that Medina was the center of hadiths.

Medina was a unique city. Almost all the legal decisions (*tashri'*), as well as many political decisions, made during the time of the Prophet were made in Medina. After the death of the Prophet, the four caliphs also spent most of their lives in Medina.

Many *ulamas* considered Malik to be a supporter of the traditional school in Islam. Actually, he was not a pure traditionalist, but there was an assumption that, while Iraq was the rationalist center, Medina was the center of traditionalist thought. Abu Hanifa was the leader of the rationalist school, while Malik was leader of the traditionalist one. This geographically-based division is an oversimplification though.

Although they used many hadiths, *fiqh* experts in Medina, such as Said ibn al-Mushayyab for example, also used ratio (*ra'yu*) when issuing *fatwa*. Many *ulamas* would not use hadith before they had checked the Qur'an, Sunna of the Prophet, and agreements among the *ulamas* of the time. Rationalism was used by Rabi'a when he prioritized a deed (*amal*) of Medina experts over a single hadith, since he thought the agreement of a thousand people was better than the opinion of a single person. He said: "*alfu an alfin khairun min wahidin an wahidin,*" or, "One thousand against one thousand is better than one against one." This showed the efforts towards rationalism in the Medina School, although it was in a relatively simple manner, the contents of hadiths were not taken for granted, but reinvestigated.[25]

Evidence of Malik's rationalism is evidenced by his dissatisfaction with learning only from the *tabi'in*. Malik also learnt *fiqh* from the experts of

---

[24] *Ibid*, p.34.
[25] Abu Zahra, p.392.

the rationalist group (*fiqh al-ra'yi*), such as Yahya ibn Said, and Rabi'a ibn Abdurrahman, who were part of the Rabi'a al-Ra'yi (the rationalist Rabi'a) in Medina. Rabi'a was one of the teachers chosen by Malik's mother.

There were differences between rationalists in Iraq and rationalists in Medina. Rationalist *fiqh* in Iraq used *qiyas* (analogy) and *mantiq* (logic), while rationalist *fiqh* in Medina concentrated more on adjustments between texts, and their varying usefulness. Although Malik was a pioneer in traditionalism in *fiqh*, Ibn Qutaiba classified Malik, along with Abu Hanifa and Shafi'i, as defenders of rationalism. When Ibn Qutaiba was asked by the *ulamas*: "Who is still using ratio after Yahya ibn Sa'ad?" he replied, "Malik."

Although he had been given the status of absolute (*mujtahid mutlaq*), Malik's *istinbat* methodology (serious effort in formulating the law from basic sources of Islamic law) was not codified during his lifetime. But his followers developed his method through the problems of *fiqh* happening. Al-Qadi Abu Iyyad, in *al-Madarik*, and Ibn Rushd, in *al-Buhja*, systematized the *istinbat* principles used by Malik in his legal decrees.

According to them, Malik's methodology relied firstly on the Qur'an as a source. If he did not find the appropriate reference in the Qur'an, he referred to Sunna, hadiths and religious decrees from the Prophet's aides and experts of the Medina school. Study of Sunna was followed by the use of *qiyas* (analogy), *maslaha al-mursala* (public interest), *saddu dzara'i* (prevention), *'urf* (custom) and *'adda* (tradition).[26]

Like Abu Hanifa, Malik also classified the Qur'an as the principal source and main basis of *shari'a*, above all other legal sources. For him, its laws are applicable until the end of time.

He rejected interpretation (*ta'wil*), preferring to use literal meanings (*dzahir*), because there was no reason given in the Qur'an for using *ta'wil*. In his understanding of the Qur'an, he used stronger meanings (*fahw al-khitab*). Sunna, in Malik's legal perspective, was the second level of legal source. He used the hadith *mutawatir*, a hadith which was narrated by a reliable group of people. He also used the hadith *mashhur*, which was narrated by one or two of the companions, but which was not classified as *mutawatir* (transmitted by a group of honest people). Malik's view on the hadith ahad (hadith with

---

[26] Abu Zahra, p.414

single narrator) was different to that of Abu Hanifa, who questioned its validity. According to Malik, the important point was that the hadith should be *sahih* (valid) or at least *hasan* (of a quality one level below *sahih*).

It was likely only Malik who considered local traditions (*'amal ahl al-madina*) to be an important aspect in the consideration of Islamic laws. But it should be remembered that the tradition refered to by the Medina school was a tradition that originated with the Prophet. Malik went as far as to say that the Medina tradition should be prioritized over the *khabar ahad* (hadith with single narrator).

If the deeds of Medina's experts were not viewed as a general agreement (*ijma"*), but only a majority, they were still prioritized over the hadith *ahad*. According to Ahmad Amin, there were many activities of Medina's experts that were interpretive. If there was a *khabar ahad* that contradicted Medina traditions, it was considered to be *mansukh* (abrogated). Malik considered that the legal decrees of the Prophet's close aides were obligatory. According to Ahmad Amin, it was this point that limited Malik's use of rationality. This is not to say, however, that Malik rejected rationality altogether, although he placed its use below the use of texts.

Other legal principles he used include *qiyas*, *Maslaha al-Mursala*, and *Istihsan*. Malik considered *qiyas* to be a method of analogizing a problem which had no legal basis in the Qur'an, to another similar problem (*illat al-hukm*). In his implementation of *Maslaha al-Mursala*, Malik worked through a matter which had no legal basis in the Qur'an or the Prophet's traditions, but as it applied to public welfare. This theory was later applied by Al-Shathibi in his *Muwafaqat*.

The final legal principle was *dzara'i* (prevention). Malik's conception of *dzara'i* was all that tended towards illegality were to be considered illegal, while all that tended towards legality was to be considered legal. Things that were purposeful were permitted, while things that created loss were forbidden.

Malik's *fiqh* developed in Egypt due to the contribution of his students, such as Abdurrahman ibn Qasim, Ushman ibn Al-Hikam, Abdurrahman ibn Al-Khalid, Ashab and others. It was very popular before the emergence of Shafi'i school. Malikite school also developed in Tunisia, although it was less popular than the Hambali school. In Andalusia, Malikite school became the official school of the authorities.

Besides being known as an *imam* of *fiqh* and a *muhaddith* (expert on hadith), Malik was also a theologian. His theological thought took a firm position on many matters, which was understandable given the socio-political conditions he lived under. In Malik's time, a conflict of ideas could trigger a civil war. For example, there was an opinion that only the descents of Ali had the right to become caliphs, whereas others maintained that the Caliphate should not only be the prerogative of the Arab nations.

In dealing with this issue, Malik refered to Sunna and *salaf al-salih* (previous pious generation), as well as appealing to theological arguments. He called on people not only to depend on rationality, but to return to the sources of the Qur'an and Sunna. In his view, if the problem contradicted the Qur'an, it was automatically contradictary to rational thought.

In Malik's view, belief, or faith, was a matter of *saying, believing* and *doing*, a definition taken from the Qur'an and Sunna. In contrast to Abu Hanifa, Malik maintained that belief could only increase, and was not decreasible. His thought was always based on *manqul* (texts), and he refused to speculate on a rationalist basis.

Malik fully believed in good and bad destinies, although he also considered human beings to be independent of God, and therefore responsible for their own actions. Thus, sinners would be punished for their sins.

Malik differed on the view of the Mu'tazila school that the Qur'an was a creation. He also rejected the Mu'tazila stance on *ru'yatulla*, that people who reached heaven would be able to see God (an ability to see God), as written in the Qur'an. But Malik did not elaborate on how they would be able to see God.

In politics, Malik accepted the authority of the four caliphs (*khulafa al-rashidin*), and opposed those who undermined these four aides of the Prophet. He maintained that this was an ideal method of leadership, legitimate since the support (*bai'at*) was not forced. He maintained that political leadership should be based on justice and public welfare.

This political stance was different from Abu Hanifa's. Malik did not hold revolutionary views against the authorities, and prefered to avoid these kinds of conflicts. He opted to stay silent when Sultan Umar ibn Abdul Azis refused to appoint an intelligent, wise man as his successor, but instead installed Yazid, who was a known authoritarian. This decision was based on the need to maintain stability and avoid casualties, and was thus in keeping with Malik's views on society and politics.

Malik lived under the rule of Abu Ja'far al-Mansur, the second caliph in the Abbasid dynasty. He involved in an important *mihna* or inquisition in 146 H. Malik had released a *fatwa* denouncing *mut'a* (temporary contract marriage) and stating that it be forbidden (*haram*). This was considered slanderous of the authorities since Ibn Abbas, the grandfather of Ja'far, had legalized *mut'a*, although the story was rejected by Abu Zahra.

Another story announced that Malik prioritized Uthman over 'Ali, a stance that created difficulties for descendents of 'Ali (*allawiyyin*). According to Shaykh Muhammad Abu Zahra, this was not the reason that Al-Manshur's anger was triggered, but rather that they were angry about the deportation of Muhammad Al-Nafs Al-Zakiyya to Medina, and his brother's deportation to Baghdad in 145 H.[27]

The most logical reasoning, according to Abu Zahra, was the issuing of a hadith that stated: "A pledge made by force is not legitimate." The *Allawiyin* group, who migrated together with Nafs al-Zakiya, considered that the pledge (*bai'at*) for authority was forced, not voluntary. The issue of the hadith was considered to be a counter against the authority of Al-Mansur. The governor of Medina, in the name of Al-Mansur, banned Malik from issuing the hadith.

Muhammad Amin takes a different stance on the issue. According to Muhammad Amin, there were two different versions of the story. First, Malik issued a *fatwa* stating that forced divorce was illegal, supported by a hadith that stated: "It is considered illegal, people who was forcibly to divorce." The decree shocked Abbasid, who thought it could make their power illegitimate. So Al-Mansur banned Malik from issuing the hadith. Second, Malik was considered to be jealous of Ja'far ibn Sulaiman while he was in Medina. People reported that Malik refused to support Ja'far's pledge on forced marriage. It is said that Ja'far ibn Sulaiman was so angry that he beat and caned Malik until his arm was broken. This incident, however, did not decrease Malik's reputation among the common people of Medina.

---

[27] Muhammad Abu Zahra, p. 408.

Malik wrote two important works – *al-Muwatta'* and *al-Mudawana* – which were the first legal works to be written by an *imam* and made into book form. The hadiths cited in this book were narrated by ninety-five narrators; all but six of whom were residents of Medina (*madiniyyun*). Of these six, two were from Shiryan, and the others from Mecca, Khurasan, Jazri and Sham, respectively. Their contribution to the text was relatively minor, but according to Ahmad Amin, some parts of the book don't even mention the six non-Medina people.

Al-Muwatta has two versions: the Yahya ibn Yahya version and the Muhammad ibn Hassan al-Shaybani one. The most representative is the Yahya ibn Yahya's version.

Malik's second work was *al-Mudawana*, which was not actually written by Malik himself. Instead it is a collection of Malik's, and his students', decrees. According to Norman Calder, in his *Studies in Early Muslim Jurisprudence*, *Al-Mudawanna* was written by Abd Al-Salam ibn Sa'id Al-Tanukhi, who was known as Sahnun. He was born in Qayrawan, 10 H, and traveled to Egypt and Tunisia in his youth to meet *fiqh* experts. Sahnun became a *qadhi* (jurist) in Qayrawan under the reign of Governor Muhammad ibn Aghlabid in 234 H.[28] Besides Sahnun, Ibn Qasim also contributed to the writing of *al-Mudawana*. There are other works attributed to Malik, including *al-Mujalasa*, on the proceedings of Malik's *fatwa*, which was written by Ibn Wahhab. There are also theological works and personal letters which have not been released.

MUHAMMAD IBN IDRIS AL-SHAFI'I

The third main school of *fiqh*, which is followed by Sunnite Muslims was founded by Muhammad Idris Al-Shafi'i (150H-250H). He was born in Gizzah in the year that the great Iraqi teacher of *fiqh*, Hanafi, passed away. In several stories, including that maintained by Al-Khayyal, Shafi'i's birth was intended by God to keep the knowledge of *fiqh* in the world. Al-Shafi'i was to replace Hanafi.

Shafi'i's father was an Arab of the Quraish tribe, while his mother had Yemeni roots. Shafi'i's birth name was Muhammad ibn Idris ibn Al-Abbas ibn Uthman ibn Shafi' ibn Ubaid ibn Abdi Yazid ibn Hashim ibn Mutalib ibn

---

[28] Norman Celder, *Studies in Early Muslim Jurisprudence*, p.1

Abdi Manaf. According to reliable opinion, Shafi'i's genealogy was connected to the Prophet Muhammad through his grandfather Mutalib. Mutalib was one Abd Al-Manaf's four sons: Hashim, Abd Al-Sham (the grandfather of Umawiya) and Naufal (grandfather of Jabir ibn Ma'tam). Mutalib took care of Abd Al-Mutalib, the grandfather of the Prophet.

Shafi'i's father passed away when he was young and he grew as a poor orphan from a respected descent. His poverty made him closer to the poor people, and made him seek a noble goal. Shafi'i started his studies in Gizza by memorizing the Qur'an. He learned hadiths from noted teachers when he visited Mecca. Besides the Qur'an and hadiths, he also memorized poems and tribal stories, including Hudzail's poetry. Al-Asma'i, a noted poet of the *jahiliyya* period, conferred his verses to the youthful Muhammad Idris Al-Shafi'i, saying: "*sahhatu ash'ar Hudzail 'ala fata Qurayshin ismuhu Muhammad ibn Idris.*"

At twenty years of age, Shafi'i heard about Malik ibn Anas of Medina. He wanted to meet the Imam and learn from him. His desire was almost fulfilled when he read Malik's book, *al-Muwatta'*, brought by someone who had just visited Medina. He still wanted to meet Malik, however, which he finally did during a scientific discussion.

Shafi'i was intellectually very strong, and during his youth he memorized all the contents of *al-Muwatta'*. He used clear language to express himself and was known for his oral recitation abilities. Malik listened to his whole recitation of *al-Muwatta'*.

During Shafi'i's lifetime, the Islamic world was marked by differences in opinion between various sects. Theology (*kalam*) emerged, bringing with it questions such as whether *kalam Allah* was an attribute adjective; whether the Qur'an was a creation; and other topics that attracted people's attention. Shafi'i studied the development of the debates, although he generally avoided discussing theology. He was more interested in the study of *fiqh*.

Shafi'i developed a methodology that was different to that of his two predecessors. Although he learnt *fiqh* from Hanafi and Malik, he did not imitate their methodologies. Generally, Shafi'ite *fiqh* methodology was based on five legal sources as it was mentioned in *al-Umm*.[29] According to Syafi'i:

---

[32] Muhammad Ibn Idris al-Shafi'i, *al-Umm*, vol. VII, p.246.

Knowledge has several degrees. First, the Qur'an and Sunna, if they have decided it. Second, *ijma'* (concensus), if it can not be found in the Qur'an and Sunna. Third, the opinions of the Prophet's companions, among whom there are no differences. Fourth, differences between the companions, about the different opinions. Fifth, *qiyas* (analogy) can be conducted, if it was not found in the Qur'an and Sunna, since from these two the knowledge was taken.

This statement was considered to be the legal source for Shafi'i's consideration of *fiqh*. Operationally, Shafi'i used *nusus* (texts, the Qur'an and hadiths) as his primary source. These texts were the main sources of *fiqh*, and within them all necessary material was contained. An *ijma'* would not be considered sufficient, if it was contradictory to the Qur'an and Sunna, the primary sources.

Shafi'i's pattern differed from those of other *imams*, such as Hanafi and Malik, as well as the others who came after them. Most of them considered the Qur'an to be the primary source. If they did not find what they sought in the Qur'an, then they used the Sunna as the second source. This pattern was also applied in a hadith by Mu'adz ibn Jalal in a hadith, one of the Prophet's companions, when answering the Prophet's question about how he would decide the solution to a problem if he was far way from the Prophet. Mu'adz said that, hierarchically, he would refer first to the Qur'an, and then the Sunna. If a solution could not be found in the Qur'an and Sunna, and then he would conduct a search for meaning (*ijtihad*).

By placing the Qur'an and Sunna on the same level, Shafi'i did not mean that they were the same; he viewed them as substantially different. The Qur'an was *mutawatir* (*yaqin*), those who read it received blessings. Sunna was not God's word, so people who read it would not be rewarded by God. Shafi'i maintained that Sunna's function was to explain the Qur'an's general statements, to clarify statements that seemed illogical, and to interpret Qur'anic verses. Thus, these explanatory texts were not to be placed on the same level as the Qur'an.

In order to avoid misunderstanding his position, we should refer Professor Abu Zahra's notes as follows:

1) When Shafi'i placed the Qur'an and Sunna on the same level in deciding a law, he still viewed the Qur'an as a pillar of the religion, whereas Sunna

was derivative (*far'un*). Sunna's strength came from the Qur'an, but was positioned with the Qur'an because it explained the Qur'an.

2) In explaining branches of law (*furu'iyya*), Shafi'i put the Qur'an and Sunna on the same level in order that the process of *istinbat* ran correctly and fluently. However, it should be remembered that not all the narration from the Prophet, has the same level of authority as the Qur'an. Hadith *ahad* (hadiths with a single narrator) were not be categorized as the same as hadith *mutawatir*.

3) Shafi'i did not view the above as equal to *aqida* (theology).[30] Shafi'i, a firm believer in Sunna, was forced to confront those who challenged those groups that questioned the validity of Sunna. These groups were the *Inkar al-Sunna*, who acknowledged that the only legal source was the Qur'an; a group that acknowledged Sunna if it was also found in the Qur'an; and a third group that only acknowledged *Sunna Mutawatir*. The first and the second groups rejected Sunna, which they did not view as an independent basic principle. The third group, that rejected hadith *ahad*, was strongly rejected by Shafi'i.

According to Shafi'i, the other legal source was *ijma'* (concensus), which he said was *hujja* or religious argumentation. *Hujja* was a concensus among the *ulamas* of a certain era on a practical law upheld on reasons they all agreed on. The first, and possibly only, *ijma'* that Shafi'i accepted was made among the Prophet's companions.

A few considerations should be remembered about *ijma'*:

1) Shafi'i placed *ijma'* after the Qur'an and Sunna. This meant that if there was a concensus that contradicted the Qur'an and Sunna, it should be considered *hujja* and, in reality, there were no *ijma'* that actually contradicted the Qur'an and Sunna. There were two main kinds of *ijma'*. Firstly, *ijma'* which had been agreed by the Islamic world and that *ulamas* viewed as being already known by all Muslims, such as the five calls to prayer, the number of *rakaat* or prayer positions, pilgrimage procedures, the giving of alms, and so on. These were assumed because they were mentioned in many Qur'anic verses

---

[30] *Ibid.* p.452.

and the *mutawatir* narration of the Prophet. This kind of *ijma'* was based on texts and the understanding of them (*ijma' ala nusus wa fahmiha*), as termed by Abu Zahra.[31] Secondly, there was *ijma'* about laws which were still being debated among *ulamas*, such as 'Umar's decision about people receiving land as the spoils of war (*ghanima*). This *ijma'* was based on texts, but those who rejected it were not considered infidels.

2) Shafi'i only considered *ijma'* agreed by *ahl al-madina* (the community of madina) to be true *ijma'*. This view was different to Imam Malik's. In fact, the *ahl al-madina* never reached a consensus (*ijma'*) on any matter that had not been generally agreed in the Islamic world, such as the number of *rakaat*: four in ashar prayer, three in *maghrib* prayer, etc. If there was diffrences, it also happened in *ahl-al-madina*. Although, conceptually, Shafi'i was different from Malik, they were only practical differences.

3) Shafi'i said that if people admitted that something was *ijma'*, it could not be considered as such, since the aknowledgement of *ijma'* after it had been reached often happened during the time of the *imams* of the legal schools.

4) According to Shafi'i, the fourth source of Islamic law was the opinions of the Prophet's companions (*aqwal al-sahaba*). According to some Shafi'ite *ulamas*, Shafi'i only used the opinions of the *qadi*m (the oldest). In his school of *jadid* (the new), he did not use *aqwal al-sahaba*, but in his *al-Risala*, according to a story by Rabi' ibn Sulaiman, Shafi'i did use it. According to Abu Zahra, Shafi'i used both *qadim* and *jadid* in his work.[32]

   Asides from the notes above, it is clear that the *aqwal al-sahabah* (opinions of Prophet's companion's) used by Shafi'i was dominated by the male *aqwal al-shahaba*, because the popularity of using female companions as hadith narrators decreased sharply at that time.

5) The other legal source which became Shafi'i's trademark was the use of *qiyas* (analogy). Shafi'i was still categorized as *mujtahid* in relation to the earlier sources, since he used the method of *tarjih* (selection) to find meanings by comparing one hadith with others, and the opinions of one

---

[31] *Ibid.* p.453.
[32] Imam Shafi'i, *Al-Risala*, p.506, Ahmad Shakir's edition.

companion and others. He considered the process of *qiyas* to be true *ijtihad*, an Islamic legal principle for uncovering the hidden meanings (*sarih*) in the Qur'an and Sunna.

However, Shafi'i was not the first expert to use *qiyas*. His predecessors, such as Hanafi and Ibrahim al-Nakha'i, also conducted *ijtihad* based on *qiyas*. But Shafi'i was known to have perfected the method, by improving requirements, clarifying limitations, and the kinds of *qiyas* to be used to avoid the misuse of the method by the *mujtahid*.

According to Shafi'i, there were two reasons why *qiyas* was required. First, *shari'a* law could not be separated from its context in time and space. We should be aware of the context in which the *shari'a* arose. If it was not written in the texts, *qiyas* could be used to form an explanation.

Secondly, Shafi'i divided *shari'a* into two parts: *qat'iy* (certain) and *zhanniy* (uncertain) knowledge. Knowledge of *qat'iy* was based on texts which had clear meanings, while *zhanniy* was based on strong assumption (*al-zhanni al-rajih*) and should ideally be backed up with textual material. Hadith *Ahad* was included in the category *al-zhanniy al-rajih*. According to Shafi'i, *qiyas* was part of *al-zhanniy al-rajih*, meaning that when exact knowledge could not be established, *mujtahid* should seek it through *al-zhanniy al-rajih*. Shafi'i said people should obey *qat'iy*, both mentally and physically, whereas *al-zhanniy al-rajih* should be followed in actions. People should strive to obey it, but if they rejected it, they still were not to be classified as infidels. Shafi'i considered *qiyas* to be very important, saying: "When the Prophet orders people to conduct *ijtihad*, meaning to seek something, and to seek it deeply, they need reason (*dalil*) and that is *qiyas*." [33]

Long before Shafi'i, Abu Hanifa and the Iraqi school in the era of Al-Nakha'i also used *qiyas* for *ijtihad*. But, in contrast to his predecessors, Shafi'i clarified the limitations which could help *mujtahid* avoid making mistakes.

The process of Shafi'i's *ijtihad* can be divided into two periods. The first was Baghdad period, the results of which can be seen in *Risalah al-Usuliya*, *al-Umm* and *al-Mabsut*. These books were written up by his close friend, Zaghfarani. The second period was the Egyptian period (199 H), during

---

[33] *Ibid.* p.453

which two books of *al-Mabsut* written in Bahgdad were revised. In the revision, some parts were cut, while others were added to and improved. The books written in Baghdad replaced the books written in Egypt.

Shafi'i's followers, who were usually called *ashab al-Shafi'i*, spread to many areas, including in Iraq, Mecca, Egypt, Sham, Nishabury and Khurasan. Among the followers, there were those of *mujtahid muntasib* status and those of *mujtahid mukharij* status.

According to Western orientalist, Noel J. Coulson, early on, Shafi'i was not someone directly involved in the evolution of Islamic law. Coulson said that Shafi'i was a *deus ex machina* – a figure introduced suddenly to resolve particularly difficult problems. Shafi'i developed the progress which had been achieved by Shaibani, one of Hanafi's closest students.

Coulson's opinion was not completely true. Shafi'i did not emerge suddenly, but was rather an individual who prepared himself to become a legal expert. He made contact with Malik when he was just fifteen years old, and he also made contact with Abu Hanifa, indirectly, through his students. Their influences are visible in the system of jurisprudence he developed. Shafi'i's key contribution was his achievement in developing a new discipline, *usul fiqh* (the principle of jurisprudence). Shafi'i's skill was his ability to manage the hadiths of the Prophet.[34]

Although Shafi'i contributed much to the field of Islamic jurisprudence, his rational approach was much influenced by Imam Abu Hanifa, and by the traditionalist approaches of the group of experts led by Malik. Shafi'i tried to place himself as the thesis and antithesis to the processes developed by his predecessors.

AHMAD IBN HANBAL

The fourth major school of *fiqh* in Sunnite Islam was established by Ibn Hanbal (164-241 H). He was born, grew up and passed away in Baghdad, Iraq. Hanbal was also his grandfather's name. His father was Muhammad ibn Hanbal ibn Hilal. His grandfather was a follower of the Umayyad disnasty, but later became a follower of Abbasid. His father was a military commander.

---

[34] Montgomery Watt, *op. cit.*, p.127-8.

Ibn Hanbal followed the same learning process as other *imams*, starting with memorizing the Qur'an, learning Arabic, memorizing hadiths, and the legacies of the Prophet's companions (*akhbar*), and the *tabi'in* (*athar*). His first concern was to learn hadiths, but this interest soon led him to study *fiqh*. So, to his mind, hadith and *fiqh* were connected. Ahmad ibn Hanbal was the first expert, after Shafi'i, who used *fiqh* in from both its *diraya* (textual) and *riwaya* (historical) aspects.

In the field of hadith, Imam Ibn Hanbal collected many hadiths from Abu Yusuf, a noted student of Hanafi. Despite this, Ahmad claimed that his *fiqh* was not influenced by Hanafi. On Abu Zahra's analysis, however, the fact that Ahmed collected *fiqh* from Abu Yusuf meant that Ahmad's *fiqh* was rationalist.[35] This said, the rational *fiqh* were not that developed since Ahmad actually took more of Abu Yusuf's hadiths, rather than *fiqhs*.

Ahmad started his journey in the study of Sunna when he was fifteen years old, between 179 and 186 H, in Baghdad. There, he learnt much from many noted experts, before going on to Hijaz, Bashra, Kufa and Yemen. He then met Shafi'i in Haram Mosque in Mecca. Shafi'i was a great influence on his style of *istinbat* (making legal decisions).

Although he faced difficulties in his studies of hadith, he remained enthusiastic. He collected many hadiths, especially those related to *fiqh*. In other words, he collected fiqih Sunna, meaning *fiqh* taken from the hadiths of the Prophet, opinions of the Prophet's companions and *tabi'in*. Thus his *fiqh* are very closely related to hadith.

According to Ibn Qayyim, Ibn Hanbal's *fiqh* decrees were generally based on the following five principles:[36]

1) *Nas* (text), the Qur'an and Sunna. If Ahmad could not find a law in based in *Nas*, he would not give a decree. He prioritized *Nas* over the opinions of the Prophet's companions. For example, ruling on the topic of 'idda (period of waiting) for pregnant women whose husbands had passed away, he did not base his opinion on Ibn Abbas, Muawiyya, or Abu Sufyan, who all had different opinions.

---

[38] Muhammad Abu Zahra, *Tarikh Madzahih al- Islamiya*, p.470.
[39] Ibn Qayyim, *I'lam al-Muwwaqi'in* , vol. I, p.22.

2) Undebated opinion of the companions of the Prophet, over other, contradictory *fatwa*. These he treated as *ijma'*.

3) If there were differences in opinion between the companions of the Prophet, Ahmad used those opinions that were not in contradiction to the Qur'an and Sunna. But if these opinions contradicted the Qur'an and Sunna, he would explain the differences without mentioning how he based his choice. Unlike Shafi'i, Ahmad did not apply a process of selection, *tarjih* or *qiyas*.

4) He used hadith *mursal* and hadith *sahih* as long as there was no indication that these hadiths were concocted or rejected. Ibn Qayyim explained that what was meant by hadith *dha'if*, according to Ahmad, was not bad (*batil*) or doubted (*mungkar*) in terms of the history of its narration, but more to do with the degree of belief (*thiqqa*) not reaching the level of *ittiham* (assumption).

5) *Qiyas*, which Ahmad used when he found no legal basis in the Qur'an and Sunna, opinions of the Prophet's companions and *tabi'in*. But *qiyas* was used only in an emergency situation.

According to Abu Zahra, Ibn Qayyim's analysis was not really perfect, since he did not include *ijma' masalih mursalah*, *dzara'i*, *ishtisan* and *istishab* – methods that Abu Zahra maintains were used by Ahmad in his works. Abu Zahra added the following to Ibn Qayyim's explanation:[37]

1) Ahmad actually never rejected *ijma'*. He just neglected *ijma'* from after the era of the companions of the Prophet. According to Ahmad, *ijma'* was divided into two levels: *ijma'* of the companions, which referred to the Qur'an and Sunna; and *ijma'* that had become popular public opinion and had not been rejected. These were not hadiths, but their position was higher then *qiyas*. If an *ulama* rejected them, they should be dropped.

2) [He used] *qiyas* (analogy) of the kind used by the pioneers, Hanafi and Shafi'i. Qiyas "Juristic methodology that relies on the use of analogy for unprecedented cases in which the source text do not provide a conclusive legal decision.

---

[40] Muhammad Abu Zahra, p.516.

3) *Masalih al-mursala*, a problem which had no legal basis, but was considered to be a good thing. Ahmad borrowed this method from Malik, with the requirement that its implementation should fulfill the following requirements: a) It was in accordance with the aims of *shari'a*; b) It refused difficulties; c) It was not in contradiction with the religious texts (Qur'an and Sunna). Hanbali's group considered *masalih al-murshala* to be *qiyas* since, in substance, it was a public good, which had been mentioned in the Qur'an and Sunna. Ahmad used this method, and maintained that the Prophet's companions had also done so. *Masalih al-mursala* was usually applied in religious politics (*al-siyasa al-shari'yya*), such as policies made by state leaders to improve people's welfare. Many members of Hanbali's group followed Ahmad's method. Ahmad viewed masalih as one of many means of *qiyas*, to be used only after the hadiths had been explored. The principle of *qiyas* was only applied in an emergency.

4) According to Ahmad, *istihsan* was "deciding law on a problem based on another problem which has legal basis in *Nas* (texts), *ijma'*, or an emergency situation because of a contradiction between physical *qiyas* and spiritual *qiyas*." Actually, *istihsan* was first developed by Hanafi, and was then used in the *usul fiqh* of Ibn Hanbal. According to Malik, however, *istihsan* was basically a kind of *mashlala* theory, a position also adopted by Hanbali. The Hanbalite group clearly stated that they adopted this stance on solving problems which had no legal basis in *nas*, as it had also been conducted by prior *ulamas*, Khulafa al-Rashidin and *fiqh* experts among the companions of the Prophet.[38]

5) The method of *al-dzara'i* was upheld by the Hanbalite group as evidence that they followed Ahmad. It is difficult to define *al-dzara'i* in precise terms. An illustration we can use is that God, as maker of *shari'a*, whenever He wanted something, everything should be refered to His will. Whenever God forbade something, everything referring to this thing would also be forbidden. *Al-dzara'i* is probably best defined as an accompanying media (*wasa'il*). Among the four schools, the Hanbalite school defended the method of *al-dzara'i* more than the others.

---

[38] Abu Zahra, p.520.

6) *Al-istishab* is a kind of law which is valid until changed by another law. changed it. Some, though not all, of the Hanbali group used this method as a legal basis. The principles of *usul al-figh* were taken from the *istishab*: (1) law is the origin of things, things are allowed, until there is textual basis for banning them; (2) the law from water is pure, until proven dirty; (3) If a husband wants to divorce his wife, but is doubtful of whether he divorced her once or three times, it was considered that he divorced her once.[39]

Ahmad ibn Hanbal did not write a complete book on this the development of his thought on *fiqh*, like Shafi'i's *al-Umm*. Some suggest that Ahmad prohibited people from writing down his ideas in book form. According to Ahmad, only the Qur'an and Sunna should be written down in book form, so that we would not forget the two legal sources.

The largest contribution to the codification of Hanbali law was made by his students. They systematically reconstructed his sayings, deeds and answers to requests for *fatwa*. According to Abu Zahra,[40] the first person who spread Ibn Hanbal's thoughts was his son, Salih. As his son, Salih knew his father's *fiqh* very well, and he answered many queries via correspondance. When he received a letter asking about a legal matter, Salih replied, based on his father's opinion. Salih was also a judge, and was therefore able to spread his father's work through his court. Salih passed away in 266 H.

Ahmad's other son, Abdullah ibn Ahmad, also contributed to the dissemination of his father's thought through the *Musnad Ahmad* for his generation and those that followed.

Besides his two sons, Ahmad's students also took on this role. One was Abu Bakar Al-Athram (d. 261 H), and another was Abd Al-Mulk Al-Maimun (d. 274 H), who accompanied Ahmad for twenty-two years. These people helped to document Ahmad's thoughts, although he, himself, sometimes prohibited their work. Another student and close friend was Abu Bakar al-Mawardi (d. 275 H) and Harb, who, although he did not accompany Ahmad for a long time, learned much from him about *fiqh* and was a firm follower.

---

[39] Abu Zahra p.523
[40] Imam Abu Zahra, *Tarikh al-Madzahib*, p.524.

The last key student was Ibrahim ibn Ishaq Al-Harabi (d. 285 H), who also disseminated Ahmad's hadiths. With his humbleness and cautious attitude, he was similar to his teacher, once refusing ten thousand *dirham* offered to him by a king in payment.

These were the first, select people who had the initiative to collect Ahmad's *fiqh* thought. This generation of collectors and developers made a special contribution to the emergence of some big ideas.

Ahmad's thought on *ijtihad* was very progresive. He maintained that the door of *ijtihad* was never closed. The Hanabali group was open to people who were able to conduct *ijtihad*, maintaining that every era should have its own *mujtahid mustaqil* (independent thought).[41]

Some of the other people who studied with Ahmad include Salih ibn Ahmad ibn Hanbal (d. 266 H), the oldest son of Ahmad, Abdulla ibn Ahmad ibn Hanbal (d. 190 H), Abu Bakar Al-Athram, Abd al-Malik ibn Abd al-Hamid ibn Mahran al-Maimuni (d. 274 H), Abu Bakar al-Murdzi (d. 274 H), Harb ibn Isma'il al-Handhali al-Karmani (d. 280 H), Ibrahim ibn Ishaq al-Harabi (d. 185 H), Abu Bakar al-Khahal (d. 311 H), Abd Qasim al-Baghdadi (d. 344 H) and Abu Bakar Abd Aziz ibn Ja'far (d. 364 H).[42]

Besides the four schools (*madzab al-arba'a*), other schools of Islamic law also developed in the Sunnite community. Abu Sulaiman Dawud ibn Ali Al-Asfihani Al-Zhahiri (202-272 H) founded the Zhahirite school, which was developed further by Ibn Hazm. Dawud was an independent *mujtahid* in Baghdad after Shafi'i. The principle of his school was the practical implementation of Islamic teachings, based on a literal approach to the Qur'an and Sunna. If there was no textual basis, they used *ijma'* of the companions of the Prophet. If there was no textual basis and *ijma'*, they used *istishab*.

There were also several legal schools among the Shi'ah community, including the Zaidite school, founded by Zaid ibn Ali Zainal Abidin ibn Husain (d. 122 H), the Imamite school, founded by Abu Ja'far (d. 290 H), and the Ibadiyah school, founded by Abu al-Shuatha Al-Tabi'i Jabir ibn Zaid (d. 80 H).[43]

---

[41] Al-Zuhaili, *op. cit.*, p.39.
[42] *Ibid*, p.40.
[43] *Ibid*, p.44.

The efforts of these schools have made it easier for Muslims in the world to practice their religion. We do not have to conduct our own *ijtihad*, since it is available in the books. Books that were not originally intended for the building of Islamic practice, later became binding legal products, a body of legal codes that must be followed. Life should be led according to the rules of one of the recognized opinions of Islamic laws; if this is not possible, we should return to the Qur'an and hadiths with our own *ijtihad*. Historically speaking, the *imams* of the schools never declared that they should be followed, fearing that this would lead to deviation from the Qur'an and Sunna, closing the door for *ijtihad*. Normatively, they depended on the statement of the Prophet that there was no best generation after the Prophet, except the era of the companions, *tabi'in* and *tabi'it al-tabi'in* (third generation of early Muslims).

This attitude about the closing of *ijtihad* can be understood because later generations, epistemologically and intellectually, could not reach the same levels as the previous *imams*. The schools were prominent at a time when Islam was starting to decline, thus fatalism was characteristic of the era.

The negative aspect of the closing of *ijtihad* was the stagnation of Islamic thought, including *fiqh*. The freezing of orthodoxy into closed discourses could halt the entry of new thoughts; every new thought would be framed in terms of the school's particular way of thinking (*ijtihad al-madzhab*). So the *ulamas* of usul *fiqh* established degrees of *mujtahid* in order to protect the status quo, rather than giving the opportunity to develop *fiqh* further. The obligation to uphold the schools of law could close the development of new thoughts or cause a process of the sedimentation of layers of tradition, which would then fossilize. The development of *fiqh* only took place in the era of the legal schools, after which, it stopped and died. In the present era, there is no single work that can make us proud like those that came out of this early period.

CRITICAL NOTES

If we consider the history and the creative processes of the top *ulamas* who established *fiqh* – from Abu Hanif to Ahmad ibn Hanbal – it seems that they were not yet aware of the issue of gender equity.

This was possibly because, intellectually, they had no interaction with women. Indeed, women had no visible role in their scholarly activities. None amongst Hanafi, Malik, Shafi'i and Ibn Hanbal ever pointed out a female teacher. It is still unclear whether the transmission of their history never recorded the role of female teachers, or whether the *imams* truly had no female teachers. But women's role on the map of Islamic thought decreased at that time. Hanafi's thinking, however, was slightly turned towards women, but it was not followed up by his students, almost all of whom were men. Although they were men, it should not have precluded them placing women fairly and proportionally in their *fiqh*, or at least developing Hanafi's ideas about women. If indeed they had female teachers, their concern was not based on gender equality, so that the existence of the female teachers influenced nothing.

In criticising all the above issues, there at least a few things to consider: 1) the genealogy of knowledge; 2) the transmission of knowledge; 3) the cultural aspects; and 4) the androcentric writing of history. I will briefly explain these four aspects for clarity:

1) Genealogy: there was no awareness of gender issues during the birth of this knowledge. However we view it, the development and growth of *fiqh* was handled by men, in relation to male power. From a philosophical perspective, there is always a dominant discourse and a non-dominant one. Usually, the dominant discourse is influenced by public discourse. Conversely, less dominant discourses were not recorded in the monitoring of history. During the development of *fiqh*, the dominant discourse was male. Actually, it is possible that the actor's masculinity was not considered to be an issue at all, and gender was not considered at all.

   It must be noted that the first *fiqh* were developed by men, at least as far as th history books record it. So, naturally, the grand narrative of *fiqh* was dominated by male discourse. The methology already had a gender bias, which can be seen in the final products.

   Moreover, the creation and development of *fiqh* was a male trademark of male *imams* and writers. As stated by Masdar F. Mas'udi, an Indonesian Muslim intellectual affiliated with NU (Nahdlatul Ulama) the current *fiqh* is a patriarchal *fiqh*, dominated by rules that came from men. Since the era of the Prophet, the companions and *tabi'in*, there has been no exposure of female writers. According to Masdar, *fiqh* was the product its time, of medieval Islam, which was dominated by the very patriarchal cultures of the Middle East.[44] This meant that although individual women lived their lives, their activities were limited by the 'rule of the father'.

2) The transmission of knowledge: the process of disseminating *fiqh* was generally dominated by men; all the four *imams* discussed above learned from male teachers. Then they memorized hadiths which were all narrated by men. They transmitted the hadiths to their male students. Of the thousands of students that an *imam* might have, the majority were always male.

3) Cultural aspects: the *ulamas* that developed *fiqh* lived in territories that had patriarchal patterns in cultural, political and social life. According to Scovill, Islamic teachings should ideally uphold egalitarianism. But the teachings were affected by the patriarchal Middle Eastern cultures where the *imams* developed their *fiqh*.

According to Hamilton A.R. Gibb, many of the *fiqh* on women have no basis in the Qur'an, but rather on hadiths that reflected Arabic tribal traditions. This is despite the fact that the laws on women in the Qur'an are generally for the improvement of women's rights and the correction of pre-Islamic traditions that were discriminatory against women.[45]

In general then, it can be said that discriminatory laws against women have a complex background, and these stances caused the injustices in *fiqh*.

4) Androcentric historical writing: Since history was written down by men, patriarchal ideas also influenced the representation of women in written discourse.

---

[44] Masdar F. Mas'udi, "*Perempuan di antara Lembaran Kitab Kuning*," in Lies Marcoes-Natsir and J.H. Mouleman, *Wanita Indonesia dalam Kajian Teks dan Kontekstual Islam*. INIS, 1993, First Edition,. p.172.

[45] Martin van Bruinessen,"*Kitab Kuning dan Perempuan, Perempuan dan Kitab Kuning*" in Lies Marcoes-Natsir and J.H. Moeleman, *Wanita Indonesia and Kajian Tekstual and Kontekstual Islam*, Jakarta: INIS, 1993, First Edition, p.172.

BURIED DISCOURSES

The four issues listed above give us at least some idea why *fiqh* became male biased (patriarchal). The lack of women's involvement in the development of *fiqh* meant the serious underestimation of issues that should have involved women. Even issues such as menstruation, childbirth, and the blood of afterbirth (*nifas*) – issues that should have involved women in their discussion – were ruled on by male *ulamas*.

But the problem was not only that there were too few female *ulamas* with an understanding of law, during the development of *fiqh*. The problem was the absence of a wider social, cultural and political viewpoint that sided with women. One Jewish female writer, Ruth Roded, for instance, has offered some very interesting information on the number of female Islamic legal experts. In the first and second centuries H, we know of A'isha, Amra bint 'Abdurrahman, and Hafsa bint Sirin as three women, from two different generations, who all had a high propensity in matters of Islamic law.[46]

In the fourth century H, in Baghdad, there were two women who became *mufti* (legal advisers): Isa bint Ibrahim (d. 328 H), and Amma al-Walid (d. 987 H), who was the daughter of the judge, Abu Abdilla al-Husain. Amma al-Walid studied with her father as well as other *ulamas*. She studied Shafi'i's jurisprudence and *Faraid* (the science of inheritance) deeply. Amma Al-Walid once issued a *fatwa* (religious decree) together with a male *mufti*.

Another female legal expert came from Allepo. Fatima came originally from Samarqand and lived in the sixth century H. Fatima studied the *fiqh* of the Hanbali school, and memorized Hanbali's compilation of hadith. She was very close to her father and they once issued a *fatwa* together. She married one of her father's students, whose own legal understanding was inferior to hers. Fatimah's biographer claimed that she corrected *fatwa* issued by her husband.[47]

Ruth Roded has impressively described many historical facts, which have never before been revealed. Besides becoming hadith narrators, many women studied and became teachers of noted *ulamas*. Ibn Hajar, according to Ruth

---

[46] Ruth Roded, *Kembang Peradaban: Citra Wanita di Mata Para Penulis Biografi Muslim*, Bandung: Mizan, 1995. p.148.
[47] *Ibid.*

Roded, studied with fifty-three women.[48] Many other great *ulamas* in the field of hadith and *fiqh* studied with female *ulamas*. Even Shafi'i learned from a noted intellectual and female *ulama*, Nafisa bint Al-Hasan ibn Zaid ibn Ali ibn Abi Talib (145-208 H). Ibn Hanbal once visited her too.[49]

Unfortunately, of all these female *ulamas*, none of them wrote religious texts that we can access, and to this day religious dicourses have been dominated by male *ulamas*. Of course, in the creative processes of these male *ulamas* – when creating religious texts – there is a kind of subjective experience, both implicit and explicit, of gender bias that had been internalized. Whether they realized it or not, this gender bias influenced how they interpreted the Qur'an and hadiths.

---

[51] *Ibid*. p125.
[52] Abdul Rasul Abdul Hassan Al-Gafar, *Wanita Islam dan Gaya Hidup Modern*, Jakarta: Pustaka Hidayah, 1993, First Edition P.70.

PART TWO

UNCONSIDERED ISSUES IN RELATION TO WOMEN AND FIQH

CHAPTER FOUR

REVIEWING THE PATRIARCHAL PATTERNS IN FIQH: A DECONSTRUCTIVE STUDY

WOMEN IN THE *FIQH AL-MUNAKAHA*

One of the important aspects of *fiqh* is the discussion of marriage (*Fiqh al-Munakaha*). This is evidenced by the long explanations on the matter in Islamic classical literatures. The noted *ulama* Ibrahim Al-Badjuri, in his *Hashiya Al-Badjuri*, stated that the marriage *fiqh* was the third obligation among the several obligations in *fiqh*. More explicitly, he explained the matter as follows:

> The chapter on marriage is the third pillar in *fiqh*. *Fiqh* prioritizes the matter of worship, as it is important because it relates directly to God. After the *fiqh* on worship, the *fiqh* on *mu'amala* (on human relations) is a primary need compared to others....Then, the *fiqh* about marriage because, after fulfilling the needs of our stomachs comes the need for sex (*farji*). Only then comes the *fiqh* on crime, since criminal law occurred after the needs for stomach and sex; and then courts and witnesses, people asked the judge and needed the witnesses and released, and finally hoped to God for release from the fires of hell.[1]

---

[1] Ibrahim Al-Badjuri, *Hashiya al-Badjuri ala Ibn Qasim al-Ghuzi*, Vol. II p.92.

Muhammad Ibrahim Al-Badjuri's statement was precise. If we note many standard *fiqh* works, we find the *fiqh* on worship occurs very early on in the text. This is followed by the *fiqh* on *mu'amala*, which was put in second place, because of its importance. Usually, it would start with a discussion on inheritance (*'ilm al-fara'idh*), which was then followed by a discussion on marriage (*fiqh al-munakaha*). Although the format can be seen in almost all *fiqh* literatures, it was not an absolute standard form – there were still variations in structure. This said, even contemporary *fiqh ulamas* tend to follow this kind of structure in their works, such as *al-Fiqh al-Islami wa Adillatuhu* by *Wahba al-Zuhaili*.

In almost all *fiqh* books, we find a chapter on marriage (*Kitab al-Nikah*). *Kitab al-Nikah* does not only discuss marriage, but also other related matters such as divorce (*talaq*), remarriage (*ruju'*), and the approved period between divorce and remarriage (*'idda*). In terms of *usul fiqh*, this kind of structure is called *qadhi*yah (one chain of explanation).

For example, I will quote the structure of a book (chapter)[2] in from the *Sharh Ibn Qasim* in the book *Ghaya al-Taqrib* by Abu Shuja.[3] In this book, the topics listed in the *Kitab al-Nikah* included: articles on custody, things forbidden in marriage (*maharramat al-nikah*), dowry (*mahar*), wedding parties (*walima al-'ursh*), the rotation of wives for polygamists, rebellion against the husband (*nushuz*), divorce proposed by wives (*khulu'*), divorce (*talaq*), other forms of divorce, the ways of divorce for free people and slaves, remarriage (*ruju'*), pledges (*ila*), *zhihar*: (Oath of continence taken by the husband which result in making marital intercourse illicit) law, accusations of adultery, *li'an* pledges, *'idda* (waiting period) laws, the various kinds of *'idda*, liberation (*istibra*)', breast-feeding, income, and articles on childcare.[4]

But, of course, different *fiqh* may have different structures, and may discuss matters at greater or lesser length and detail. There were *ulamas* that put

---

[2] In classical books of *fiqh*, the term of "*kitab*" (large chapter) and "*bab*" (chapter) have different meanings. *Kitab* usually refers to books discussing *fiqh*, while *bab* are the various sections within them.

[3] Abu Shuja's book is the most important literature book in *fiqh*, especially for Islamic boarding schools (*pesantren*). Almost all *pesantrens* in Indonesia use this book as their main reference before discussing other larger *fiqh* books in more detail. The book entitled *al-Ghaya al-Taqrib* was extended in other several larger books, for instance *Fath al-Qarib* and *Hashiya al-Badjuri*.

[4] See the contents list of Ibrahim Al-Badjuri, *Hashiyah Al-Badjuri ala Ibni Qasim Al-Ghuzi*, Ma'arif: Bandung, Second Edition. p.398.

an explanation on divorce in their book, but others did not give it a special chapter. For example, Ibn Rushd in his *Bidaya al-Mujtahid*, gave the topic of divorce a separate chapter.

Islamist John L. Esposito classified *Fiqh al-Munakaha* as Muslim family law, in which he also discussed marriage, divorce, *'idda*.[5] Although the texts vary in structure, many law books, especially in the Shafi'i school, share a similar character in the section on *Kitab al-Nikah*.

In the chapter, I will briefly discuss some, though not all, of the key topics related to *Kitab al-Nikah*. One of the main aims of this book is to see whether the influence of patriarchy has been absorbed into the concept of marriage in Islamic *fiqh*. The discussion will focus on those articles in *Fiqh al-Munakaha* that are patriarchal in nature and need to be reviewed. These include, for example, requirements for marriage such as *ijab qabul*, witness, and dowry.

Clearly, the institution of marriage institution has strong potential to create patterns of imbalance in the relationship between husband and wife. Especially in formalistic and legal matters, the husband usually has a special position in terms of rights, compared with his wife. But the imbalance or hegemonic relationship between husband and wife was influenced by the marriage agreement (*akad*). More concretely, there is an assumption about the subordinate position of women in marriage because the marriage process involved the ceremony of handing over the woman to the man. In the language of *fiqh*, this process is called *ijab qabul*, which can be said to be the essence of marriage.

With the agreement of *ijab-qabul*, man's position becomes like that of a buyer and the woman's like that of a commodity to be sold. So it is not surprising that, during arguments, men might shout at their wives, with inappropriate words such as: "I already bought you; you have to serve anything I want." Although it was not always presented in such vulgar language, the subordinate position of women was demonstrated in everyday behavior in family life. Unfortunately, this situation was to an extent legitimized by our literatures of *fiqh*. The chapters on marriage rules, in particular, put women in the corner.

---

[5]   See John L. Esposito, *Women in Muslim Family Law*, Syaracuse University Press, 1982.

FAMILY AND THE PRE-ISLAMIC SYSTEM OF MARRIAGE

To understand the Islamic concept of marriage, it is necessary to explain the marriage system of the pre-Islamic period, especially in Mecca and Medina. Studies have been conducted by various *ulamas of Figh*, but these have mainly concentrated on theology without considering other approaches such as anthropology, history and sociology. As a result, the studies resulted in the production of a normative theological construction of the system of marriage in Muslim family life.

The discourse on marriage occurs in all religious traditions. This was known by many *fiqh* experts, such as Ibrahim Al-Badjuri, who stated that marriage had been known since the creation of the first human beings. Marriage has existed in law since the time of Adam.[6] It is said that God led the marriage of Adam and Eve, with the angel Gabriel as the witness. Although the validity of this story is unclear, the story demonstrated that marriage was a key part of human history.

People carry out their marriage traditions according to the norms of their various cultures. In ancient China, for example, men could choose any woman they wanted, anytime they wanted. If the woman gave birth to his child then their would be a discussion of marriage. This situation continued until King Fu Hi set out marriage regulations, allowing men to take as many wives as they liked.[7]

The situation in ancient India was not much different from that of the ancient Chinese. A man could choose whichever woman he wanted, until the era of King Asfinako, who regulated the marriage system. But the system still allowed men to have an unlimited number of wives.

The form of marriage in ancient Egypt was very different. A man was allowed to have more than one wife, as it was believed that God had many wives. The belief was strengthened by the fact that kings and religious leaders, who were considered to be the sons of God, also had many wives, and could expect to receive God's blessings on this matter.[8]

---

[6]   Ibrahim Al-Badjuri, p.90
[7]   Mahmud Abd Al-Hamid Muhammad, *Huquq al-Mar'a*, Maktabah Madbouli:Egypt, 1990. p.142.
[8]   *Ibid.* p.43-144.

In ancient Greece, it was understood that a woman could be owned by anybody, because she was considered to be public property. In the *Republic*, Plato said it was necessary for women to make themselves freely available, especially during times of war. On this basis, he also said that the education of children was the responsibility of the state. The condition ended during the reign of Caesar Sikarobus, who established marriage regulations that still allowed men to have unlimited wives.[9]

The state of marriage in ancient Rome was rather different. Men were only allowed to take one wife – an ethos that has influenced Christian thought to this day.

So what was marriage like in Arab tribes before the coming of Islam? In one hadith the Prophet once said: "I was born from a marriage, and I was born not in adultery. So I was moved from good material to a pure womb. I was not touched at all by the influence of *jahiliyya* style adultery."

Based on the statement above, we can see that *safah* (marriage made out-side the rules of valid *Shari'a*) was a pre-Islamic form of marriage in Arabia. *Safah* was not only conducted between a man and a woman (in monogamy), but also between a woman and many men (polyandry). When the woman delivered her child, she then decided which of her lovers would become her husband. In this marriage system, the woman was the decision maker. Many Arabic leaders were born through the *safah* system. There is even a story that says that 'Amr ibn 'Ash was born through this system. It is said that Nabighah, his mother, was engaged by several men, including Abu Sufyan ibn Harb, Al-Ash ibn Wail and Abbas ibn Muthalib. When Nabigha delivered her son, she directly appointed Al-Ash as his father. When asked why she selected Al-Ash as the father, instead of Abu Sufyan who came from a respected family, she replied that Abu Sufyan was a stingy (*bakhil*) man.[10]

Besides the kind of marriage system described above, there were various other forms of marriage during the time of jahiliyya (era of darkness). For example, *al-rahti* was a form of marriage that involved a group of men

---

[9]   *Ibid.*

[10]   Muhammad Abd Al-Hamid Muhammad, *Huquq al-Mar'a*, p.147.

[11]   During the era of Isaac, the religious life was controlled by Isaac's law. After Isaac's law was installed, there was a vacuum until the presence of the Prophet Muhammad. During the vacuum, many teachings were distorted.

with one woman, whereas *al-mukti* was a marriage between a man and his stepmother after his father died or divorced. The Qur'an states: "Do not marry a woman who has [already] been married to your father, as was conducted by people in the past. It is a really bad and ugly deed" (Al-Nisa' (4): 22).

The verse prohibits people from imitating the deeds of people in the past, meaning those who lived in the era before Islam and after the Prophet of Jesus (the era of *fatra* (transition)).[11] During this time, marriages were conducted in all these ways, although they should have followed the way of Jesus. But many religious leaders manipulated Jesus' teachings and moved from God's law.

According to several forms of evidence, the kinship system in the pre-Islamic era was matrilineal. Sons and daughters belonged to their mother, and became the leaders of their tribe or mother's group. Wealth belonged to the matrilineal group and was managed by a female group leader. This form of marriage involved the wife staying in her family household, while her husband could visit the house if he wanted to make love with her.[12]

The matrilineal system was generally dominant in Arab society, although some historical sources suggest that patrilineal systems was also applied in some areas, such as in Mecca, the birthplace of the Prophet. In patrilineal systems, the family consisted of members from male line, a fact that can be seen in the use of inherited male names used as family names. Wealth also belonged to men's clans, and if land belonged to individuals, it was inherited by their sons or brothers. The form of marriage was still uxorilocal, but a woman only had one husband.

After the migration (*hijra*) of the Prophet Muhammad from Mecca to Medina, both the matrilineal and patrilineal systems were still being implemented. But as time passed, the patrilineal system replaced the matrilineal system, which was considered to be a remnant of the times of *jahiliyya*, whereas the patrilineal system was considered more Islamic.

It was at this point that the patriarchal discourses started to develop. When the Prophet was still alive, he could maintain the balance and maintain justice and equality. After his death, patriarchal tendencies became increasingly strong in the Islamic world.

---

[12] Montgomery Watt, *Muhammad at Medina*, Oxford University Press, 1972, p.272.

DECONSTRUCTING THE DEFINITION OF MARRIAGE

The term *al-Nikah* (marriage) comes from the Arabic root "*nakaha, yankihu, nikahan*" which literally means "*al-dham, al-wat'u* and *al-aqdu*." For example, when we say "*tanakaha al-ashjar*", the meaning is that "*idza tamayalat wa dhamma ba'dhun ila ba'dhin*," meaning "when the trees lean against each other, they go on to gather."

In Islam, marriage was one of the *shari'a* recommended by the Prophet. Marriage was God's order to regulate the relations between men and women, in a family full of love and blessings (*mawadda wa rahma*). Through marriage, both man and woman could do things that had previously been forbidden, such as having sex.

According to the Prophet, marriage was only a recommendation, rather than an obligation. A recommendation could also change, and become obligatory or just arbitrary (*jaiz*), depending on the situation. The Prophet once said: "*Nikah* is my recommendation, and whoever dislikes my recommendation, dislikes me." This hadith showed that although marriage was just a recommendation (not an obligation), those who didn't follow it were not true followers of Muhammad. If we use a different logic, (*mahfum mukhalafa*), we can consider the recommendation of marriage as approaching the status of an obligation.

Is there a patriarchal perspective in the Islamic system of marriage? The question is both tendentious and controversial if viewed from the perspective of *fiqh*. It is tendentious because it suggests that there may have been social engineering based on patriarchal ideology in defining marriage in the classical literature. And it is controversial because the term was never in the vocabulary of either classical or contemporary *fiqh* scholars. In order to assess whether there was a patriarchal pattern in discussions on marriage, we should look at definitions given by the old *ulamas* from the four main schools of *fiqh*:

1) The Hanafite *ulamas. Ulamas* from this school generally defined marriage as an agreement that resulted on the possession of sex (*budh'*) by intention. The possession of sex meant than a man would have ownership over the woman's genitals as well as the rest of her body, which was his to enjoy.

Of course, true possession was the sole right of God, but nonetheless, this view gave men the right to have sex (*istimta'*) with their 'possessions'. [13]

2) The Shafi'ite *ulamas*. *Ulamas* from this school viewed marriage as an agreement which resulted on the right of men to have sex by using the terms *ankah* (to marry someone off), *tazwij* (marriage) or other phrases to that effect. In essence, this definition gave men the right to benefit from the woman's genitals. Some *ulamas* said that the marriage gave the right for a man to have sex, but not the right of ownership. [14]

3) The Malikite *ulamas*. The *ulamas* of this school, especially Ibn Arafa, defined marriage as an agreement to have sexual pleasure, without mentioning the price beforehand. In simple terms, the *ulamas* said that marriage was an agreement that allowed the man to own and enjoy the woman's genitals and the rest of her body. [15]

4) The Hanbalite *ulamas*. The *ulamas* of this school defined marriage in a practical way. Marriage was defined as a contract made verbally, using the terms *ankah* and *tazwij* in order to have sexual pleasure.

Although the above definitions seem varied, if we observe them carefully, they have strong resemblances: marriage was basically a contract to regulate *intifa'u zaujin bi bidhi'i zaujihi wa sa'iri badaniha min haithu al-taladzudz* (the use by husband over his wife's genitals and the rest of her body for sexual pleasure). Through the marriage contract, the husband gained the right to enjoy his wife's whole body. Some *ulamas* differentiated between *milk al-intifa'* (temporary possession) from *milk al-manfa'a* (permanent possession), but this distinction does not detract from the man's fundamental right of ownership.

If we look at the details of the definitions, we find patriarchal assumptions, although they may not have been made intentionally by the *ulamas*:

1) The objectification of women by men. The definitions above are a step towards men's ownership of women. The terms *milk al-mut'a* (the possession of sex), *milk al-budu'* (the possession of the vagina) and such,

---

[13] Abd Al-Rahman Al-Jazairi, *al-Fiqh 'ala Madzahib al-Arba'a*, Dar al-Fikr, vol. IV. p.2.

[14] *Ibid*

[15] *Ibid*. p.2-3.

have pejorative implications. It seemed that marriage was only defined in terms of its sexual and physical aspects. In reality, we can not pass up the importance of these aspects, but there are more important ones too, such as the primary mission to form a family which is full of love and blessings (*mawwada wa rahma*), following God's will.

2) Due to this objectification, women's position was subordinate to and controlled by men, and this included her sexual life. The Hanafi school argued that men rather than women had the right to sexual pleasure, meaning that men could force their wives to satisfy their sexual desires, even when their wives refused them.[16]

3) *Ijab* (submission) and *qabul* (acceptance) in marriage, although they did not imply a straight buying-selling transaction, were often treated as such in practice. This was reinforced by the system of dowry, which seemed to be a tool for a sales transaction and made women seem like objects.

It is important to review the definitions offered by the *ulamas* of these four schools of *fiqh*, to see if the patriarchal biases can be avoided. Although there is no guarantee that the issues can be resolved, it is an apt place to start.

REVIEWING THE ESSENTIAL MEANING OF MARRIAGE

The problems of the subordination, marginalization and impoverishment of women in family life would not happen if we properly understood the essential meaning of the marriage contract. The highest principle of a marriage was expressed delightfully in the Qur'an: "He has created you from a single person, from whom He created his wife so that he would feel happy with her. After he made love with her, his wife fell pregnant and she felt light (for some time). When she felt heavy, the husband and wife beg to God and said, "Truly, if You give us children who are good, we will become among those who give thanks to You," (Al-A'raf (7): 189).

According to the above verse, a marriage is the reunification of the most essential form of human beings, *nafs wahida*, at a worldly level. God uses

---

[16]   Abd Al-Rahman Al-Jazai'ri, *al-Fiqh 'ala Madzahib al-Arba'a*, vol. IV. p.4.

the term of *nafs wahida* to show that marriage is the reunification between a man and woman, on a practical level, after the initiation of the process during the Creation. Through marriage, as a means of reunifying humanity, there should no longer be issues of one sex being dominant or subordinate to the other. Man and Woman should consider themselves to connected and unified, without distinction or subordination, let alone 'ownership'. This is in line with the Prophet's statement: "*al-mar'atu shaqa'iqu al-rijal*," which means "woman is the twin sister of man."

As such, marriage should be understood as essential to humanity; wives and belong to husbands, and husbands belong to wives.

In another Qur'anic verse, God said: "And among the signs of His authority, He created wives from the same material as you in order you be happy with her and He gives love and mercy between you. Truly, those who think will get these signs." (Al-Rum (30): 21).

This verse also emphasizes the relation of the essential unity of human beings (*min anfusikum*) on the ideal and practical levels, a marriage full of love and mercy. Marriage, as a practical institution on this religious level, is the definition closest to the generic definition of marriage, *al-dham*, meaning 'to gather'. The gathering of a man and a woman in a unity of essence and practice, without hierarchy, is the purpose of this contract.

In this sense, there is no clear centralization of the male role in the contract of marriage. There is also no suggestion of the dominance of one sex over the other. So it was right and timely that Wahbah al-Zuhaili defined marriage as a binding relationship backed up by lawmakers (*shari'*) that allowed a man to enjoy sexual pleasure (*istimta'*) from his wife, and conversely that the wife should enjoy sexual pleasure from her husband. Wahbah's definition was a breakthrough in the effort to redefine the understanding of marriage maintained by the *ulamas* of the past, particularly those representing the main schools of *fiqh*.

DECONSTRUCTING THE CONCEPT OF GUARDIANSHIP IN MARRIAGE

In discussing marriage discourses, the concept of guardianship can not be separated from that of marriage, as it is one of the requirements of that contract. The four schools of *fiqh* decided that a marriage would not be religiously valid without a guardian. The requirement referred to a hadith narrated by Al-Daruqutni, which recounted that the Prophet said: "*There is no marriage without a custodian and two witnesses.*"[17] *Ulamas* viewed the hadith as legal evidence for the requirement for there to be a guardian for the bride in the marriage. I will now elaborate on the role of the guardian and its patriarchal implications.

The term *wali* (guardian) was a derivative from the root *wilaya*. *Wilaya* contains several etymological meanings: First, it can mean helping (*nusra*), as it was used in the Qur'an: "*Whoever helps Allah and His Prophet, the believers, truly, those helpers are lucky people.*" (Al-Maidah (5): 56). Secondly, *wilaya* means love (*mahabba*), as it was used in the Qur'an: "All believers, male and female, love each other. (Al-Taubah (9): 71).[18]

Besides these two meanings, *wilaya* can also mean *al-sulta* (power and ability). It can be said that *wali* are people who hold a certain power (*sahib al-sulta*), whereas in *fiqh*, *wali* refers to people who have the power to spend wealth (*tasarruf*) without depending on other people's permission.

Imam Abu Hanifa divided custody into three levels:

1) Power over the soul (*wilaya ala al-nafs*), which included personal affairs (*shaksiya*), such as marrying and teaching. These came under the authority of the father or grandfather.
2) Power over wealth (*wilaya ala al-mal*), which included the authority to spend wealth, to use (*tassaruf*) the wealth. This was also the prerogative of the father and grandfather, or other people who had been authorized.
3) Power over both soul and wealth, both of which both fell under the authority of the father and grandfather.[19]

Our discussion will concentrate on *wilaya al-nafs*, which comes under two categories. First, is power by force (*wilaya al-ijbar*). And secondly, there is power without force, where people have the full right to choose. The power of force is by definition based on four issues: kinship relations, ownership, slavery and leadership. Meanwhile, democratic authority (*ikhtiyar*) referred

---

[17] "*La nikaha illa bi waliyyin wa shahiday adlin.*"
[18] The verse: *Wa al-mu'minuna wa al-mu'minati ba'dhuhum auliya'a ba'adh.*
[19] Wahba Al-Zuhaili, *al-Fiqh al-Islam wa Adillatuhu*, Dar al-Fikr, vol. VII, p.187.

to the right of the guardian to marry off their daughters, based on the daughter's free choices.

According to Malik, there were two kinds of custody; *khassa* (specific) and *'amma* (general). Specific guardianship belonged to the father, grandfather and state leader. General guardianship was connected completely with Islam, and every Muslim male. A good example of the application of general guardianship would be a situation where a woman wanted to marry, but she did not have a father, or other male family members. Or she may have been a *dani'a*, a woman without beauty, wealth or social standing,[20] and has no family origin[21]. In such cases, any Muslim man should help her to arrange her marriage.

According to Imam Shafi'i, there were two concepts of guardianship (*wali*). The first was *wali ijbar*, which refers to those who are given the power of force. The second was *wali ikhtiyar*, who does not have the authority to force. The authority of *wali ijbar* belonged to the father and then the grandfather or other member of the male lineage, if the father was deceased. A guardian had the right to arrange the marriage of his daughter, even if she was underage, without her permission. *Wali ikhtiyar* was a concept of guardianship where authority was given to a *wali 'asaba* who had the right to arrange the marriage of a woman who was not virgin. A *Wali ikhtiyar* can not arrange a marriage without the permission of the woman. The permission did not only mean her silence; it required a verbal answer.

The last imam of the four schools of *fiqh*, Ibn Hanbal also offered a concept of guardianship that was not so different from those of the other *imams*. Ibn Hanbal stated that *wali ijbar* was the right of the father or, if there was no father, of a judge. This is similar to Malik's position, which did not include the grandfather as a potential *wali ijbar*. On *wali ikhtiyar*, Ibn Hanbal agreed with the other *ulamas* that the role could be taken by all kinds of *wali*.

So, who has the right to be a guardian? In *fiqh*, the concept of guardianship is based on the concept of *'asaba*, which maintains that people with the right to become guardians are those who descend from the patriarchal lineage:

---

[20] I use the term poverty to interpret the term *al-khaliya min al-hisbi* meaning those who do not have good ethics, such as mastering sciences, the destination of their lives, and so on.

[21] I use "tuna nasab' Indonesian term (having no origin) as a translation for *al-khaliya min al-nasabi*, meaning people who do not have a line of origin, the children of adultery or slaves.

father, grandfather, brothers, stepbrothers, cousins, step-cousins, nephews, uncles, step-uncles and, if lacking all of these, a judge.

There are resemblances between the stances on the concept of guardianship between the four schools of *fiqh*. Three of the four schools, except Hanafi, agreed that the right of guardianship belonged only to men. This becomes even clearer if we look at the requirements to guardianship agreed upon by classical and modern *ulamas*. Wahbah al-Zuhaili, a noted contemporary *fiqh* expert and profuse writer, said there were five requirements which were agreed in consensus (*ijma'*) by the *fiqh* experts. The most important of these are:

1) *Kamal al-ahliya*, meaning that people who have the right of guardianship are adult, mentally healthy, and free. Conversely, children, the mentally impaired, and slaves can not become *wali*.
2) The guardian and the person given guardianship must share the same religion. So, non-Muslims are not allowed to become guardians for Muslims.
3) A guardian must be a man. This opinion was held by almost all the *ulamas* of the four schools, except the Hanafite school.[22]

Sayyid Sabiq was more progressive than Al-Zuhaili in defining the requirements of guardianship. Although it was not entirely explicit, it is clear that he maintained that there were four requirements for guardianship: they should be adult, mentally healthy, free (not slaves) and Muslim.[23] But he still maintained several controversial points on the guardianship of women. In his subtitle: "*I'tibar Wilaya al-Mar'ah ala Nafsiha*," he said: "The majority of *ulamas* believe that a woman has no right to arrange her own marriage or that of others."[24]

Why is this so? In determining the requirements for men (*al-dzukura*) in marriage guardianship, *fiqh* experts usually used Al-Nisa, verse 34, as their legitimating argument. Jalalludin Al-Mahalli, in his *al-Mahalli*, said that the prohibition against women being guardians in marriage was for two reasons. First, it was not suitable in the context of local customary

---

[22] The requirements are fairness, *istiqama* and intelligence in practicing religion.
[23] Sayyid Sabiq, *Fiqh al-Sunna*, Dar al-Fikr, vol. III p.3.
[24] *Ibid*.

tradition. And secondly, there was no legal basis for it in the Qur'an and hadith. In fact, the Qur'an states: "*al-rijalu qawamuna ala al-nisa'i,*" and in hadith narrated by Ahmad, Ibn Hibban and Hakim said: "there is no marriage without a guardian." Also, in a hadith from Ibn Maja, it is stated: "A woman is not allowed to arrange the marriage of others or her self."[25]

Shaykh Shihab Al-Din Al-Qalyubi said that verse 34 of Al-Nisa' and the hadith suggested that guardianship was the right of men. Any effort to change this should be rejected, since it violated the [authority] of the hadith from Ibn Maja.[26]

Supporting the prohibition against women becoming guardians, some *ulamas* legitimated their position based on Al-Baqara, verse 221, which reads: "Do not marry a polytheistic woman (musyrik) before she has become a believer. Truly, a Muslim female slave is better than a polytheistic woman, although she may be attractive to you. *Do not arrange the marriage of a mushrik man with a Muslim woman before he has become a believer. Truly, a Muslim slave is better than them. They will lead you to hell, while Allah asks you to Heaven and His forgiveness. And Allah gives his orders [in these verses] to human beings in order that they can learn.*"

Secondly, they used the chapter, Al-Noor (24), verse 32, which states: "*And marry those among you who are alone, and who have already been prepared among your slaves, between male slaves and female slaves. If they are poor, Allah will help them afford it. Allah has the greatest knowledge and He knows all.*"

Some *ulamas* interpreted these two verses to mean that only men could give the order to arrange a marriage, rather than women.[27]

If we analyze the bases of legitimization used by the *ulamas*, Shihab Al-Din Al-Qalyubi, Jalal Al-Din Al-Mahhali and the others, there was no definite legal reason why the guardian of a marriage should be a man. I will briefly review the legal basis through an interpretive approach; a more complete explanation of these verses will be explained in a separate chapter.

---

[25] Jallal Al-Din Al-Mahali, *Al-Mahalli Sharh of Minhaj Talibin al-Nawawi*, Dar Al-Kutub Al Arabiyah, vol. III, p.221.

[26] Shihab al-Din al-Qalyubi, *Qalyubi wa Umaira Dar al-Kutub al-Arabaiya*, vol. III, p.221. We need to know that *Qalyubi wa Umairah* was a *Sharah* (larger explanation) to *al-Mahalli* as written by Shaykh Jalal Al-Din Al-Mahalli, while *al-Mahalli* is a larger explanation of *Minhaj al-Talibin* by Al-Nawawi.

[27] Sayyid Sabiq, *Fiqh al-Sunna*, vol. II, p.122.

1) The chapter Al-Nisa', verse 34, actually shows that the basis of male leadership was due to sociological and economical factors, and that men are responsible for the income of the wife and family. The verse did not describe a historical event that should become normative in religion, but rather a historical socio-economic event. During this time, Arab culture was under the hegemony of a materialistic, economic culture. So it is not unusual that people with those material or economic qualities thought of themselves as leaders. This also happened in the household. When the husband owned the material and economic resources, he became the leader of the family.

2) The chapters Al-Baqara, verse 221, and Al-Nur, verse 32, do not overtly proscribe women from becoming the guardians of a marriage. The verses issue an order for marriage, but it was for both men and women. The verse does seem to issue an order to men, but this is due to male leadership patterns in the local culture. In a situation where women could become leaders, the verses would be interpreted differently.

Then, where did the concept that guardianship should only be applicable to men come from? Montgomery Watt, in one of his books, said that many Arabic-Meccan traditions were adopted into Islamic law. Based on Montgomery's statement, we could say that the adoption of guardianship and male lineage from Arabic traditions into Islamic *fiqh* was part of an effort to preserve the tradition, because the Qur'an and hadiths never mentioned these concepts explicitly.

DECONSTRUCTING POLYGAMY

Al-Nisa' (4), verse 3, states: "*And marry the women you like; one, two, three or four; but if you can not make it fair, just marry one.*"

One of the crucial and most widely discussed problems in *fiqh munakaha* is polygamous marriage. Polygamy is a complicated problem faced by women and Islam. Some Islamists have even said that the acceptance of polygamy suggests that Islam neglects democracy and human rights in married life. Polygamy, according to these experts, is discrimination against women's rights.

On polygamy, there was an interesting statement from Al-Bajuri quoting from 'Abd Al-Salam:

> In the past, during the era of Moses, women were allowed to be married without limitation for the welfare of men. During the era of Jesus, it was forbidden to marry more than one woman for the woman's welfare. During the era of our Prophet, the two traditions were maintained. The teachings are as follows: during Moses' time, the welfare of men was prioritized, as Pharaoh's regime had killed many boys and let the women live. So, it was normal that during Moses' time, men were prioritized since their number was less than the number of women. During Jesus' time, women's welfare was prioritized, since Jesus was created without a father (*bila abin*), so it was normal that Jesus' law prioritized women. Meanwhile, during the time of Muhammad, the wisdom of giving men permission to marry four women was because every person has four characters, and marriage means love and mercy, and this could be lost if there are more than four characters.[28]

Is this true? From the above quote, Al-Badjuri seems to want to show the justice of Islamic law, which synergized the guidelines for public welfare in Islam, and corrected pre-Islamic laws that did not lead to public welfare. Abdis Salam's opinion also seems to be a rationalization of the stance of Islamic law on polygamy. But, historically speaking, the statement is not backed up by strong evidence. This opinion is contradictory to the stance that the Islamic laws on polygamy were a correction of the pre-Islamic practice of marrying as many women as one wanted to. During the time of the Prophet, there was a close companion called Ghilan Al-Tsaqafi, who had ten wives. This was reported to the Prophet and He ordered him to take only four of the ten. This shows that polygamy was the Qur'an's sociological and anthropological response to the community at that time. The number four should not be interpreted as a maximum number for today; it was the maximum for the past. We often judge history unfairly.

Generally, in discussing polygamy, almost all works of *fiqh* focused solely on the aspect of permission (*mubaha*), without criticizing the assumptions

---

[28] Shaykh Ibrahim Al-Badjuri, *Hashiya al-Badjuri libni Qasim*, vol. II, p.93.

it was based on, anthropologically and sociologically. Ibn Qasim Al-Guzi, for instance, allowed all men to marry four free women, without considering the requirements which should be fulfilled in polygamy, as laid out in the Qur'an. This type of thinking is found not only in *Mukhtasar* by Ibn Qasin, but also in other *mu'tabara* texts (recognized as strong literary references). According to Fazlur Rahman, this phenomena shows the *ulamas'* misunderstanding of the concept of justice in Al-Nisa', verse 3.

These principles were underlined by Muhammad 'Abdu when he issued a religious decree (*fatwa*) that was very controversial for its time. His *fatwa*, which was issued in 1298, was quoted in its entirety by Ali Ahmad Jurjawi in his important book, *Hikma al-Tashri' wa Falsafatuhu*. According to this book, 'Abdu said the Muhammad's law allowed a man to marry four women, if the man knew himself to be capable of fairness. If he was unable to be fair, he should not marry more than one wife. In this situation, 'Abdu quoted this verse: "*fain khiftum alla ta'dilu fawahidatan.*" According to 'Abdu, if the man could not maintain his wife's rights, he would ruin the structure and welfare of family life. Actually, the main pillar in the house hold was a love among the members of the family.[29]

Quoting Al-Jurjawi on 'Abdu's *fatwa*, it appears that 'Abdu emphasized the importance of qualitative concepts of justice that can not be measured, like love and mercy. This concept was in line with the term '*adala* used in the Qur'an, which carries a more qualitative meaning. The concept of justice usually used by the *ulamas* was more quantitative, and closer to the meaning of the term *qistun*. This quantitative understanding justice was more fragile since it was liable to change. This version was seen in the *fiqh* on polygamy that discussed matters such as the equal sharing of income, the equal sharing of time between the wives and so on. The *ulamas* did not consider the qualitative factors, such as love and feelings of unfairness. Qualitative justice should have been prioritized by the *ulamas*, because it can not be automatically assumed that those who can conduct quantitative justice can conduct qualitative justice too.

The mistakes of the *ulamas* in defining qualitative justice could be seen, for instance, in Abdurrahman Al-Jazairi's famous work, *al-Fiqh al-Madzahi*

---

[29] Ali Ahmad al-Jurjawi, *Hikma al-Tashri wa Falsafatuhu*, p.12.

al-Arba'a. He said that the offering of equal rights to multiple wives was not compulsory for people in polygamous marriages because, as human beings, they would be unable to conduct this fairly. Love was instinctive affair. For example, a man might feel more love for wife A, while being far more sexually aroused by wife B; and the control of such injustices was beyond the capacity of human beings. According to *fiqh* experts, this teaching came from God in the phrase: "And you will not be able to be fair among your women." The verse was interpreted as establishing the man's inability to equally share love and mercy and, since it was therefore deemed impossible, the *fiqh* experts did not include love and mercy in their rulings on the requirements for husbands in polygamous marriages.

Of course, this was an arbitrary interpretation. If we read the verse carefully, it is actually God's warning about the importance of qualitative justice. Polygamy is clearly permitted as is shown in Al-Nisa', verse 3, but it holds a requirement of justice. However, justice was difficult to implement because husbands may not have the ability to distribute qualitative needs (love and mercy) and quantitative needs (income, home, etc.) equally between their wives.

This was the real concept of true justice (*'adala*) discussed in Al-Nisa', verse 3. But the *ulamas* prioritized the aspect of permission (*mubaha*), over justice (*'adala*). However, the aspect of *'adala* should have been equally prioritized as a requirement in polygamy. If the requirement of qualitative and quantitative justice was not, or could not be, fulfilled then polygamy would be difficult to justify, even though it was allowed in religious law. But the emphasis on quantitative justice was in keeping with the prioritization of men over women.

Furthermore, the *ulamas* interpreted that the numbers two, three and four in Al-Nisa', verse 3, were not final rulings (*ihdad*), only valid during the time of the Prophet. The verse's meaning can be revealed sociologically, historically, and economically. As mentioned above, the number four (as the total number of wives permitted) should be viewed as a brave correction by Islam of the tradition of unlimited polygamy practiced by people at that time.

If polygamy was to be allowed, then, it should be based on the perspective of the Qur'anic exegesis theory: *munasaba ayat bi al-ayat* (Qur'an exegesis based on verses to verses), meaning that it could be conducted with widows who have fatherless children. In this case, polygamy is a part of charitable action. But, in reality, the verse is often misused for self-interested gains. People often say that they conduct polygamy because it was allowed by the Qur'an and was also conducted by the Prophet when, actually, they would just like to have more than one wife. They often forget they are not the Prophet, but merely fallible human beings.

Although he quoted 'Abdu, Al-Jurjani gave different reasons on the legality of polygamy, which was never proven scientifically.[30]According to him, there were four teachings on polygamy, although I only list the three most relevant ones below:

1) Human beings consist of four substances that formed the structure of the body. So it was deemed right that men should have four wives. The issue is why this was only deemed fitting for men. Women are also human after all.

2) Four also referred to four kinds of employment: administration, trade, farming and industry. The problem is that these days there are dozens of kinds of jobs available. Based on this logic, are men to be allowed to have more than four wives?

3) A fair man who has four wives has three days a week to share out his love between them. But how can this love be measured in temporal terms? The problem is how to measure the love. This idea has absolutely no basis in the Qur'an and Sunna.

Besides this, many *fiqh* take the male perspective when discussing polygamy. They suggest that if polygamy was forbidden, there would be adultery and moral decadence. Sa'id Talib Al-Hamadani, an Indonesian writer and leader of Al-Irsyad, said that polygamy was permitted in Islam in order to enlarge the number of followers (*umat*). Furthermore, he said that the developing world required more human resources and that men have a longer reproductive capacity than women, who experience the menopause. Polygamy was a better solution than the husbands' having sexual relations eslewhere.[31]

---

[30] This opinion was not only Al-Jurjawi's, but was also shared by most *ulamas* to rationalize polygamy. But the rationalization is questionable.

[31] H.S.A. Alhamdani, *Risalah Nikah Hukum Perkawinan*, Jakarta: Pustaka Amani, 1989, vol. III, p.80-1.

This kind of monolithic interpretation often occurred in *fiqh*. *Ulama* should conduct preliminary studies that include women's as well as men's perspectives. In terms of the phenomenologist approach, the *ulamas* should take an emphatic approach to the matter. Women are also human beings with their own interests and inner feelings. They should be loved by their husbands without the disruptive presence of three other women.

In my view, we should review the matter of polygamy as permitted by religion, because in daily life it is something which has been exploited for the mores of human lust. Polygamy appears to create more losses than benefits.

If we view the social and theological history of polygamy, it seems that the system was actually aimed at helping widows with orphaned children. We should consider Muhammad Shahrur's book, *Al-Kitab wa Qur'an: Qira'a Mu'asira*. He tried to reinterpret Al-Nisa', verse 3, etymologically, in a way different to that of the earlier *ulamas*. He maintained that the words *qastun* and *adlun* have two contradictory meanings. *Qastun* can mean 'justice' as mentioned in the Qur'anic chapters, Al-Ma'ida, verse 42, Al-Hujurat, verse 9, and Al-Mumtahana, verse 8. Secondly, *qastun* can mean tyrannical cruelty and sin as mentioned in Al-Jinn, verse 15 (*wa ammal qasituna fa kanu li jahannam hataba*). *Adlun* also has two contradictory meanings. It can mean both *istiwa'* (equal) and *a'wajaj* (crooked). While *qastun* means justice in only one branch, *adlun* means equal justice in two. This double meaning, according to Shahrur, is the essence of this meaning of justice.

Besides those developments, other options could be considered, such as applying the theory of *munasaba* in deciding the laws for polygamy. Through this theory, the above verse on polygamy, as a 'joining term'('*ataf*), relates to the earlier verse as follows: *Wa atul yatama amwalahum wala tabaddalahu al-kabitha bi al-tayyib wala takulu anwalahum ila amwalikum innahu kana hubban kabira*, which refers to fatherless children whose fathers have passed away. So, polygamy is only tolerated to help orphans. But in helping fatherless children, why must we marry off their mothers? The correct answer would be that we should help such children without involving any outside interest, such as engaging in polygamous marriage.

DECONSTRUCTING DIVORCE

Before discussing the topic further, we should clarify that the 'deconstruction of divorce' does not refer to the question of whether or not divorce (*talaq*) is needed or not in Islam. Rather, it focuses on how and why divorce became the prerogative of men, giving them the authority to divorce their wives, without a clear progress of bargaining. This kind of divorce does damage to both parties, but is especially damaging for the woman.

If we look at the histories of major religions besides Islam, almost all have a concept of divorce. Of the three Semitic traditions, only [some branches of] Christianity forbids divorce. This prohibition is still very influential in many parts of the world; marriage can not be broken up except by the death of one party. On the one hand, this may help to maintain marriages, but it is problematic when there is a problem that seems irresolvable except by divorce. We face a real dilemma when religion may outlaw divorce, but individual demands can not be avoided. It may help to suggest that they decision is delayed and discussed, but if this process amounts to nothing, specific divorce regulations are required.

The firmness of Christian theology on this matter resulted in tension in the West, and consequently many rejected the Church's rulings on the matter. They argued that human beings can not be expected to be perfect creatures, given the fallible nature of their very humanity. Western society sought new legislations that were more in keeping with their way of life.[32]

Of course, divorce was not only known within Islam. Divorce also happened in ancient times, although marriage relations occurred instinctively, like the mating of animals. Both marriage and divorce were more a matter of instinct.

During the Babylonian era, the code of Hammurabi maintained that husbands had the right to divorce their wives, but that wives were only given the right to request a divorce based on the fault of the husband. If a wife asked a divorce, but she was in the wrong, she would receive the death penalty for having the nerve to ask for a divorce.[33]

---

[32] See the explanation of the concept of divorce and social and cultural change in Qasim Amin, T*ahrir al-Mar'a*, Ain Sham, vol. III, p.161-185.

[33] Mahmud Abd Al-Hamid Muhammad, *Huquq al-Mar'a baina Islam wa al-Diyanat al-Ukhra*, Madbouli: Kairo, 1990, p.208.

In ancient Greece, a man had the right to divorce his wife whenever and wherever he wanted. But during the classical period, women also gained the right to ask for divorce.[34] In pre-Christian Rome, men could also divorce their wives wherever and whenever they wanted.

So how does Islam view divorce? In *fiqh*, divorce is known as *talaq* – a word with the etymological root *tallaqa*, which can mean *hillu, alqaidi al-irsal, al-tarqi* or *fakka*, all of which mean 'to release the bonds'. These 'bonds' could be either physical, in the sense of actual ropes, or psychological or spiritual. The etymological meaning is usually wider than the terminological one (*ma'na shar'iyya*). Imam Malik wrote this poem on the topic of *talaq*:

Al-ilmu shahdun wa al-kitaba qaiduhu

Qayyid shuyuduka bi al-hibali al-wathiqa

Fa min al-humaqa an tashida ghizalah

Wa tufakkiha baina al-khalai'iqi taliqa

Science is like a hunted animal, and writing is its bond

So, tie the animal with a strong rope

And it is foolish to hunt baby deer

And you release it among other free creatures

Malik was the using meaning of *talaq* in a literary way. Terminologically (*shar'iyyah*), as was usual in *fiqh* literature, such as the work of Shaykh Ibrahim Al-Badjuri, *talaq* referred to the cutting of the marriage ties voluntarily. Etymologically, *talaq* had both psychological and physical meanings, while terminologically, it had only psychological meaning.[35] Abu Bakar Syatha, in his *I'anah Al-Talibin*, used the term *talaq* in a similar way, implying that the ties of marriage could be released through the use of words that indicated this kind of meaning.[36]

---

[34] *Ibid.*

[35] Shaykh Ibrahim Al-Badjuri *Hashiya ala Ibn Qasim Al-Ghuzi*, Bandung: Shirka al-Ma'arif, vol. II, p.139.

[36] See Muhammad Shata al-Dimyati, *Hashiya I'anat al-Talibin*, vol. IV, p.2.

From the way it is proposed, *talaq* can be divided into two parts:

1) *Talaq sharih*, which means proposing divorce using clear language, rather than connotation.
2) *Talaq kinaya*, which means to propose divorce using language with a single meaning (*yahtamilu ghairahu*).

There are two kinds of *talaq*: *talaq ba'in* and *talaq raj'i*. *talaq bain* is divorce that can not be reconciled because it has been spoken three times, while *talaq raj'iy* still offers the possibility of reconciliation.

In terms of *fiqh*, a divorce is considered legal if it is conducted by mature people (*taklif*) without force. It was, however, illegal if conducted by those without legal witness or those who are mentally impaired. The divorce would also be invalid if it was achieved by force (*mukra*). If the divorce statement was conducted by intoxicated people, its validity was assessed on the cause of the intoxication – being intentionally intoxicated was acceptable, while divorce statements made while unintentionally intoxicated were invalid.[37] In the former case, the divorce would be seen as a punishment for drunkenness.

Jurists had varied views on divorce law. The jurists of the Hanbali and Hanafi schools considered divorce to be *haram* (forbidden), except in emergency situations. Their legal basis was a hadith of the Prophet: "*Ia'aanalahu kulla dawwaqin mithlaqin*," which means, God dislikes people who often marry and divorce."

According to the jurists, a divorce was an action that did not demonstrate gratitude to God's gift of marriage as a pleasure. This is why divorce could only be conducted in an emergency situation, such as the suspected infidelity of the wife or because the husband no longer loved her.[38] The opinion was basically good, but the status of an 'emergency situation' was determined only in terms of men's interests, rather than women's. It is always an abstract evaluation and a matter of degree – suspicion without clear evidence should not be sufficient reason for divorce because then men could divorce as often

---

[37] *Ibid.*
[38] Sayyid Sabiq, *Fiqh al-Sunna*, translation, al-Ma'arif, Bandung, vol. III, p.2.

as they liked. No longer loving a wife is also insufficient to be classified as an 'emergency situation'. Why shouldn't the husband strive to rekindle the love, as his wife would be urged to do?

The main problem that needs further discussion is why the proposal of divorce was only conducted by men. Men had the right to divorce their wives, even in the absence of a serious reason. A husband could threaten to divorce his wife whenever he wanted to remarry and couldn't get the permission of his first wife. Although the wife has the right to *fasakh* (destroy the marriage), it was a passive right. *Fasakh* can only be conducted in an emergency situation, and the woman will receive none of the compensation she would receive in a normal divorce.

Sayyid Sabiq, in his book *Fiqh al-Sunna*, said that Islam gave men the right to divorce because they would strive to preserve the marriage, having paid an expensive dowry in the first place. If they wanted to remarry, they would need funds to do so. They also had to earn income for the family and pay compensation to the ex-wife following divorce. Sayyid Sabiq also stated that men were more rational and patient in dealing with their wife's behavior, so that they would not easily divorce their wives in haste. He also said that women were easily angered, harsh, and did not bear the burden after divorce.[39]

Sayyid Sabiq's psychological and material reasons are logical enough, but his argument has weaknesses. Once again, his reasons were gender biased and monolithic (from the husband towards the wife). Not all spouses fit his psychological gender profiles. Not all husbands have willingness to maintain the marriage and patience to face their wives and many of the husbands could not think rationally. Material responsibility which should be given to the ex-wives following divorce was no longer a burden if the husbands wanted to remarry.

In order to attempt a deconstruction of divorce, we need to reconstruct how divorce has been conceptualized and implemented. Some initial thoughts include:

1) A divorce should be based on clear, urgent reasons. Both the husband and wife must agree on the emergency of the situation. If the husband

---

[39] *Ibid.* p.17.

suspects his wife of infidelity, he must prove it before a court. Medical reasons must be validated by a medical expert.

2) During the process of divorce, the husband should be democratic (*shura*) and fair (*'adala*), meaning that he should consider the opinion of his wife. If the husband has no strong argument and the wife wants to maintain the marriage, the husband can not carry through the divorce. This is an implementation of the Islam teaching, "*wa amruhum shura bainahum*". The wife should have rights, not only in terms of compensation and income during the period of *'idda* (the one-hundred day waiting period before a widow or divorcee can remarry), but also in terms of a bargaining position during the process of divorce itself.

3) The husband should have a clear guarantee of material responsibility for income, such as clear employment, as demanded by the Islamic jurisprudence in order to avoid objections in the future.

If the divorce must be carried through, and it is still the full right of the husband, there should be tight regulation of the process. It is useful here to see the opinion of a contemporary interpreter of the Qur'an, Dr Muhammad Shahrur. In his *al-Kitab wa Qur'an: Qira'a Mu'asira*, Syahrur suggested a judicial solution to the process of divorce that avoided losses to women. He suggested than men and women should be given the same rights to ask for a divorce. Verbal requests for divorce were not to be taken seriously. To avoid trivialization, divorces should be conducted in court, so that the wife would be given a transparent legal guarantee.[40] He maintained that a divorce could be cancelled by the husband if he found that his wife was pregnant. This was in order to protect the welfare of the woman and child.

DECONSTRUCTING 'IDDA

Some years ago, a discussion group in Situbondo, East Java, conducted a *Bahthul Masa'il* forum on the theme of: "The Implications of the Global Transformation of the Concept of *'idda*".[41] This was a courageous move

---

[40] Muhammad Shahrur, *al-Kitab wa Qur'an: Qira'a Mu'asira*, Al-Uhali, 1994, p.626.
[41] The *Bahthul Mathail* was conducted by a women's study network, Sakinah, under the supervision of the non-governmental organization, P3M, Jakarta, Indonesia. The program was held on Sept. 2, 1997.

because the teachings on 'idda had not been challenged for fourteen centuries. Moreover, the forum was held in an Islamic boarding school which still firmly upheld the values of *fiqh*. Why has 'idda (the one-hundred day waiting period before a widow or divorcee can remarry) become a serious matter now?

Firstly, 'idda as a religious concept is actually more of a cultural construction than a religious saying. '*Idda* was designed to detect pregnancies for the purpose of piety and the rules of worship (*ibada*). But, as a cultural construction, 'idda was viewed as imprisoning women in the domestic domain. So, there is a dilemma or contradiction between its theological and socio-cultural functions in relation to Islamic teaching.

Secondly, if 'idda was designed to detect pregnancy, it is no longer valid or useful in this age of advanced medicine.

It is useful to analyze the meaning of the term 'idda, both etymologically and terminologically. We will also look at its use in classical *fiqh* and assess why it is still maintained in the present. Etymologically, 'idda derives from the Arabic root adad, which means number. The root (*masdar*) is from the verbs (*fi'il*) *i'tadda* and *i'tidad*. The term 'idda was used because it carried the meaning of 'number [of months]', because it illustrated the notion of the waiting period (*tarabus*) in which it could be determined whether a woman was pregnant or not.[42]

Another, broad definition was made by Zainuddin 'Abd Al-'Aziz Al-Malibari, who claimed that 'idda was a waiting period to determine whether a woman was pregnant, for the purposes piety, or for adjustment after the death of her husband. But, according to the true purposes of Islamic law, 'idda was applied to avoid the mixing of sperm [from different men].[43] In his definition, Zainuddin 'Abd Al-'Aziz Al-Malibari added 'piety' (*ibada*) as the legal basis for 'idda. According to Muhammad Syata, the author of *Fath al-Mu'in*, this definition is related to the position of very young and post-menopausal women, for whom 'idda only means piety, but is nonetheless legally obligatory. However, this reasoning is not logical and, according to many experts in *fiqh*, there was no basis for this ruling on 'idda in Islamic law (*shar'iyya*).[44]

---

[42] See *Hamish al-Badjuri*, vol. II, p.168.

[43] See *Hashiya I'anah al-Talibin*, p.38.

[44] Muhammad Shata, p.38.

According to *fiqh*, *'idda* is divided into two kinds:

1) *'idda* following the death of the husband or *mutawaffa anha zaujuha*.
2) *'idda* not following the death of husband or *ghairu mutawaffa*.

After the death of a husband, a wife may or may not be pregnant (*bara'tu rahmiha*). If the woman is pregnant, the *'idda* is extended until she gives birth. If she is not pregnant, the waiting period lasts four months and ten days.

Meanwhile for a pregnant woman whose husband has not died, the *'idda* lasts until the baby has been delivered. If the woman is not pregnant, but is still of childbearing age, the waiting period depends on *aqra* (periods between menstruations). The jurists of the Malikite and Shafi'ite schools had different accounts of the correct duration of *'idda* period. The Maliki school uses the measurement of menstruation (three periods must pass), while the Shafi'ite *ulamas* used the measurement of cleanliness (three periods between menstruations). However, both amount to more or less three months. For very young or post-menopausal women, the waiting period is three months.

According to these explanations, *'idda* is still very relevant as a religious ritual, and can be maintained despite modern discoveries in the fields of medicine and science that can ascertain a woman's pregnancy in a matter of minutes. But if *'idda* is understood in terms of piety and time for adjustment after the loss of a husband, it can still be said to be relevant.

However, what we are questioning here is the implication of the implementation of *'idda*. According to classical *fiqh*, women undergoing *'idda* were not allowed to leave their houses except in an emergency. As a result, the waiting period was viewed as the forced domestication of women using a religious excuse. There were many rules to follow during *'idda*; the woman could not go out, wear good clothes or use perfume. How does Islam actually view this waiting period?

To answer the question, it is better to go directly to the Qur'an: Ia tukhrijuhunna min buyutihina wa la yakhrujna illa an-ya'tina bifahisyatin mubayyinatin (Al-Talaq [65]:1). This verse is viewed by almost all the *fiqh* jurists as a prohibition against women going out during the period of *'idda*.

The prohibition is also supported by a hadith narrated by Malik, Al-Thauri, Shu'bah and others Prophet: When Fura'ia binti Malik's husband died, the Prophet said, "Stay in the house until the duration of the agreement ('idda) has passed." Fura'ia replied, "I have undergone 'idda for four months and ten days."[45] According to the consensus of the *ulamas*, this hadith was evidence for the ruling banning women from leaving their houses during 'idda. And in the *fiqh* books, they use this kind of approach.

There are two strong, basic arguments used to justify the seclusion of women during 'idda. But is there another way of deconstructing the above interpretation of the Qur'an and hadith?

1) Let us look at Al-Talaq, verse 1. It clearly states three important things in the verse: a) The divorcing of wives should be conducted properly and promptly, according to the religious laws; b) After the divorce, they should not be removed from their home, except in cases of depravity; c) This is God's decision (*hudud*), which must not be violated. This was the usual interpretation of the jurists.

It is important to note that, in Arabic, the process of interpreting a sentence depends very much on how it is read (*nahwiyya*). The sentence, *wa la yakhrujna* (and they don't go out), in relation to the sentence, *mabni ma'lum* (active form), could also be read as: *wa la yakhrujanna* (and don't [let] them go out). The latter sentence strengthens the one that precedes it, *la tukhrijunna*, which bans the women from going out.

This way of reading Arabic uses the 'tool of exceptions', or *adat istitsna*, which is called *illa ayya'tina bifahisatin mubayyina*. This may have been the case because during the Uthman era, the Qur'an had not yet been given clear reading signs (writing).

So, on this reading, the verse is not a prohibition against women leaving their homes during 'idda, but is rather a protective measure to ensure they are not thrown out.

2) The hadith banning women from going out of their homes during 'idda was viewed by Dawud Al-Zhahiri as weak because it was only narrated by one narrator. On this basis, Al-Zhahiri allowed mu'tadah (women undergoing 'idda) to go outside.[46] This hadith was also challenged

---

[45] "*Imkithi bi baitiki hatta yablugha al-kitab 'ajala*", Furai'a replied ,"*fa'tadtu fihi arba'ata ashhurin ashra.*"

[46] *Tafsir Al-Qurthubi*. vol. III, p.176.

by another hadith, which stated: "*Tuliqat khalati wa aradat an tajida nakhlaha fa zajaraha rajulun an takhraja fa atat an-nabiya fa qala la bal fajdi nakhlaki fa innaki asa an tashddaqi au taf'li ma'rufan*" (narrated by Muslim, from Jabir).

Based on this alternative hadith, *fiqh* experts such as Malik, Shafi'i, Ahmad and Al-Laith allowed mu'tadda (devorced women) to leave the house, but only during daytime. Malik, however, allowed both mu'tadda that could be remarried (*raj'iya*), and those who could not be remarried (*ba'in*) to go out, while Shafi'i only allowed for *mu'tadda ba'in* to go out.[47]

Without asserting whose opinion was the strongest, it is clear that the prohibition was not a legal requirement, but only a means to an end (*wasila*). *Wasila* leans more towards the maintenance of social ethics, whereas the theological aspect leans more towards the legal discussion cited above, that is to say: *lima'rifati bara'atu rahmiha, li ta'abudiha* and *littahayia*. This creates the possibility of remarriage and recall.

The issue is whether we prioritize the means of the law over the objective of the law. The prohibition was a medium to reach the legal goal. But this kind of law is difficult to fulfil – it's fine for the *mu'tadda* who feels protected by the ruling to stay at home, but what about mu'taddah who has go out and work to feed her family and children?

I think it is better to be flexible on this matter, which is not black and white. If a *mu'tadda* can not stay at home for the duration of *'idda* because of specific needs as mentioned above, she should be allowed to in emergency situations. Moreover, the prohibition could be waived for those without an urgent need to go out, as long as she still respected the objectives of *'idda*. After all, the point of *'idda* is not about whether you stay home or go out, but about how the purpose of *'idda* can be fulfilled.

DECONSTRUCTING *IHDAD*

Ihdad is closely related to *'idda*. In *fiqh*, *ihdad* was included in discussions of *'idda*. *Fath al-Mu'in* and its larger derivative, *I'anat al- Talibin*, for example,

---

[47] *Al-Qurthubi*, 18. p. 154

discussed *ihdad* in a single series with *'Idda*. This was also the case with *Hashiya al-Badjuri* by Ibrahim Al-Badjuri.

But is *ihdad* really an Islamic teaching? Is it not a cultural construction designed to limit women's mobility, using religious language?

Historically speaking, *ihdad* was part of pre-Islamic tradition. Arab women whose husbands had died, were secluded in a cell, isolated, contained and prevented from wearing good clothing. One hadith tells of how women who were undergoing *ihdad* smelt so bad that people would avoid them and, upon leaving seclusion, they would be surrounded by crows because the smell was like that of a corpse.[48] At this time, *ihdad* had a very long duration.

The tradition was then adopted by Islam, with a change in the length of time required. In a hadith narrated by Bukhari, the Prophet said: "It is not allowed for women who believe in God and the final day of *ihdad* for people who died in three days, except if it is for a dead husband, and then it is for four months and ten days."

According to *fiqh*, *ihdad* applied to all widows, free women and slaves alike. According to the hadith above, the period for a normal family member would be three days, while for a husband, the woman would undergo four months and ten days of seclusion – the same as the duration of *'idda* as undergone by women whose husbands had left them.

Jurists viewed the term *la yahillu* (not allowed) in relation to its opposite – obligatory. Using the logic of *usul fiqh*, something that had once been banned, but was now allowed, became an obligation.[49]

The next question is how should *ihdad* be implemented in Islam?

On the procedure of *ihdad*, Shaykh Muhammad ibn Qasim said:

Etymologically, *ihdad* was taken from the word *had*, which means *al-man'u* (to prevent), and terminologically, means the prevention of the wearing of accessories and colorful clothing of yellow or red, for example, in favor of plain clothes made from cotton, wool or silk. This also included the avoidance of perfumes on the body, clothing, in food – this was called *ghairu* muhrim.

---

[48] Masdar F. Mas'udi, *Ihdad and 'idda in the Change of Religious Life*, a paper presented in the seminar "Implications of Global Transformation in "idda, Situbondo, Feb. 27, 1997.

[49] Shaykh Ibrahim Al-Badjuri, *Hashiya al-Badjuri ala Ibn Qasim al-Ghuzi*, Bandung; Shirka al-Ma'arif, Vol. II, p.175.

This also included the wearing of eyeliner, unless there was a good reason like sickness, and even then it should only be worn by night and erased during the day.[50]

This description of *ihdad* is not so different from those found in other literature of *fiqh*. It involved an extreme ban on accessories or self-adornment of any kind. In Al-Badjuri's account of Ibn Qasim, all accessories like gold, silver, and other jewelry that could beautify face was prohibited, except under special circumstances at night time. Even then, it was permitted, but not recommended (*makru*), unless there was a serious need for it.[51]

Besides the ban on wearing accessories, the hardest requirement of *ihdad* was the prohibition against leaving the house. Women were not allowed to be involved in public life. Widows were stay in and mourn their husbands for four months and ten days, whereas mu'taddah were not obliged to undergo *ihdad*, although it was recommended.

In the contemporary world, *ihdad* is a serious problem for women due to the limitations placed on their social lives. The current structure of the community is very different from when the laws were formulated. Women require [access to] the public sphere for self-realization. Of course there is still a skeptical position in Islam that maintains that it would be better if the contemporary world became more like the world in which those regulations were first made by the *ulamas* of the past.

It is fine for those who feel that they can live under the old rules, but many others are seeking ways to live that are more conducive to the modern era, and to reconstruct or even deconstruct the old rulings of the *ulamas*. One principle of *usul fiqh* states: *al-hukm yadurru ma'a illatihi wujuhan wa adaman*. Moreover, there is no clear regulation of *ihdad* in the Qur'an, which only mentions '*idda*.

To this purpose, we could reinterpret *ihdad* according to the context of the present times, while returning to the aim of the law (*shar'ia*). *Ihdad* was designed for the condolence of husband and members of the family. Before Islam, *ihdad* was expressed through mourning and not wearing external

---

[50] *See Taqrib* by Ibn Qasim al-Ghuzi in Hashiya al-Badjuri, vol. I, p.176.
[51] Ibrahim Al-Badjuri, *Hashiya*, Vol. II, p.176.

self-adornment. Islam changed the duration of *ihdad* but it retained the way it was done. In order to demonstrate condolence, it is not necessary to stay in a darkened room and express it through physical appearance. In the present, relatives and neighbors may visit us during mourning. But this does not mean that we should wear "impolite" dress and accessories. One modern legal expert suggested that the implementation of *ihdad* should be carried out according to ethical norms, but must also respect the dignity of women.

DECONSTRUCTING *IJBAR*

The term *ijbar* refers to forced marriage, which is still popular among Muslims. Etymologically, the term derives from the Arabic root: *ajbara, yujbiru, ijbar*an, meaning 'to force'. In Islamic law, especially the *fiqh* of Shafi'i, *ijbar* meant the right of the father or grandfather to arrange the marriage of the daughter forcibly. Ibrahim Al-Badjuri clearly stated that a father or grandfather (if there was no father) had the right to force the marriage of a daughter.[52] For a widow, the parents had no right to force the marriage. Shafi'i's position was shared by many other *ulamas*.

Due to the factor of force, *ijbar* is considered as a symbol of undemocratic and unfair relations in Islamic family life, particular in father-child relations. The mainstream understanding of *ijbar* is that the daughter can be married off to the partner preferred by her father. This practice should be reviewed in the context of the development of the era, as it was during the discussions held at the International Conference on Population and Women (ICPD) in Cairo in 1994, which concluded that women should control their own reproductive rights, such as choosing their own life-partner. In classical Islam, such choices were limited by the concept of *ijbar*. Can *ijbar* be conducted without any compromise at all?

There are actually several requirements that must be fulfilled before *ijbar* can be carried out: 1) There must be no animosity between parents and daughters, either physical or mental; 2) The prospective husband should be of the same level; 3) The prospective husband should be a man who can be expected to make his wife happy in the future; and 4) That there is

---

[52] Ibn Qasim al-Ghuzi, *Hashiya 'ala Ibn Qasim al-Ghuzi*, Vol. II, p.109.

no animosity between the man and woman.[53] A guardian (or parents) is permitted to arrange the marriage of a daughter without her consent after meeting the following requirements: a) Must be married with a *mahar mithl* (dowry); b) The dowry should be paid in cash, if there is no tradition of payment by installments; and c) The dowry should be paid in the official currency of that country. Some *ulamas* added another requirement – that the guardian could not force to arrange the marriage of the daughter with someone inappropriate for her, such as a blind or elderly man. But many considered this last requirement to be weak and, as such, it was not made a legal requirement of *ijbar*.[54]

Although the requirements above are all good, they only take account of the parent's interests. But, the daughter has no power of self-determination. This may not be problematic if she does not feel that she is being coerced, but clashes can occur if father and daughter do not share the same opinions on prospective partners. Who is the winner in cases like these? Is it wrong to reject *ijbar*? According to Cairo's ICPD document, isn't it the woman who has the right to choose?

Of course, this is a complex problem. On one hand, *ijbar* has its legal basis in *fiqh* (religion), but on the other, it is contrary to the demands of democratization, both in the family and society.

We should think maturely and clearly about our understanding of *ij-bar*:

1) It is true that parents have the right to force the marriage of their daughters according to a hadith narrated by Al-Daruqutni, which quotes the Prophet as saying: "*al-shaykhu ahaqqu bi nafsiha wa al-bikru yuzawijuha abuha*", or "a widow has the right to arrange her own marriage, while the marriage of a virgin is arranged by her father." But in the language of *fiqh*, the father's and grandfather's rights are viewed as authority (*yajuzu*), but not obligation. Rejecting *ijbar* is not rejecting an obligation, and nor is it a sin, although it may be impolite or unethical to refuse a parent's order.

---

[53] *Ibid.*
[54] Al-Badjuri, Vol. II, p.109

2) Good parents should conduct *mu'ashara bi al-ma'ruf* (good attitude treatment) with all family members. Although a father has the right to force their daughter's marriage, they would not use it. They would respect their daughters' choices.

3) Ultimately, the marriage is carried out by the daughters, not the parents. The parents have to take responsibility for their children, but only the daughter knows if she is happy or not in the marriage, so the choice of partner should be handed over to the daughter. The obligation for the parents is to arrange and fund the marriage. It is according to the Islam regulation that the parents have the obligation for the income for the whole family.

4) Reinterpretation of the concept of *ijbar* should not be viewed as an effort to adjust to the ICPD agreement, but as an effort to value our daughters. By giving them the right to decide their own fates, and to train them to be responsible within their own choices.

DECONSTRUCTING *NUSHUZ*

Home life is not always harmonious; even during the preparation of the marriage, it is suggested that a husband and wife should strive to create love and care (*mawadda wa rahma*), according to the teachings in the Qur'an on marriage and family life. In reality, however, human beings do not always act in keeping with the aims of the Qur'an and there are often misunderstandings between spouses. Sometimes these can be resolved amicably through discussion, as recommended in the Qur'an. Sometimes, though, the outcome is seen as unfair from the wife's perspective, and she goes back to her family home to seek sympathy. In *fiqh*, this is called *nushuz*. On the topic of *nushuz*, the Qur'an states: "And the women whom you fear will conduct *nushuz*, advise them; and sleep separately and beat them, if they obey you, do not overreact against them" (Al-Nisa' [4]: 34).

Etymologically, *nushuz* means 'to challenge' (*al-isyan*), and is derived from the word *al-Nashaz*, meaning the highest part of the earth (*ma irtafa min al-ard*). This is close to the meaning that is implied in Al-Mujadila [58], verse 11, "*wa idza qilaa unshuzu fan shuzu.*" Terminologically, *nushuz* means to disobey Allah's orders to obey one's husband. In *fiqh*, the first step that should be taken by the husband if his wife commits *nushuz* is to advise the wife, but still keep sleeping together. Sleeping together is a symbol of the harmonious relationship between the husband and wife. If this fails, the next step is for the husband to sleep separately from his wife. If this second step also fails, the husband can sleep separately and has the right to beat her.

According to the jurists, the above steps can be taken by the husband whenever he suspects that his wife has committed *nushuz*. As one classical *fiqh* states: "If it is feared that a wife may conduct *nushuz*, advise her; if she refuses the advice and still does *nushuz*, sleep separately and, if she is still doing *nushuz*, separate and beat her; in the case of *nushuz* – especially if she is in a polygamous marriage – her turn to share his nights and her right to income is cancelled."

On reading this statement, we see that the husband could claim that his wife was doing *nushuz* purely on the basis of suspicion. It is clear that the wife's position is very fragile. She has no opportunity to defend herself, let alone to correct the husband's behavior, because whatever action she takes could be determined to be *nushuz* by the husband. In contrast, the husband has the highest position and can decide whether an action can be considered to be *nushuz* or not.

In addition, as mentioned in *Hashiya al-Badjuri*, a respected book in Indonesian Islamic boarding schools, it is stated that even a change in the wife's facial gestures can be categorized as *nushuz*. Her face changing from bright to angry, or going out without an urgent need – to chat, or study, or request a *fatwa* (religious decree) from an expert because the husband could not give one – could be considered to be *nushuz*. If the husband is capable of giving a *fatwa*, the wife should ask the husband.

The issue is whether it should be as easy as this to accuse a wife of *nushuz*. In facing a problem, we should not make the accusation of *nushuz* rashly. The Prophet said that hurried actions are an act of evil. Before we make accusations, we should search for the reasons behind her act of *nushuz*, in order to avoid misjudgments and mistakes.

People often relate *nushuz* with domestic violence against women. And it is true that in Islamic law the husband is allowed to beat a wife who fails to give an explanation. But such beatings are often made on the basis of a wife's actions that can not be called *nushuz*. We should give clear boundaries to the meaning of obedience to the husband. Is this absolute obedience or just obedience in response to good things?

There were some *ulamas* who interpreted that what was meant by 'beating' was a physical beating, but that it should fulfill several legal requirements – that it should not hurt or disable the wife, for example. If the beating does cause disability, the husband must cover the costs of medical treatment until the wife recovers. The husband is not allowed to beat his wife using stick, strike her face or beat any part of her body that could cause death. This suggests that *fiqh* did not demand violence, but that beatings were for the purpose of giving a 'lesson'.

Al-Qurtubi, in his masterpiece, *al-Jami' li Ahkam al-Qur'an*, said the beating mentioned in this verse was of a kind that did not hurt (*ghaira mubarrih*), and did not cause broken bones or wounds to the skin. According to Al-Qurtubi, the purpose of the beating was to teach wives a lesson. If it caused physical damage, the husband should bear the medical treatment.[55]

However, whatever legal requirements are fulfilled during a husband's beating of his wife, *nushuz* is still a medium of violence against women, both physical and psychological. Moreover, the verse could be interpreted in many ways. Literalist groups, for instance, interpret *wadhribuhunna* as a physical beating. Because of this, it is very important to reinterpret the verse on *nushuz*, to consider the interests of husband and wife proportionally in order to avoid suffering for both of them. This new perspective has entered Islamic thought in Indonesia. This new perspective is a perspective based on gender justice. Without taking this perspective, women's position in relation to *nushuz* will remain weak.

So, before accusing a wife of *nushuz*, the husband should investigate the reasons behind her actions. Is it the really the wife's intention to disobey the husband? Or is she just trying to claim her right to something the husband is not willing to give her? These matters need to be viewed clearly to avoid accusations of *nushuz* against the wife.

Islam positions women on an equal level with men. The rights and duties of both husbands and wives have been clearly formulated in the Qur'an, in the frame of equality and balance. On this basis, Islam does not regard sexual

---

[55]   Al-Qurtubi, *Jami' li Ahkam al-Qur'an*, Vol. III, p.133.

difference as problematic issue. The Qur'an tells us: *wa ashiruhunna bi al-ma'ruf* (Al-Nisa' [4]:19), meaning "treat all of your wives well." Considering this verse, it seems unlikely that a woman would be driven to commit *nushuz* if her husband treated her well, as suggested by his religion.

Everywhere, opposition occurs in response to unjust treatment – unfulfilled rights or duties – by either husband or wife. However, if a wife makes a mistake, her husband is given the right to correct it; if the husband errs, his wife does not share this right. *Uqud al-Lijain* states that a wife who is patient in the face of her husband's bad behavior will go to Heaven. This statement is clearly contradictory to the Qur'anic teaching on good treatment of wives. A wife is a human being who can be hurt or offended, so even the most patient of wives will react to her husband's bad behavior. A reaction against a husband whose behavior violates the rules of his religion can not be construed as 'opposition'.

If we read the Qur'an carefully on the topic of *nushuz*, we will find its true meaning. This is found in part of Al-Nisa', verse 34. Apart from explaining *nushuz*, this verse discusses male leadership in matters of income, and the value of pious, God-fearing women. Many *ulamas* viewed this as a description of Arabic communities at that time. So the verse has flexible meanings, sociologically and historically.

In my view, our *fiqh* experts have not been fair in the reconstruction of the concept of *nushuz*. It seems that *fiqh* only consider the interests of men, which results in the weakening of women's bargaining position. They are several important considerations in the matter of *nushuz*:

1) The principle of fairness – we believe that the Qur'an always takes a fair and just position on all life's problems. So, if a wife commits *nushuz*, we should strive to understand the reasons behind her action. We should not only look at the women's alleged disobedience, but also assess whether the husband's treatment of her was fair.

2) The principle of *mu'asyara bil ma'ruf* – the general principle that both spouses should treat each other well in the marital relationship. If this principle is carried out to the full, there is very little possibility that a wife would commit *nushuz*.

CHAPTER FIVE

WOMEN IN POLITICAL FIQH

Generally speaking, political issues are only discussed in a small portion of *fiqh* literature. Usually political topics (*siyasa*) are given space in the chapter entitled '*Muamala*' (human relation)and in the *Ahwal Shakhshiyya* (personal laws).

With the passing of time and social change, probably due to the demand for specialization of knowledge and the widening of Islamic discourse, political issues were given more space in *fiqh* literature. However, *fiqh* literature dealing with politics remains rare.

The resurgence of political *fiqh* was sparked at various times by the increasing discussion of the political ethics of power in Islam by *ulamas*. Al-Mawardi, Al-Ghazali, Ibn Khaldun and others started to write about administration, leadership and other political regulations. These became the basis of political *fiqh*. One of the best works is Al-Mawardi's book, *al-Ahkam al-Sultaniyya* (The Law of the Kingdom). This book was not the first, but it was a pioneering effort in the emergence of the systematic documentation of political discourse.

In any discussion of politics, we should we need to talk about the human being as politician – as the subject and object of politics. All Islamic discourse about politics is rooted in *fiqh*, but women have been, perhaps intentionally, marginalized in *fiqh* books. As a subject of politics, it seems that women have no place in Islamic political discourse. Whether one wants to admit it or not, in the domain of Islamic political discourses, such as the *fiqh* pertaining to matters of state leadership (*imama*), parliament, ministers (*wazir*) etc. – appear to be closer to male, rather than female, activities.

Thus, the position of women in political *fiqh* should be treated in a separate agenda. The issue is not only whether a woman is allowed to become a [state] leader (*imam*) or not, but about the political role of women in general, and whether they can acquire political rights equal to men's.

In this chapter, we explore the political role of women from an Islamic perspective. We will also look at how far *fiqh siyasa* addressed women's rights, such as the right to become a state leader (*imam*), a member of parliament, or even to participate in general elections.

WOMEN'S POLITICAL RIGHTS IN DEBATE

Do Muslim women have political rights? If they do, how far do they reach? Women's political rights in Islam have been debated for a long time, as they have in other religions. In Islam, the debate is centered on the problem of whether Islam puts forward and teaches about women's political rights or not. Mainstream Islamic discourse maintains that women should remain in the domestic sphere, while politics is part of the public domain managed by men.

There are three mainstream opinions regarding women's political rights:

1) The conservative opinion maintains that Islam, and *fiqh*, prohibits women from being involved in the political domain, since its emergence in Mecca and Medina.
2) The liberal-progressive opinion maintains that Islam put forward women's involvement in politics from the beginning.
3) The apologist opinion maintains that some aspects of politics can be handled by women, while others can not. According to this group, women's political arena is motherhood.

THE CONSERVATIVE GROUP

This first group maintains that Islam does not acknowledge equality between men and women in political practice. *Ulamas* who supported this position, such as Al-Ghazali, said that women could not be elected as leaders of state (*imam*). How could a woman to be a head of state when she had no right to make big decisions or give testimony in legal problems (in his *Fadha'ih al-Batiniya wa Fadhail al-Mustazhiriyya*, pp. 180-1).

Al-Qalqashandi maintained a similar opinion, stating that women were not permitted to become a state leader because of an innate lack, indicated by their inability to arrange their own marriages, let alone, be given the authority to rule over other people.[1] This group did not give women the opportunity to be involved in political life, in general.

The Conservatives also maintained that the world was divided into two aspects: the public sphere (*al-wilaya al-amma*) and domestic sphere (*al-wilaya al-khassa*). The public sphere, which comprises social matters, such as legislation and conflict resolution in the community, leading the administration and so on, come under men's authority, whereas the domestic sphere, including household duties, education and rearing of children, and handling the husband's income in relation to the home, are handled by women. From the Conservative's perspective, Islam has historically excluded women from political matters. Since the era of the Prophet, they say, not even one woman was directly involved in political affairs.

The above position is argued to have legal basis in the Qur'an, hadiths, *ijma'* and *qiyas*. In particular, Al-Nisa', verse 34[2], Al-Baqara, verse 228, are often referred to[3] Based on these verses, Ibn Katsir claimed that men had the superiority to handle public matters, especially politics. Then, Al-Ahzab, verse 33, was interpreted by some experts as an obligation for women to stay in the home.[4] Women was not allowed to show themselves it was recommended that they cover their bodies with a veil (*ihtijab*), to avoid the gaze of the outside world, especially men.

The basis of the second argument used to ban women from being active in the public sphere was taken from the hadiths of the Prophet. In Islamic discourse, the hadiths that undermined women or, as Riffat Hasan called them, the 'misogynistic hadiths'. These included:

---

[1]   See Al-Baghdadi, *al-Farqu bain al-Firaq*. p.90.
[2]   Al-Nisa' (4) verse 34.
[3]   Al-Baqara (2): verse 228.
[4]   Al-Ahzab (33) verse 33.

1) The hadith, *la yufliha qaumun walau amrahum imra'atan*,[5] which said that women were not allowed involvement in the public sphere because they were bound to fail and even cause damage.

2) The hadith, *al-nisa'u naqisatu 'aqlin wa dinin*,[6] which was used by the *ulamas* to support the argument that women's faith, biologically and theologically, lacked rationality and piety. Women were excluded from politics because they lacked the required rationality.

The third argument had its legal basis in *ijma'*, a consensus among *ulamas* on a certain legal problem. The Conservatives agreed that during the era of the Prophet, *khulafa' al-rashidin*, and the generations that followed, women were never invited to be involved in dealing with political problems. Of course, at that time, there were many bright women, including the Prophet's wives, but they never joined or were asked to get involved with politics.

The fourth legal basis is *qiyas*, meaning 'to consider'. In Shafi'i's *fiqh* tradition, *qiyas* was an important basis for formulating Islamic law. For instance, women are not allowed to be state leaders because women are not allowed to be leaders (*imam*) of prayer. Women were also not allowed to move around unaccompanied by her brothers or other male relative. This topic will be discussed later.

THE LIBERAL-PROGRESSIVE GROUP

In contrast to the first group, a group of liberal-progressive *ulamas* did not hinder women's involvement in politics. They explicitly stated that women had full rights in political life. Women were allowed to bear as heavy a political burden as men do. Some of the *ulamas* in the group allowed women to hold any political position, but some were still half-hearted and allowed women to take up positions, except for head of state.[7]

The *ulamas* of the Khawarij and Mushabbiha groups can be included in the liberal-progressive group, while the 'half-hearted' *ulamas*, who can be

---

[5]   Al-Shaukani, *Nail al-Autar, Bab al-Halabi*, vol. III, p.273.

[6]   *Mukhtasar Bukhari*, vol. I, p.32; *Nail al-Autar*, vol. I, p.3; and *al-Mawaqif Sharh al-Jurjani*, vol. VIII, p.249.

[7]   See Al-Baghdadi, *al-Farqu bain al-Firaq*, p.90.

considered as moderate, but with conservative leanings, were the *ulamas* from the Sunni sects, such as Al-Mawardi and Ibn Taimiyyah.

Normatively, the liberal-progressive group took the Qur'an and hadith as the source of their legal basis. This group did not use *ijma'* and *qiyas* since both of them were still controversial among *fiqh* schools. Some *ulamas*, such as Malik, accepted the *ijma'*, but some, like Shafi'i, refused it, but accepted *qiyas*. Others rejected both *qiyas* and *ijma'*.

The Liberal-Progressives used the Qur'anic principles of justice (*'adala*) and equality (*musawa*). They often cited Al-Taubah, verse 71,[8] which they said explained that men and women had the same rights in politics and to rule in the public domain (*wilaya al-am*). They had the same rights to promote goodness and avoid evil deeds, and to become judges and conflict mediators. This group also used Al-Hujurat (49), verse 10,[9] and Al-Isra' (17), verse 70.[10] The substance of these verses is that Islam honors the position of men and women equally and allows no discrimination between human beings, male or female.

In establishing legal basis, the group also quoted hadiths that upheld women's rights, especially the right to talk in public. There was a popular story about the Prophet's close friend, Umar ibn Al-Khattab, and a woman who debated with him. Umar once led a sermon in a mosque, calling people not to give expensive dowries to women. 'Umar's sermon was quickly interrupted by a woman, who quoted Allah's commandment: "*Wa in aradtum istibdala zaujin makana zaujin wa utitum ihdahunna qintaran fala ta'hudzu minhu shai'an ata khudzunahu buhtanan wa isman mubina, wa kaifa khudzunahu waqad afda ba'dhukum ila ba'adh wa akhadzna minkum mithaqan ghalizha.*" After listening to the hadith, 'Umar admitted that the woman was correct.

According to this group, this story showed 'Umar's agreement and accommodative stance towards women's public role, and that Islam allows women to be involved in political affairs. It can also be understood as 'Umar's return to the non-discriminative attitudes held by the Prophet. Many other stories also supported 'Umar's stance.

---

[8] Al-Taubah (9) verse 71.
[9] Al-Hujurat (49): verse 10.
[10] Al-Isra' (17): verse 70.

THE APOLOGIST GROUP

I call the third grouping the Apologists. In viewing women and politics, this group maintained that women's political rights had nothing to do with religion and *fiqh*. Women's political rights were social, political and cultural matters. Furthermore, they said it was a mistake to consider the limitations on women's political rights to be a problem of religion or *fiqh*. It was also a mistake to use a Western approach to analyze and rectify the matter – indeed, we would be considered as Western cohorts for using this approach to solve our internal Islamic problems. The group said that women's only political role was to become a mother. Women being active in the public domain was deemed to be a negative and damaging thing. They also believed that women were proportionally more emotional rational. Actually, these three opinions follow the thought patterns of the Conservative *ulamas*.

WOMEN'S POLITICAL RIGHTS IN CONTEMPORARY *FIQH* DISCOURSE

Women's political rights in contemporary *fiqh* are still under debate, although many perspectives have changed. But the perspective remains similar to those of the classical *ulamas*. There are at least two groups who still debate women's position in politics. The first disagrees with political rights for women, and the second suggests that women's political rights should be secured as a matter of course.

THE FIRST GROUP

This group believes that Islam prohibits women from entering politics. Usually they base this on the following arguments:

> Women are basically different from men in terms of biology, rationality and civilization. Biologically, women are weak. Rationally, women tend to prioritize emotion over rationality. According to this group, women's role in building civilization was not as visible as men's contribution, or even that it was an entirely male creation. On this basis, women are not permitted political rights.

The division between male-female activities is the bottom line for this group. They maintain that, culturally and religiously, women's role is in the home, rearing children, cooking and cleaning. Social and political roles are reserved for men (husbands).

According to this group, if the women were politically active in politics, it would create a negative impact on their families, causing friction in the family, especially where husband and wife had different political affiliations. Furthermore, women's involvement in activities outside the home would create a crisis in the family, subverting her role as mother. A woman's duty is to create harmony and morality in the family. This perspective is usually professed by Islamic fundamentalist groups. But even in contemporary Islamic *fiqh* discourse, this perspective is sometimes seriously accomodated.[11]

THE SECOND GROUP

This group maintains that the equalization of the political positions of men and women is unavoidable, for the sake of 'good' and democratization. Women make up over fifty percent of humankind, meaning that they hold half the potential for goodness in the world. Muslim intellectuals who could be considered among this group include Asghar Ali Engineer, Fatima Mernissi, Riffat Hassan and many others. The above was a brief discussion of various views on women's position in political Islam. The following sections raise some crucial issues in *fiqh*, such as *imama* (leadership) and representative institutions.

STATE LEADERSHIP

Imam Abu Ya'la Muhammad ibn Husain Al-Fara' Al-Hanbali (380-458 H) maintained that the choosing of a state leader (*imam*) was a religious obligation. Abu Ya'la's opinion was based on Ahmad's claim that it is as bad as slander if an *imam* is incapable of managing human's affairs. This kind of position on leadership is based on *al-sam'u*, or textual references – meaning the Qur'an and hadiths, rather than pure rationality. Rational thought alone

---

[11] See, for instance, Wahbah Al-Zuhaili, *Al-Fiqh Al-Islam wa Adillatuhu.*

could not define whether something was an obligation, a recommendation, or forbidden. Choosing a leader is categorized as a public obligation (*fardu kifaya*). The object of this obligation was addressed to two groups. Firstly, religious experts (*ijtihad*), because this group had voting rights and secondly, leadership candidates (who were legally capable of becoming a *imam*).

The *ijtihad* experts, known as *ahl al-ikhtiyar*, should fulfill three requirements: 1) They should be '*al-adalah* (just); 2) They should be know how to evaluate who could become a good imam; 3) They should have the rational ability and foresight to choose the best candidate (*aslah*) for leader.

According to Abu Ya'la, a leadership candidate should meet the following requirements: 1) The state leader should come from the Quraish tribe as Ahmad had claimed that: "There is no caliph except from the Quraish line." But some interpreted this to mean that the leader should come from the majority group. 2) The leader should have the attitude of a judge: free from intervention, mature, mentally healthy, knowledgeable and just. 3) The leader should be able to handle war commands and all other political affairs. 4) The leader should have a deep knowledge of religion.

On the issue of *imama* (leadership), Al-Mawardi (d. 450H) said that an imam was a successor of the Prophet, protecting the religious and political world. Installing a leader was an obligation according to *ijma'*. In contrast to Abu Ya'la's position, Al-Mawardi maintained that there were two opinions on how to install an imam – based on *shari'a* (law) or on the basis of reason. The first said that this choice was an imperative of *shari'a*, whereas the second said that the use of rationality could protect people evil and avoid conflict. Al-Mawardi tended towards the first opinion, maintaining that rationality did not have the authority to choose a leader, but could be used to avoid disputes.[12]

Al-Mawardi maintained that it was a *fardlu kifaya* (public obligation) to choose a leader, but, similarly to Abu Ya'la, that only two groups were responsible for performing this function: the community group (*ahl al-ikhtiyar*) responsible for the decision; and the group of candidates themselves. The *ahl al-ikhtiyar* should fulfill three conditions: 1) They

---

[12] Al-Mawardi, *al-Ahkam al-Sultaniya*, Dar Al-Fikr, p.5.

should be fair; 2) Have the knowledge to enable them vote for the appropriate *imam*; and 3) Have the depth of vision and forethought to select the best candidate.[13]

Al-Mawardi stated that there were seven requirements to be a leader: 1) fairness; 2) ability to face up to problems as they arise; 3) sighted (not blind); 4) able-bodied; 5) ability to rule and maintain goodness; 6) courage; and 7) from the Quraish tribe.[14]

Ibn Hazm, a *fiqh* expert from the Zhahirite school, had different thoughts on leadership. For him, a Muslim was not allowed to allow a vacuum of leadership to occur for more than two days.[15] Ibn Hazm's opinion was based on Nafi's story from Umar, which said: "I heard from the Prophet, 'Whoever releases themselves from obedience, they will meet God [on the day of judgment] without a grip. Whoever dies without a *bai'at* [pledge for a leader], they would die in the darkness." Clearly, the issue of leadership is very important, but the issue we want to discuss is how it would be if state leadership was held by a woman.

Based on the above opinions from the founding fathers of Islamic political theory, we can see that there was an indication of gender bias, but it was not really explicit. Abu Ya'la, Al-Mawardi, and Ibn Hazm did not mention it explicitly. Related to this matter, there are two possibilities: 1) that it was considered 'common sense' among the *ulamas* at the time that women could not become leaders; and 2) that they intentionally did not mention that only men had the right to become leaders, because they did not want to open the corridor for women to do so. But the first possibility is the strongest. Although Al-Mawardi did not mention men explicitly, he quoted a hadith in *al-Ahkam al-Sultaniyya*, which stated: "*La yufliha qaumun wallau amrahum imra'atan*," or, "No group will be happy if they surrender to the rule of women."

The issue of women as state leaders was often viewed subjectively and in black and white terms, as shown in the case of Benazir Bhutto. When Benazir achieved her position in Pakistan, many *ulamas* did not support her. When

---

[13] *Ibid.*, p.6.
[14] The requirements were stated by Al-Mawardi, who said that the status of the Quraish was the reality at that time. It could also be interpreted as meaning that they were the majority.
[15] Ibn Hazm: "It is forbidden for a Muslim to go for two nights without a legal leader." See *al-Muhalla*, vol. X, p.504.

she was replaced by Nawaz Sharif in the 1997 general elections, the Islamic fundamentalists viewed this as ammunition for their argument that women were weak and unsuitable for leadership positions. But if a male leader failed, the *ulamas* viewed it as a normal part of political process.

Pejorative images of politically active women were also shown during the meeting of the International Parliamentary Union (IPU) in New Delhi. The five-day meeting of IPU, which was attended representatives from seventy-seven countries, discussed men and women's partnership in politics. The meeting, which was entitled "Towards Partnership Between Men and Women in Politics", stated that female politicians often received unfair treatment, especially from the mass media. Female politicians were called "wild" and hysterical, while male politicians were depicted as wise politicians.[16]

The failure of a leadership is not based on the personality of the leader, especially in a modern system where success is the collective responsibility of everyone involved. So it is unfair to claim that Benazir's leadership represented the general leadership of women. Why isn't the success of Margaret Thatcher be taken as representative of the success of female leadership as whole?

The issue of female leadership was not only discussed in the classical *fiqh* books, but also in contemporary *fiqh*. Wahba Al-Zuhaili, a modern *fiqh* expert, listed the seven requirements for the head of an administration in his book, *Nidzam al-Islam*. An *imam* should have perfect leadership, and be Muslim, free, mature, mentally healthy and, finally – a man. According to Al-Zuhaili, becoming an *imam* required qualities that were too cumbersome to be borne by a woman, who would not be able to manage wars and other high-risk duties. It seemed that Al-Zuhaili used physical requirement to prohibit women from becoming state leaders. Related to the matter, he cited a hadith, narrated by Abu Bakra: "It is not fruitful for a group to surrender their problems to a woman."[17]

Although supported by a hadith, al-Zuhaili's argument was not strong enough to prohibit women from becoming leaders. But it did show that

---

[16] Mahesh Uniyal, 'Women Politicians Given Bad Press Coverage', *The Jakarta Post*, 2 February 1997, p.4.

[17] Wahba Al-Zuhaili, *Nidzam Al-Islam* (Beirut: Dar Qutaiba, 1993), Third Edition, p.19. The requirement to be *al-dzukura* (maleness) was stated by Al-Zuhaili and Al-Mawardi in his *al-Ahkam al-Sultaniya*.

political *fiqh* was gender biased. Al-Zuhaili did not see that physical differences are God-given and unavoidable. Refusing the faith means refusing God's authority. Physical difference does not mean that capability is also different. In the present day, leadership does not require physical strength, but good management skills. A strong leader is someone who can organize people, assets, markets etc. If a woman has these qualities, why should be prohibited from becoming a head of state?

How should female leadership in Islam be understood? As we have seen, state leadership or *imama* is very important. The issue of female leadership is still being debated. Each Muslim group teaches their own doctrines on this matter. The question is whether Islam really does prohibit women from becoming leaders? Benazir Bhutto of Pakistan and Khalidah Ziyah of Bangladesh have responded actively. Long before them, in the time of the early prophets, God told a tale about Queen Balqis of Saba, an area in South Yemen. If God prohibits women from being leaders, why does the Qur'an tell this story without undermining the queen?

It seems that argument used as the basis for banning women from leadership is a hadith narrated by Abu Bakra. To explain this hadith, I will explore it and its narratives as collected in the book, *Sahih Bukhari*.

In *Sahih Bukhari*, there were two versions of the hadith's narratives. The first version is in the *Kitab al-Maghazi* (Book of War),[18] and the second version is in the *Kitab al-Fitan* (Book of Slander).[19] Both versions share the same narrators: Uthman ibn Haitham, 'Auf and Hasan, but have slightly different structures.

Commenting on the first version, which is related to the Camel War, Ibn Hajar Al-Asqalani said that Zubair and Talha went to Mecca after Uthman was murdered. They met Ai'shah, who was on pilgrimage (*hajj*). The three agreed to find out who had killed Uthman. Ali heard about this, and met the three people and their group. Then the Camel War started. (It took its name

---

[18] See Ibn Hajar Al-Asqalani, *Fath al-Bari*, in the chapter of *Al-Maghazi*, Dar Al-Diyan li al-Shirka: Cairo, vol. VII, p.732.

[19] See Imam Bukhari in *Sahih Bukhari*, the chapter *al-Fitan*, vol. IV, p.2843. "Uthman ibn Haitham told us from 'Auf from Abu Bakra: Truly, Allah gave us purpose with a statement from the Prophet after he heard at the time of the Camel War that the King of Persia had installed his daughter as his successor. The Prophet said: "A community that is led by a woman is unfortunate.""

from the camel A'isha to call for peace.) In the second version, however, Ibn Hajar claims that there were about eighteen different versions of the cause of the Camel War.

If we look at it's the context, this hadith was not aimed at A'isha in the Camel War, but rather towards the daughter of King Kisra, who had replaced her father as monarch. This is shown as follows:

1) There is a definite sense of *asbab-al-wurud* (the moment when the Prophet made the hadith) in this hadith, as demonstrated by the words *lamma balagha*, meaning "when the Prophet arrived" and so on.

2) How it was possible that the Prophet responded to A'isha if the accident happened twenty-five years after his death? The point has been mentioned by Fatima Mernissi, who conducted a historical and methodological critique of this hadith. She criticized both its *matn* and the personality of Abu Bakra.[20]

According to Mernissi, Abu Bakra was controversial. In the beginning, Abu Bakra was a close and loyal aide to the Prophet Muhammad. He faced a dilemma when conflict arose between Ali and A'isha. Should he support Ali (the son-in-law of the Prophet) or A'isha (the wife of the Prophet)? Abu Bakra decided not to take sides with either of them. But, following A'isya's defeat in the Camel War, Abu Bakra suddenly issued a hadith from a different context and situation, which had been kept in his mind for twenty-five years.[21]

If the Prophet expressed the hadith in response to the succession of King Kisra of Persia by his daughters, Abu Bakra used the hadith to respond to A'isha. In addition, Abu Bakra's family background unclear, which caused Ibn Hanbal not to use his hadiths. Abu Bakra was once caned by 'Umar for giving false testimony in an adultery case.[22]

The fact that the hadith was issued by the Prophet to respond the leadership of King Kisra's daughter was supported by another hadith narrated by Ibn Abbas on the Prophet's letter to the King.[23] The hadith told that the

---

[20] Fatima Mernissi, *Wanita di Dalam Islam*, p.62.
[21] *Ibid.*
[22] *Ibid.* p.76.
[23] The hadith of Bukhari was placed precisely after the first version by Abu Bakra.

Prophet had asked Abdulla Ibn Khuzafa Al-Sahmi to write a letter to King Kisra, and to send it to the leader of Bahrain so that he could pass it to the King. But, when the King received the letter, he tore it up.[24]

Another story about the hadith of Abu Bakra came from Muhammad Anas Qasim Ja'far in *al-Huquq al-Siyasa li al-Mar'a*. He maintained that the hadith referred to a specific event, the Prophet's response to the installment of the daughter of King Kisra, who he felt did not fulfill the proper leadership requirements. According to Anas Qasim Ja'far, this hadith was a hadith *ahad* (narrated by a single person) and could not, therefore, be used as convincing evidence. Although hadith *ahad* contain solid information (*dzanniy*), they still need to studied in depth, particularly in relation to their chain of narration. This type of hadith can not be used as a legal basis for important problems.[25]

Muhamad Ismail Al-Kahlani, in his *Subul al-Salam*, a commentary treatise on *Bulugh al-Mar'am* by Ibn Hajar Al-Asqalani, revealed the different opinions among jurists about the understanding of this hadith. Abu Hanifa allowed women to be leaders, except in the case of criminal law (*hudud*). But Ibn Jarir allowed women absolute rights to be leaders.[26]

Whatever happened with Abu Bakra and Abu Huraira, we should still respect them as close companions of the Prophet, but we should not hesitate to criticize them. As companions, they are highly esteemed, but as human beings, they were fallible.[27] Rejection of the companions' positions can be done without accusing them of lying and such. Criticism should be based on the argument that the hadith was defective (*ma'lul*) or corrupted (*shadz*). The criticism should not be aimed at the companions as the founding figures of Islam (*al-sabiquna al-awwaluna*), but at the contents (*matn*) of the hadith.

WOMEN AND GENERAL ELECTIONS

Perhaps, in Indonesia, there is no real issue about women's rights to vote in general elections. But in many Islamic countries, it is a sensitive and hotly-

---

[24] Kisra was the general name for all Persian kings, while the Caesar was Heraclius.

[25] Muhammad Anas Qasim Ja'far, *al-Huquq al-Siyasah li al-Mar'ah fi al-Islam was al-Fikr wa al-Tashri' al-Mu'asir*, Egypt: Dar Al-Nahda al-'Arabiya, pp.46-7.

[26] Muhammad Ismail al-Kahlani, *Subulus al-Salam*, vol. IV, p.123.

[27] Interview with Quraish Shihab, Saturday 8 June 1996 at the office of IAIN, Jakarta.

debated issue. The basic problem is not whether women can be involved in elections, but how their involvement is carried out.

This problem can not be separated from the bigger picture of women's political rights in general. In Egypt, women were given their voting rights for the first time in 1949. Why were women not given voting rights earlier? If we acknowledge women as human beings and as a part of the nation, we must acknowledge their political existence. But, nonetheless, many nations still prohibit women from involvement in general elections, using religiously-based excuses.

There are several reasons that are frequently cited to legitimate women's exclusion:

1) During the Prophet's time women were never involved in politics. The Prophet never invited women to discuss matters of warfare. The deeds or 'tradition' of the Prophet (*Sunna*) suggest that He didn't invite their direct participation.

2) Theologically, the main Islamic sources, the Qur'an and hadiths, seemed to put women behind men. These sources were often interpreted too literally by the *ulamas* of the past. Because *fiqh* was familiar to the people, the *fiqh* corpus was often viewed as a representation of Islam as a whole. As we have seen, *fiqh* does not generally empower women as it was developed in a male-dominated culture.

In this context, it was understandable that some Muslim countries did not give voting rights to women; it was considered fine for them to be represented by men. This perspective should be critiqued. We should review legal products which forbid women from involvement in politics, particularly as neither the Qur'an nor hadiths prohibited their participation.

The notion of a general election, as the key to democratic and modern nationhood, has been developed since the French Revolution. During the time of the Prophet, there was no electoral mechanism of this sort. Even in Athena, the home of classical democracy, elections were very rudimentary. However, in the Prophet's time, there was a mechanism for succession. Islamic intellectuals and historians, including Mohammed Arkoun, viewed that the Medina experience was ideal and unrepeatable. In Medina, women could convey their aspirations directly to the Prophet, thus demonstrating that Sunna accommodated women's political interests, though in a simple way.

And what about women's political right to vote? The prohibition against women voting was not based on the reasons cited above. Some argued that women were banned from voting to avoid their entering public spaces without their *muhrim* (legal accompaniment). But if the issue was really about *mahram*, then these escorts could be replaced with security guards, for example. The problem of how to avoid contact with non-*mahram* could be resolved by setting up separate voting booths for women. But there is a more comprehensive solution: it requires the good will of both men and women, following God's will. As the Prophet said: "*Innama al-a'malu bi al-niyyat*," or, "In truth, all actions depend on their intentions."

To close the discussion, I will cite the position of Al-Siba'i, a former Dean of Al-Azhar University in Egypt who, after long discussions, proclaimed that Islam does not prohibit women from participating in general elections, and that those elected by these means are there to represent the populace and their rights. He said that Islam never banned a woman from voting for her representatives, or from conveying her aspirations as a member of society.[28]

WOMEN AS MEMBERS OF PARLIAMENT

This discussion deals with the further implications of women's right to vote.

If women are allowed to use their vote, why shouldn't they be able to become members of parliament? Isn't membership of parliament a real form of women's participation in general elections? There were no direct indications in either the Qur'an or hadiths that prevented women from becoming members of parliament.

According to Abd Al-Halim Abu Shuqqa, the fact that there was no prohibition meant that it was effectively *permitted*. This is similar to Al-Siba'i's opinion, which also maintained that parliamentary duties, such as law-making and administration, were the basis of this right. If we study it closely, Islam

---

[28] Professor Mohammad Al-Siba'i, *al-Mar'ah baina al-Fiqh wa al-Qanun*, p.155.

never excluded women from participating in legislation and supervisory duty (as related to *amar ma'ruf nahi munkar*: the implementation of good deeds and the avoidance of bad ones). In the context, Al-Siba'i maintained that women were permitted to become members of parliament.

Furthermore, Abd Al-Halim Al-Shuqqa said that was a woman's right to become a member of parliament. Although some conservative groups suggested that these rights should not be taken up, this stance is no longer valid in the current time.

Similarly, Dr Yusuf Qardhawi argued that there should be no such ban, because it would be against the social interest. Society needs women's participation.[29] On this basis, there is no valid reason or justification in Islamic teachings to reject women as members of parliament.

---

[29] Quoted by Mohammad Halim Abu Shuqqa in *Tahrir al-Mar'a* (Freedom of Women), vol. II, p.542.

CHAPTER SIX

WOMEN'S POSITION IN THE FIQH OF WORSHIP (*FIQH AL-'IBADA*)

A s a pillar of *fiqh* (jurisprudence), *fiqh al-'ibada* has dominated the body of literature. All matters pertaining to prayer and worship in Islam are discussed in detail in *fiqh al-'ibada*.

Fiqh can be divided into three main groups: 1) The *fiqh* of worship (*ibada*); 2) The *fiqh* of business (*mu'amala*); and 3) The *fiqh* of personal law (*al-ahwal al-shakhshiyya*). Each kind of these has different characteristics:

1) The *fiqh* of worship contains regulations on worship and ritual practice which are usually closed to reinterpretation. This *fiqh* resulted in standard products that do not accept innovation or review. Any addition to this kind of *fiqh* can be considered a sin, because it is said to be an intervention against God's authority;

2) The *fiqh* of *mu'amalah* pertain to everyday human relations. This *fiqh* is usually open to reinterpretation; and

3) The *fiqh* of *al-ahwal al-shakhshiyya* is related to the courtroom. Some parts of this kind of *fiqh* can be reinterpreted, while others are closed.

In this chapter, I will focus on the *fiqh* of worship and the patriarchal bias that can be found within it. Is this patriarchal bias a 'given' (i.e. God-given), which can not be reinterpreted? Or is it a human creation, made through the interpretation process? If certain parts of it may be reinterpreted, which parts would be acceptable?

WOMEN AND AZAN

Azan (the call to prayer) was first practiced in the era of the Prophet, in the first year of Hijriyyah. The first *mu'azin* (the person who makes the call to prayer) in Islamic history was a companion of the Prophet, Bilal. Many stories were recorded about Bilal's loyalty and sincerity, as well as his role in calling people to pray. In Indonesian tradition, 'Bilal' is the term used to describe *mu'azin*, particularly for the Friday prayer.

Etymologically, *azan* means announcement (*i'lam*). Terminologically, *azan* means announcing that the time for prayer has arrived, through the recitation of sentences regulated in Islamic law (*shari'a*).[1] The theological basis for *azan* is the Qur'an, hadiths and *ijma'*.[2]

Historically, *azan* is the revised form of a previous regulation on how to call people together for worship. In the past, there were several methods to call people, such as the minaret (where a fire was lit), with flags, with drumming, and so on. But, the background to *azan* has its background in a hadith, which explained that once, when the Prophet visited Medina, people were having difficulty calling people for prayer. They discussed what sign they could use to call Muslims to pray together with the Prophet. Some suggested ringing a bell (*naqush*), but the Prophet said that this was a Christian tradition. Others suggested using a trumpet (*buq*), but the Prophet said this was a Jewish tradition. Some suggested using a tambourine (*duf*), but the Prophet said this was a Roman tradition. Others still suggested the use of fire, but the Prophet said this was the tradition of the Persian *Majusi*. Some suggested the use of flags, flown so others would spread the news. But, the Prophet said that none of these was new, so no agreement was made. Then, while Abdullah Ibn Zaid slept he remembered the Prophet. Abdullah dreamt that

---

[1]   Similar definitions can be found in many works of *fiqh*.

[2]   The Qur'anic basis of this argument is the verse: *Ya ayyuha ladzina amanu idza nudhiya li salati min yaum al-jum'ati fas'au ila dzikrillai wadzar al-aba'i* (Al-Jumu'a [62]:9) "Those people who are believers, if they are called for Friday prayer, do it quickly and remember God, leaving their merchandise." The basis of this argument was a hadith narrated by Bukhari and Muslim: *Idza hadarat al-salatu falyu 'adzadzin lakum ahadukum.* "If the time for prayer comes, make announcement among you."

an angel taught him how to conduct *azan* and *iqama* (the announcement to begin prayer). He recounted his dream to the Prophet. According to the Prophet, the dream was similar to what had been revealed to him by God, and so he ordered the practices of *azan* and *iqama* to take place.[3]

One of the Prophet's companions, Anas, stated that when the number of Muslims increased, the Prophet ordered that there be a specifically Islamic way to call the people together at prayer time. Then the Prophet ordered Bilal to conduct *azan* and *iqama*. These were established as the Islamic way to announce prayer time.

However, as part of *ibada*, *azan* can not be performed by everyone. It was only recommended for male Muslims; it was not recommended, and even forbidden, for female Muslims. It was forbidden to women because it was considered to be opening her *aurat* ('modesty', in the form of voice) in public. In Islam, *aurat* is both a physical and non-physical concept. Shaykh Al-Islam Zakariya Al-Ansari, a loyal follower of Shafi'i, wrote in his *Matn al-Manhaj* that *azan* and *iqama* were only recommended for men, even if it was conducted alone and before schedule.[4]

Zakariya Al-Anshari also emphasized the important requirement of maleness in conducting *azan* and *iqama*. In the following order, he related these requirements for those who conduct *azan* and *iqama*: they should be Muslim, intelligent, male, and punctual, except during *azan* for *subuh* (pre-dawn prayer).[5]

Another *fiqh* expert from the Shafi'ite school, Abdullah Ibn Abdurrahman Al-Hadhrami, had a similar opinion to Zakariya Al-Ansari, except that he allowed, and even recommended, that women could conduct *iqama*.[6]

In his masterpiece, *al-Fiqh 'ala al-Madzahib al-Arba'a*,[7] Abdurrahaman Al-Jaza'iri maintained a similar position to the above *ulamas*. In a special

---

[3] This hadith was narrated by Ahmad, Dawud, Ibn Majah and Turmudzi. The hadith was considered to be of the *sahih* (valid) category.

[4] Shaykh Al-Islam Zakariya Al-Ansari, *Matn al-Manhaj*, Matba'ah Al-Qahirah: n.d., p.15.

[5] Zakariya Al-Anshari, *Matn al-Tahrir*, Matba'a 'Amma: 1391 H, First Edition, p. 17.

[6] Abdulla ibn Abdurrahaman al-Hadrami, *Mukaddima al-Hadrati Fiqh al-Sadati al-Shafi'iyya*, Musthafa Bab al-Halabi, 1330 H, p. 20.

[7] The book is very popular with Indonesian *ulamas* and in *pesantrens* (traditional Islamic boarding schools) for a basic comparative study of the four main schools of *fiqh*, especially for those who can not otherwise read beyond the works of the Shafi'i school.

chapter about the requirements of mu'azin (shurut al-mu'adzdzin), he wrote: "A muazin must be a Muslim, it is not acceptable for it to be performed by a non-Muslim. They should be mentally healthy, so it is illegal for drunkards and people with epilepsy (al-mughma alaih); they should be male, so it is illegal for women or transvestites."[8]

The invalidity of women conducting azan was also expressed by Shihab Al-Din Ahmad ibn Ahmad Al-Qalyubi in his popular book, Qalyubi wa 'Umaira, where he explicitly stated that women could neither conduct azan nor become the leaders of prayer.[9]

Based on these various opinions, it seems that the ban for women to conduct azan was mainstream point of view in Islam, especially in the school of Shafi'i.[10] Despite this, azan is not forbidden to women. If we read the Qur'an and hadiths, there is no single instance of a prohibition against women conducting azan. However, there was one hadith, narrated by Ibn 'Umar, which in essence banned women from conducting azan. It said: "laitha 'ala al-nisa'i adzanun wala iqamatun" (It is not valid for women to conduct azan and iqama).[11] According to Sayyid Sabiq, this hadith was based on the opinions of Anas, Hasan, Ibn Sirin, Al-Nakha'i, Al-Thauri, Malik, Abu Thaur, and the group that supported logic (asah al-ra'yi), who decided to forbid women from conducting azan.[12] But there are other stories that permit women to conduct azan, including this one from Imam Ahmad: "It is not a problem for women to conduct azan, and it is not a problem if they don't." Imam Shafi'i and Ishaq also allowed women to conduct azan and iqama. It is also noted that A'isha, the Prophet's wife, also conducted azan and iqama, as well as leading prayers, although only amongst other women.[13]

But if we critically analyze Ibn 'Umar's statement above – which is upheld by the majority of fiqh experts – we see that, textually, the hadith is not a prohibition against women conducting azan. The word laitha is used here to mean that at

---

[8]   Al-Juzairi, al-Fiqh ala al-Madzahih al-Arba'a, Dar al-Fikr, vol. I p.315.
[9]   Shihab Al-Din Ahmad Ibn Ahmad Al-Qalyubi, Qalyubi wa Umaira, Dar al-Haya al-Kutub al-Arabiyya: Indonesia, n.d., p.129.
[10] We need to clarify that Shafi'i's fiqh was different from Shafi'ite fiqh. The former was issued by Shafi'i directly, while the latter was issued by his followers and may contain contradictions.
[11] From Ibn 'Umar.
[12] Sayyid Sabiq, Fiqh al-Sunna, Dar Al-Fikr, 1983, Fourth Edition, vol., I, p.102.
[13] Ibid. Followed by this tale about A'isha: "Really, A'isha conducted azan and iqama and she become a prayer leader among women" (Baihaqi).

that time women were not yet conducting *azan*. Ibn 'Umar's statement is more of a historical account of the situation at that time, but the *ulamas* treated it as evidence for imposing a ban on women conducting *azan*.

The requirement of maleness for becoming a *mu'azin* was indeed decided among the leaders of the law schools, except for Imam Abu Hanifa. But even Abu Hanifa said that if the *azan*, conducted by a woman, provoked lust among the listeners, it should be banned.

From the perspective of Abu Hanifa's statement, the prohibition was made because it was thought that women's voices could provoke lust in their listeners. This stance can be traced back to the pre-Islamic view of women as temptresses.[14] The assumption that a woman's voice is part of her *aurat* (something, usually part of the body, which should be covered) also applied to prayer time, when a woman's voice should be slow and lowered if she was in the proximity of men praying. Thus, the Islamic concept of *aurat* included both the body and the voice. So why does the same not apply to mean's voices, which could equally arouse women's lust? This view on the voice as *aurat* has its source in Judeo-Christian tradition, and Islam has distanced itself from this understanding, focusing instead on the body.

These matters demand further research – why are only women's voices treated in this way? Isn't a woman's voice God-given and unchangeable? Why isn't the issue about men's inability to control their sexual desire? There does not seem to be sufficient basis to prohibit women from conducting *azan*. In Indonesia, it is commonplace for women to carry out this duty.

WOMEN: BETWEEN COMMUNAL PRAYER (*JAMA'AH*) AND LEADING PRAYER

Before discussing the role of *imam al-salat* (leaders of prayer) in detail, we need to look at women's position in *jama'a* (communal prayer as recommended by the Prophet) – we can not discuss one without the other. To begin, how does *fiqh* position women in its discourse on *jama'a*?

The first *jama'a* was conducted in Medina during the time of the Prophet. When he was in Mecca, the Prophet did not perform *jama'a* as it would have provoked his enemies. The situation in Mecca was not safe for Muslims, who

---

[14] This is reminiscent of the story of Adam's fall from Heaven being caused by Eve, and her voice, as found in Bible.

were under constant threat from Quraisy infidels. After moving to Medina, and especially after the night journey (ascension), the companions prayed together with the angel Gabriel.

Shaykh Jalaluddin Al-Mahalli maintained that, according to the *ulamas* of the Malikite school, communal prayer (*jama'a*) was only an obligation for men. According to assah (more valid) opinion, *jama'a* was not recommended for women, meaning that the legal status for it was not *Sunna* (recommended), but only permitted (*mubah*); it did suggest extra value.

The issue is why *jama'a* is recommended for men but not for women. Doesn't this mean that there are limitations and discrimination against women in worship?

Questioning this issue is important as it not only relates to discrimination in *fiqh* on the value of worship for men and women, also suggests that the history of the domestification and subordination of women in Islam may stem from their absence from *jama'a* in the mosque. Performing *jama'a* in the mosque is a symbol of freedom, union and creativity for women. Restricting women to praying at home is like restricting their self-actualization and socialization.

According to Shaykh Jalaluddin Al-Mahalli, women were not recommended to engage in *jama'a* because their position was not as special as men's. To justify this stance, he cited this phrase from the Qur'an: "Men are one level higher than women." Even if we accept this view, we could ask why women, rather than men, are not recommended to perform *jama'a* so that their quality of worship and position become higher.

Jalaluddin Al-Mahalli's opinion was supported by the *Tafsir al-Jalalain*,[15] which interpreted the word *qawwamuna* as *musallitun* meaning or 'power over women'. According to Jalaluddin Al-Mahalli and Jalaluddin Al-Suyuti, male leadership was given because men were superior in matters of knowledge, reason and power. Besides this, men supported the family economically, and pious women (*saliha*) were women who obeyed their husbands.

In fact, if we examine these verses from the perspectives of both the occasion for which the verse was revealed (*asbab an-nuzul*)[16] and the method

---

[15] The interpretation was written by Jalaluddin Al-Mahalli and Jalaluddin Al-Suyuti.

[16] *Asbab al-nuzul* is an empirical history of the origins of Qur'anic verses, although there is no consensus among all *ulamas* as to whether all verses have *asbab al-nuzul*.

of interpreting it in relation to others (*munasaba*), it was not at all clear that women can not perform *jama'a*. It is clear that Al-Mahalli's statement is mistaken. Moreover, there is a hadith that states that the Prophet said that communal prayer (*jama'a*) is twenty-seven times better than praying alone, as an announcement to all Muslims, both male and female. There is absolutely no discrimination in this hadith; what is good for men is also good for women.

Another reason which was used by *fiqh* experts not recommending women for doing prayer in *jama'a* was a hadith narrated by Abu Dawud that recounted: "Do not forbid your women from going to the mosque, but the home is better for them." This hadith was used by *fiqh* experts to justify that women were not prioritized to pray in the mosque, saying it was to avoid slander. So, it was better for women to pray together in their homes. In fact, this hadith can be interpreted in many ways.

The restrictions on women praying in mosques were issued during the reign of Caliph 'Umar, who instructed the Prophet's wives not to go to mosque to protect them from the Quraish infidels. 'Umar's companions meant to protect the women from being upset by Arabic behavior against women, but this was understood differently by the *fiqh* experts. Before the 'Umar's instruction, women were allowed to go to the mosque. Unfortunately, 'Umar ibn Khattab's action was institutionalized as a standard Islamic teaching in the next Islamic generations.

Although Abu Dawud's hadith is considered valid (*sahih*), its contents (*matn*) are contextual. Its *matn* do not actually problematize women's communal prayer in mosques, but refer to a cultural situation in the Arab world that was dangerous for women outside the home. The current situation is very different. Women's safety, in Indonesia for example, is now guaranteed by the state, as it is for men. So, it is no longer a problem for women to perform *jama'a* in the mosque.

So, what is the value of *jama'a* for women? The Prophet said a prayer made in *jama'a* was twenty-seven times better than praying alone. God rewards his believers according to their deeds. This depends on whether our motivation to join in *jama'a* is sincere or just in order to be seen (*riya'*). This applies to both men and women, both of whom are susceptible to the unacceptable traits of *riya'*, to *sum'a* (wanting to be heard) and pride. In Islam, there was no discrimination in worship; there is equality (*musawa*) for men and women. But it must be underlined that worship should be conducted ethically and appropriately.

Before discussing the legal basis for women becoming leaders of prayer for *jama'a*, I would like to quote the great imam Shafi'i, in his famous work, *al-Umm*:

> [Shafi'i says], may God gives his blessings when a woman prays together with men, women, boys and girls. Woman's prayer became subordinate to men's and boys', which were not subordinate as God had decided men as the leaders of women, while women were their lovers and so on. And women are not allowed to be the imam for men in any conditions. And women are not allowed to be the imam of prayer for transvestites, as their prayers are not sufficient and should be repeated (*qada*), and repeated again (*i'adah*). These prayers are not considered full, because they were done together with those who are not permitted to become *imams*.[17]

It's clear that Shafi'i prohibited women from becoming leaders of prayer because God had created men in this role. The opinion was not only upheld by Shafi'i, but also many *fiqh ulamas*. In an extreme way, Shaykh Jalaluddin Al-Mahalli stated that men and transvestites were not permitted to follow a female imam as her being was worth half that of a man.[18]

The two examples above are representative of the other *fiqh* literature, which all shared the nuances of Shafi'i's opinions. However, as a basis for legitimization, both Shafi'i's and Al-Mahalli's positions were flawed in their implementation. The use of Al-Nisa', verse 34, by Shafi'i was not in line with its occasion of revelation (*asbab al-nuzul*) or its meaning. There are three versions of the asbab al-nuzul, none of which relate to women's leadership in *jama'a*. The verse was issued due to the disobedience (*nushuz*) of Said ibn Rabi's wife, Habiba bint Zaid ibn Abi Huraira.[19]

---

[17] Muhammad Idris Al-Shafi'i, *al-Umm*, Dar Al-Fikr, Eighth Edition, vol I, p.191.
[18] See Jalaluddin Al-Mahalli, *Qalyubi wa Umaira*, vol. I, p.231.
[19] Abil Hasan Ali ibn Ahmad Al-Wahidi Al-Nisaburi, *Asbab al-Nuzul*, Beirut: Dar Al-Fikr, p.100.

The contents of Al-Nisa', verse 34, are about men's responsibility as income earners for their families. The term *qawwamuna* should be interpreted to mean that men should be the income earners because the patriarchal situation in the Arab world at that time made it impossible for women to be income earners. The issue is why a verse about men's function as income earners was used as a prohibition against women becoming *imams*. It is clear that such use of the verse is not correct.

Al-Mahalli's reasons are also flawed. If we trace it further, the source of its legitimacy was a hadith that stated: "Abu Sa'id Al-Khudri said [that] the Prophet went out to the mosque in the morning and afternoon. One day he passed a group of women and said: "Greetings women, do much charity, as I see that you are the majority of those in hell." The women asked: "Why, oh Prophet?" And he said: "You have often disobeyed your husbands. I have never seen people so lacking in reason and religion as you – men's strong hearts are more capable of this!" The women asked: "What is our lack of reason and religion?" And the Prophet answered: "Isn't the testimony of a woman [worth] half of a man's?" The women replied: "Yes." And the Prophet said: "All this is a lack of reason. During menstruation, isn't it true that you do not fast or pray?" The women replied: "Yes." And the Prophet said again: "This is proof that you lack religion."[20]

In hadith books, this is usually included in the chapter about Al-Haidh. But why did *fiqh* experts use this hadith as the basis of their argument to prohibit women from becoming leaders of prayer? There two approaches most often used in studying hadiths: 1) The *matn* (content) approach; and 2) The *sanad* (narration) approach. In terms of *matn*, there are three interpretive models: a) literalist (*zhahiriyya*); b) metaphorical (*majaziy*a); and contextual (*makaniya wa zamaniya*).

All of these models could be implemented in interpreting the hadith above, but following Ibn Rushd, we find that most people use the literalist approach.[21]

On the literalist approach, it is true that a woman is [worth] half a man, and they lacked reason and religion because they menstruate; this is what

---

[20] This hadith is in the authoritative *Fiqh al-Sunna* by Sayyid Sabiq, vol. I, p.74. "Things forbidden to women who are menstruating or in the period of *nifas*."

[21] In one of his books, Ibn Rushd said that literalists made narrow interpretations

the words of the hadith say. This is the dominant model of interpretation used by the *ulamas of fiqh*.

However, the hadith can be interpreted differently. If women can not perform worship because of menstruation, then they do not receive God's blessings (reason and religion), received by those who worship. Isn't menstruation God-given? As such, neither the literalist nor metaphorical approaches can resolve the issue.

Looking at this hadith, we should return to God's teaching that men and women were created in the same perfect form (*ahsan taqwim*), with the same dignity.

Of course, God gave different biological signs to men and women, but these are not differentiations of value. Menstruation and childbirth were not God-given to undermine women's worth.

WOMEN AND THE RECOMMENDATION FOR FASTING

This issue is related to our daily lives. The question comes from my heart: why should a woman have to ask permission from her husband in order to perform *ibada*? Isn't this against the Islamic teaching on human autonomy, without ties, except the bond to God?

As the teaching goes, the Islamic first came to Mecca in order to free humanity from slavery to the 'secular gods', whether in the form of statues of Latta, Manna or Uzza, or the worship of ancestral deities. Besides this theological liberation, Islam also released people from human slavery. Islam emphasized this because it aimed to educate people to be responsible and autonomous in their actions.

So how does this relate to the aforementioned issue of women having to ask their husband's permission to perform the (non-obligatory) fasting? Before answering this question, let us define what this kind of fasting (*puasa Sunna*) is.

Generally, *Sunna* fasting is defined as non-obligatory fasting. A Muslim is rewarded for performing it, but not punished if they don't. There are various kinds of non-obligatory fasting, such as fasting in the months of Muharram and Shawwal, and between the days of Monday and Thursday, and so on. Muslims who are able are recommended to perform this kind of *ibada*. This is recommended for any Muslim, except married women, who should ask their husbands' permission first.

The requirement of asking the husband's permission was based on the following hadith: "A wife must not fast when her husband is present, unless she has her permission." do The narrators of this hadith were Abu Huraira, Hammam ibn Mambah Ma'mar, Abdullah, and lastly, Muhammad ibn Muqatil.[22] Besides this one, there are other hadiths that maintain a similar position.

What is the basis of this permission? In *fiqh*, a wife should ask her husband's permission for all her actions. This is the wife's obligation and the husband's right. This rule originated from the Islamic family ethic that states that the husband leads the wife (*al-rijalu qawwamuna 'ala al-nisa'i*), as mentioned in Al-Nisa', verse 34, and also other hadiths.

From the perspective of *fiqh* experts, male leadership applies both inside and outside the family. A husband should be respected as a leader by his family and, as such, his permission must be requested. In Islam, the issue of permission is important because it could erase the value of the worship conducted. Why is the husband's permission so important? Is the husband's willingness more important than the good deed of fasting? More important than worship?

In Islam, the highest deed for a woman is to obey her husband, which in turn suggests obedience to her religion. According to Islam, a husband is a reflection of God on earth. One hadith – although it is unclear whether it is a valid one or not – said that if a woman was allowed to worship another, besides God, she should worship her husband. God would ask her to pray to her husband. So the husband's position is cosnidered higher than fasting or other kinds of worship.

The issue remains why the contrary does not also apply – why doesn't a husband require his wife's permission? Doesn't prohibiting a good deed disrupt the worship of God? I am saying that although asking permission is fine, it should be conducted in proportion to the wider issues.

---

[22] Bukhari, *Sahih al-Bukhari*, Maktaba Dahlan Indonesia, Kitab Nikah/Chapter on Marriage, vol. III, p.2150. The hadith states: "*Haddathasana Muhammad ibn Muqatil akhbarana Abdullah Akhbarana Ma'mar an Hamman ibn Mambah an Abi Hurairata an al-Nabiyyi Saw., la tasumu al-mar'atu wa ba'luha shahidun ila bi idznihi.*"

The permission was required due to the fear that a wife could not serve her husband's sexual desires if she was fasting. As a wife, she should be available to serve his needs at all times. She should ask his permission in order not to disappoint him. It is a good rule that the members of a family should inform each other of their activities, but this should not only apply to the wife, but also the husband.

This permission is to demonstrate obedience. But the nature of obedience should be questioned further. Should a husband who prohibits his wife from performing good deeds be obeyed?

A good husband is one who can understand his wife's aspirations and opinions. A good husband who acts according to the rules of good conduct (mu'ashara bi al-ma'ruf), does not enforce his own will. There is no husband in the world who doesn't want his wife to conduct good deeds.

The Qur'an says explicitly that a good wife is obedient, protective and able to take care of herself when her husband is away from home. But this kind of wife should also have a good husband, who can perform his obligations.

A husband who orders bad actions should not be obeyed. So, a husband who prevents his wife from doing good deeds should not also be obeyed. For a wife, obedience to her husband is the first level of goodness, with the understanding that her husband indeed deserves to be obeyed.

CHAPTER SEVEN

WOMEN BETWEEN THE FIQH OF TESTIMONY AND INHERITANCE

The issue of women's position in the courtroom and in relation to inheritance law remains problematic to this day. The problem does not rest with the Qur'an (the primary source), which is always open to reinterpretation, but on the fanaticism of certain people towards Qur'anic interpretation (*tafsir*). Their reluctance to reinterpret is not just based on hermeneutic concerns, but also political and ideological ones – particularly the rejection of liberalized thinking, as this is often considered to be influenced by Western thought. Such people fail to see the results; but object to the process. And the anti-Western feeling is combined with a fanatic attitude towards *fiqh* itself.

This is not really the fault of the followers, but is mainly due to the *ulamas of fiqh* creating a sense of dependence on their thought. Mohammad Arkoun called this 'orthodoxy'. For instance, a follower of the Shafi'ite school could not follow the teachings of other schools of thought, even if they were included in the four main Islamic schools. Discourse needed to be undertaken in one 'package' (*qadhi*ya). In terms of Islamic legal maxims, the mixing of different schools of thought without a clear reason was called *talfiq*.

In Indonesia, *fiqh* about law courts has developed more progressively than *fiqh* on inheritance (*mawarith*). For example, it is no problem for a woman to be a judge in either state or religious courts. According to the noted Indonesian intellectual, K.H. Abdurrahman Wahid, Indonesians struggled to set up judicial training schools for women since the era of former Minister of Religious Affairs, Wahid Hasyim.

But the *fiqh* on inheritance is still controversial in Indonesia. Another former Minister of Religious Affairs, Munawir Syadzali, was sharply challenged due to his idea to re-actualize Islamic teachings, particularly the ruling on the concept of sharing of inheritance 2:1 between men and women and changing it to 2:2 or at least equal shares. This courageous idea was rejected by many Muslim groups and Munawir was even accused of having deviated from Islam. In the reality, though, the equal division on inheritance has been practiced by the people, even before Munawir's proposal.

WOMEN IN THE DISCOURSE ON WITNESS AND TESTIMONY

Problems related to testimony are usually not discussed in a separate chapter of classical *fiqh* literatures. Discourse on acting as a witness appears with connection to certain jurisprudential cases of *fiqh* that needed witnesses. In contemporary *fiqh*, testimony is usually given its own chapter.

In this part of the book, women's testimony will be discussed in relation to the discrimination against and subordination of women. How far has women's role in giving testimony changed? This will be followed by a discussion of inheritance, focused on the issue of the 1:2 ratio, which suggests that the testimony of one man is equal to the that of two women.

As we know, In Islam, men and women can both give testimony in court. But, *fiqh* experts banned women from giving testimony in certain cases, such as criminal law (*hudud*) and retaliatory law (a life for a life: *qisas*). More importantly, there is the issue that the witness of two women is considered necessary to equal the testimony of a single man.

Shaykh Abu Shuja' in his *Taqrib* wrote:

There are two kinds of this right; the rights of God and the rights of human beings. *First*, there are the rights in which only the testimony of two men can only be accepted, in cases which have no relation to property, and men are allowed to watch it. *Second*, rights in which the witness of a man and of two women; or a witness and a defendant who has been sworn in for cases related to property. *Third*, the rights in which the testimony of two men and two women, or four women in cases which men were not allowed to watch. Women are not allowed to be witnesses in the rights of God.[1]

Abu Shuja's statement is an example of the assessment of women's value and position generally found in *fiqh* literatures.

WOMEN'S WITNESSES IN MARRIAGE AND DIVORCE

Marriage (*zawaj*) is an important part of human life. It is so important that it requires a properly conducted ceremony, witnessed by two witnesses.

The majority of *fiqh* scholars viewed that a marriage is not legal unless it is legally witnessed.[2] This argument is based on certain hadiths, including one from Ibn Abbas, who said: "Adulterers are among those who marry without witnesses."[3] And another came from A'isha: "It is invalid, a marriage without guardian and two witnessses."[4]

However, some *fiqh* scholars maintained that witness was not obligatory (wajib) in marriage. These included Abd Al-Rahman ibn Mahdi, Yazid ibn Harun, Ibn Al-Mundzir, Ibn Umar, and Ibn Zubair. According Ibn Mundzir, there was no single khabar (information from the Prophet) which narrated about the need for witnesses in the marriage. Yazid ibn Harun said, similarly, that there was no obligation to have witnesses recorded in the Qur'an, but that it was a teaching from the defenders of rationalism (*ashab al-ra'yi*). The Shi'ah Imamiyah scholars said that announcement, witness and clarity were recommended but not theologically obligatory in a marriage.[5]

However, having witnesses helps to avoid the prejudices of human weakness. Also, human beings are social creatures who need recognition

---

[1]   Abu Shuja, *Taqrib*, Indonesia, Dar al-Hayat, n.d., pp.68-9.
[2]   Some of Malik's followers did not require witnesses, but maintained that an announcement was sufficient. But, Al-Zuhaili viewed that Malik's opinion on this was weak. According to *mu'tamad* opinion (upheld), Malik still required witnesses. See Wahba Al-Zuhaili, *Al-Fiqh Al-Sunna wa Adillatuhu*, Dar Al-Fiqr, vol. VII, p.125.
[3]   Hadith by Turmudzi from Ibn 'Abbas. See *Nail al-Autar*, vol. VI, p.125.
[4]   Hadith by Daruqutni and Ibn Hibban.
[5]   Quoted by Wahba al-Zuhaili in *Fiqh Al-Islami wa Adillatuhu*, vol. VII, p.82, from *Mukhtasar al-Nafil fi al-Fiqh al-Imamiya*, p.194.

from society that they have legally married according to religion. Many *fiqh* scholars decided that witness was obligatory in a marriage, and that the legal basis for this obligation was found in several hadiths.

The need for witnesses also appears when someone wants to divorce. The majority of *fiqh* scholars, both *salaf* (first generation) and *khalaf* (new) groups, thought that divorce could take place, with or without a witness. This opinion based on the principle that divorces is the husband's prerogative, so he did not need witnesses to go ahead and divorce his wife. During the era of the Prophet and his companions, there was no indication on the need of witness (*ishhad*) in divorce.

However, the above opinion was rejected by scholars from the Imamiyah Shi'ah sect, who maintained that witness is part of the validity of divorce. This was based on a verse of the Qur'an: "You testify with two fair witnesses among you, and uphold witness" (Al-Talaq [65]:2). According Al-Tabrasi, literally, the verse was evidence that witness in divorce was obligatory. According to the Imamiyah Shi'ah, this position was supported by stories from the *imams* of Ahl al-Bait.[6]

Meanwhile, among the Prophet's companions who supported the need of witnesses in the marriage were Ali ibn Abi Thalib and Imran ibn Husain, while among *tabi'in* were Muhammad Al-Baqir, Ja'far Al-Sadiq, 'Ata, Ibn Juraij and Ibn Sirin. In *Jawahir al-Kalam* which was quoted by Sayyid Sabiq, it was told that a man questioned Ali about his divorce. Ali asked the man: "Was the divorce witnessed by two witnesses according to the orders of God and His Prophet?" The man replied, "No, it was not." So Ali asked the man to return to his wife and said that the divorce was invalid.[7] Based on the notes above, we can see that many *fiqh* scholars thought there was strong basis to argue for the need of witnesses in divorce.

Having witnesses in divorce actually benefits the woman's position, which is basically weak. Witnesses might ensure that women have their legal rights legitimated. Women can call witnesses to put pressure on the husband in cases of conflict and they might even favor the wife's position.

---

[6] See Sayyid Sabiq, *Fiqh al-Sunna*, Dar Al-Fikr, vol. II, p.220. For further explanation, see Al-Alusi on al-talaq.

[7] *Ibid.*

But this raises another problem: who has the right to act as witness? Men, women, or both? In *fiqh*, there are certain requirements for a witness.[8] One of these requirements – *dzukura* (maleness) – remains controversial.[9]

Basically, there are two problems faced by women in relation to the discourse on testimony. First, women have no legal right to be a witness in either divorce or marriage. Second, although women are allowed to be witnesses, the value of two women's testimonies is equal to that of one man.

What is the legal basis of these issues? 1) The prohibition against women becoming witnesses was not explicitly stated in the Qur'an. No single verse in the Qur'an forbids women from becoming a witness. The basis of this opinion was a hadith narrated by Al-Zuhri. This hadith, which was often quoted in *fiqh* literature, said that women were not allowed to testify in *hudud* (see below), marriage and divorce.[10] So the status of the hadith's *matn* and *sanad* need to be evaluated. 2) Historically speaking, this prohibition was based on the assumption that women at this time did not have expertise in this field.

With the association to the above two statements, we can begin to question the prohibition against women as witnesses, as well as the issue of their value as witnesses only being equal to half of that of a man's.

WOMEN'S TESTIMONY IN *HUDUD* LAW

Etymologically, the word *hudud* is derived from *hadda* which means 'limit'. In terms of law, criminal law (*hudud*) refers to punishments that have been decided by human beings and by the great law maker (Shari') – God – as stated in the Qur'an. Nothing should be added or subtracted in implementing this *hudud*.

---

[8] Requirements for being a witness: mentally healthy, mature, male, able to listen to two married, Muslim people. See *Fiqh al-Sunna*, vol. II, p.50.

[9] Almost all classic and contemporary *fiqh* follow this opinion. See, for example, Shihab Al-Din Al-Qulyubi in *al-Qulyubi wa Umaira*, Zakariya al-Ansari in *Matn Tahrir*, Muhammad Abu Bakar Shata in *I'ana al-Talibin*, Abu Shuja in *Taqrib*, Wahbah Al-Zuhaili in *Fiqh Al-Islami wa Adillatuhu* and Sayyid Sabiq in *Fiqh al-Sunna*.

[10] "*Madhat al-Sunna al-Rasulillah Saw.: Al La yajuzu shahadatun al-nisa'i fi al-hududi, wala fil al-nikahi, wa la al-talaqi.*" (HR Abu 'Ubaid from Al-Zuhri)

Sayyid Sabiq, a contemporary *fiqh* scholar, claims that, etymologically, *hudud* means the separation of one issue from another, or an issue that differentiates between two others. *Hudud* can also mean prevention. So *hudud* could refer to a form of punishment that would prevent the repetition of the offence committed.

According Abu Shsuja' in his *Taqrib*, offences which could be punished with *hudud* include accusing people for adultery (*qadzaf*); drinking liquor; killing animals; conducting rebellion (*bughat*); apostasy (*ridda*); and neglecting prayers. In the cases above, women's witness is not considered legal. The sociological and theological reasons why women's testimony is not accepted in the above cases will follow. We will focus on two examples: adultery and *qadzaf* (making the accusation of adultery) because both relate to women.

ADULTERY

Adultery is one of offences that is punishable by *hudud*. *Fiqh* scholars said that adultery was the highest rank of offence to which *hudud* can be applied (*ashad al-hudud fi al-jumlah*).

All the world's religions view adultery as an offence. In Islam, adultery is punished heavily. Why? 1) Adultery is considered to be a violation against God's laws on legal marriage; 2) Morally and ethically, adultery reflects an irresponsible attitude; and 3) Adultery is damaging to women, due to the absence of formal legal regulations on their rights and obligations. If, for example, pregnancy occurred outside of wedlock, who would be responsible for the baby, if the person responsible refused to admit his role?

So what is the definition of adultery? Muhammad Ibrahim Al-Badjuri, in his *Hashiyah Al-Bajuri*, defined adultery as the entrance of a man's genitals, which were already *mukallaf* (carrying legal rights) into the genitals of a forbidden woman.[11] This definition excluded adultery committed by children and insane people. According to *fiqh*, these two groups can not be punished for adultery.

---

[11] See Ibrahim Al-Badjuri, *Hashiyah Al-Badjuri*, vol. II, p.229.

According to *fiqh*, people who commit adultery can be categorized into two types: *muhsan* adultery and *ghairu muhsan* adultery.[12] *Muhsan* adultery is adultery (fornication) committed by unmarried people, while *ghairu muhsan* adultery is committed by married people. People who committed muhsan adultery were punished by *rajam* (stoning) with medium-sized stones, while people who committed *ghairu muhsan* adultery were punished with *jild*[13] (one hundred strikes of the cane) and one year's imprisonment. This sentence was of the same length as that given to people who shirked their full duty to pray (*qasar*).

Perpetrators of *muhsan* and *ghairu muhsan* adulteries were punished with different degrees of *rajm*. But, the implementation of the punishment only occurs when the crime fits the definition of adultery, and when it was witnessed directly by four male witnesses. The status of women's testimony in such cases will be discussed below, together with *qadzaf*.

QADZAF

Another offence which is punishable with *hudud* law and requires witnesses is *qadzaf* (the [false] accusation of adultery). In Islam, *qadzaf* is a serious sin, although not as serious as *mushrik* (polytheism) or adultery. The Qur'an categorized *qadzaf as fakhisha* (a rotten deed). It was explicitly mentioned in the Qur'an, Al-Nur verse 19. In Al-Nur, verses 23, 24 and 25, God threatens people who accuse others of adultery without proper evidence. In these verses, God describes the forms of torture that people who accuse others of adultery (accusers: *qadzif*) will undergo[14] in the world and in the hereafter.

Linguistically, *Qadzaf* means *al-ramyu*, or throwing (a stone at someone, for example). *Qadzaftu* means 'I throw' in Arabic. In the Qur'an, Taha (20), verse 39, it states: "*Aniqdzi fihi fi al-tabuti faqzi fihi fi al-yammi*" or "*Put him [Moses] in the coffin, and throw it into the river.*" Etymologically, the definition *qadzaf* was taken from this verse. But *fiqh* scholars used the term *qadzaf* to

---

[12] There are four requirements for people who could be considered to have conducted *ghairi mukhsan* adultery: Mature and mentally healthy (not children or suffering from insanity); free, rather than slaves; and the adultery has been committed within a formal marriage.

[13] According to Imam Khatib, this punishment was called *jild* (skin) because the punishment should touch the skin directly.

[14] When Allah uses the term, *la'ana*, it refers to major sins.

mean 'throwing' an accusation of adultery at other people.[15] The term *qadzaf* is only used in relation to accusations of adultery.

The accusation of adultery can be made against anybody. However, in *fiqh* literature, the accusation was usually made against a wife. Why? Because the Qur'an explicitly uses the feminine term, *muhsanat*. So it is understandable that *fiqh* scholars situated the accusation of adultery in relation to women, even though the Qur'an suggested that essentially *qadzaf* could happen to anyone.

People who commit *qadzaf* are punishable with *hudud* if they fulfill three conditions, applicable to the accuser (*qadzif*), the accused (*maqzuf*), and something that can be used to make the accusation (*maqduf bihi*). In *fiqh* terminology, this is called *shart al-qadzaf*. The requirement for the accuser is that they be mentally healthy, mature, and free from oppression. The requirement for the accused is that they be mentally healthy, mature, Muslim, that they have never conducted adultery and they are free (not a slave). The requirement for maqzuf bihi was 1) That it be conducted clearly without requiring thought from the accused; and 2) It must use subtle but pointed wording. Regarding this kind of allegorical statement, Imam Malik said that its value was the same as that of a clear sentence.

Other offences were also punishable with *hudud*, such apostasy (*ridda*), drinking liquor, *hiraba* and so on. But it seemed that only the cases of adultery and *qadzaf* directly related to women. However, all offences that required witnesses should be seen in terms of the following perspective.

Neither adultery nor *qadzaf* could be punishable by *hudud* if there was no strong evidence and testimony from others. I will take this opportunity to describe the mechanisms of *hudud* in relation to female witnesses, because they have been excluded in this context. Why has this been the case?

Al-Nisa' (4), verse 15, states: "And for the women among you who commit fahisyah (adultery), there should be four among you who have witnessed it."[16] Based on this verse, it is clear that there should be four direct witnesses. According to *fiqh* literature, these witnesses must have seen the penis penetrate the vagina directly and without anything obscuring the view. This condition was made in order to respect people's dignity.

---

[15] Very similar definitions of *qadzaf* can be found in many other *fiqh*

[16] See Al-Nisa' (4), verse 15.

WHY NOT ACCEPT WOMEN'S TESTIMONY? A DECONSTRUCTION

In the two jurisprudential examples mentioned above, as well as some others, women could not be accepted as witnesses. This patriarchal bias was due to the interpretation of verses on the creation of women in the Qur'an and hadith. Women are seen as second class citizens because they are said to have been created from man (Adam). But what of adultery cases only known about by women? Don't they have the right to come forward as witnesses? Think in terms of the rape of many Chinese-Indonesian women during the riots of May 13-14 1998 in Indonesia – I think we need to deconstruct the status of the prohibition against women becoming *hudud* witnesses which has been upheld by *fiqh* up to this point.

To begin, we will investigate the Qur'anic verses that discuss women's testimony. Then, we will look at various hadiths that discuss this matter.

Al-Baqara, verse 282, explicitly states that the value of a man's testimony is equal to that of two female witnesses. However, it is important to realize that this verse deals specifically with financial contracts and nothing more. *Fiqh* scholars have applied the contents of this verse to all other kinds of legal issues besides financial contracts.[17]

Many modern Muslim intellectuals, who sympathize with women's rights, maintain that this verse does not show women's inferiority. The 1:2 ratio was established because the woman's financial skills were weaker than the man's at that time. The logic was that one woman would act as witness, while another would ensure that the witness did not forget anything.

Muhammad 'Abdu claimed that this ratio was not an obligation, but only a recommendation.[18] If the Qur'an demanded the 1:2 regulation, it would have made this clear consistently in other verses about testimony. According to Asghar Ali Engineer, at least seven other verses in the Qur'an do not state that the testimony of two women is equal to that of a single male witness.[19]

Besides, women's testimony in cases punishable by *hudud* and *qisas* have often happened in the past, such as in the case of 'Umar's wife, Naila, who testified on his murder. 'Ali then punished the murderer with the law

---

[17] Asghar Ali Engineer, *Hak-hak Perempuan Dalam Islam*, LSSPA: Yayasan Perkasa, 1994, p.86.
[18] Sayyid Muhammad Rashid Rida, *Tafsir al-Manar*, Beirut: Dar Al-Fikr, vol. III, p.124.
[19] Asghar Ali Engineer, *op. cit.*, p.89.

(*hadd*). Based on this example, we could say that women's testimony is sufficient to make a legal decision. According to Salbiah Ahmad, we often disqualified women's testimony in order to protect them from the possibility of humiliation. Nonetheless, Salbiah Ahmad concluded that whoever who had abilities to be a witness, should have that right.[20] Ibn Qayyim revealed a more progressive opinion in his *al-Turuq al-Hukmiyya*, which allowed women to testify in the two kinds of cases discussed above. Al-Tabari and Ibn Hazim gave similar opinions.

FIQH ON INHERITANCE

More evidence of women's subordination in *fiqh* is shown in the case of the unequal sharing of inheritance between men and women. *Fiqh* maintained that women could have only half of the portion accorded to a man. The regulation was drawn from Al-Nisa' (4), verse 11: *Li dzakari mithlu hazzh al-unthasayain*, or "A man's portion is like the portion of two women." According to some *fiqh* scholars, the contents of this verse were categorized as *qat'iy* – absolute and undeniable. Anyone who rejected this verse would be considered an infidel.

In fact, the discourse on inheritance has developed since the beginning of Islam and should be seen in its historical context. During *Jahiliyya* (the time of darkness), the discourse on inheritance was solely male discourse. The actors, decision makers and receivers of inheritance were men, whereas women made into objects to be given as inheritance. The discourse changed totally due to Islam. Before Islam, women were to be inherited but, under Islam, women gained the right to obtain inheritance.

In Indonesia, there was a heated discussion about Al-Nisa' (4), verse 11, a few years ago. The debate was whether the 1:2 sharing of inheritance was an absolute legal decision which could not be changed, or whether it was flexible and open to change according to time and place. Former Minister of Religious Affairs, Munawir Syadzali, expressed his views on the re-actualization of Islam and the idea that the 1:2 sharing should be adjusted to the current context.

---

[20] Salbiah Ahmad, "Evidence of Women (as Witnesses), Diyat and Apostasy," in Rose Ismail (ed), *Hudud in Malaysia: The issue at Stake*, SIS, p.43.

In early Islam, the 1:2 division was not problematic. But it has been challenged by contemporary women's rights activists as a discrimination against women. Why do women only get half of the men's portion? Aren't they both God's creations? Are the different allowances based on gender or biological differences? Islam offers many ways out of the problem:

1) The verse is the Qur'an's response to social conditions at that time – a time when women had no rights over property given to her. Gifts were to be passed on to her brothers or parents. Sociologically and historically, though, these gifts showed that both men and women had the right to property. Islam gives women two opportunities to own property – through inheritance or through dowry. So the 1:2 division was dependent on the past context.

2) On a socio-theological basis, the amount of inheritance given to men was larger because Islam does not demand that women give dowry or income to their families. However, Islam offers a solution for parents who want to give equal portions to their children, both men and women. The mechanism was a grant or inheritance which was conducted before the death of the parents. The Prophet once said: "Equalize the gifts you give among your children. If I was allowed to give more to one, I would give more to my daughter."

The two reasons above are logical enough to explain why men get more than women. They also show us that the difference in the sharing of inheritance between men and women was not based on biological difference, but socio-cultural reasons – gender. Because it is only based on gender roles, laws on this matter can be changed.

CHAPTER EIGHT

TOWARDS A NEW PARADIGM OF FIQH

THE IMPORTANCE OF CHANGE IN *FIQH*[1]

As mentioned in the previous chapters, one of the striking weaknesses of our *fiqh* literature is its lack of awareness of gender equity. When people talk about Islam's resistance to women's rights and empowerment, *fiqh* is usually cited as the main source of this injustice. In this regard, *fiqh* is understood as a religious concept that defends a situation in which women do not have full autonomy to determine their own rights.

This is unsurprising if we look at the genealogy of *fiqh* and the people who established the discipline. *Fiqh* is a product of Medieval Islam, at which time gender rights had not yet been formally recognized. Awareness of gender equity is a product of modernity. Our task now is to study the criticism directed at *fiqh*, as a vehicle for reshaping it, and to make a new *fiqh* that strives for and protects gender equity.

In this chapter, I would like explore the possibilities for making new interpretations of, or even changing, the teachings of patriarchal *fiqh*. Many

---

[1] I have written twice about this new *fiqh* agenda in the mass media. First, in *Republika* (1-2-1996) "Perempuan, Menstruasi dan Lailatul Qadr,"where I stated the need to deconstruct the configuration of classical *fiqh* that placed women in a subordinate position; and second, in *Media Indonesia* (20-4-1996) "Perempuan Butuh Fiqh Baru," where I suggested that *fiqh* be viewed as living, travelling texts.

Muslims assume that *fiqh* is unchangeable, but this is not the case, and we need to make the shift as *conditio sine quo non*. There are at least two perceptions that support the implementation of such changes:

1) Prior to making any changes, we should understand that *fiqh* (*shari'a*)[2] is not the same as the Qur'an and *Sunna* (tradition), which indeed can not be altered. As we know, among the *ulamas*, the unchangeable position of the Qur'an and *Sunna* is not negotiable; we can only reinterpret previous interpretations of the Qur'an, rather than change the Qur'an and *Sunna* themselves.

2) *Fiqh* is the result of serious human endeavor (*ijtihad*) and is open to human excesses and failings. It is also very context-specific. As the result of interpretation of the Qur'an and Sunna, even with tight methodological and intellectual requirements, flaws are unavoidable.

Human works never reach perfection. The Prophet Muhammad said in a hadith that: "Humanity is a place of error and forgetting." Thus, reinterpretation of *fiqh* is necessary – not to damage *fiqh*, but to protect and defend it.

However, some groups only acknowledge the qualities of *fiqh* and refuse to admit its weaknesses. The stance creates obstacles for change. Fundamental changes seem difficult, as even small reinterpretations are still considered taboo. These groups often question our ability, as people born in the current era, to make changes to *fiqh*. Are we capable of thinking like the past *ulamas* did? Haven't we sinned greatly? A whole range of questions are raised.

And these questions have become a psychological burden for those who want to make changes because, even if they really have the ability, people would not trust them. Muslim traditionalist groups still think of the results of *ijtihad* by the *ulamas* of the Islamic schools of the past as a legal source that can not be changed. *Fiqh* is treated as a product of interpretation that

---

[2] I intentionally put the terms *fiqh* and *shari'a* in bracket because they are often treated as the same the thing, although some place *fiqh* lower within the wider context of *shari'a*, as in Al-Zuhaili's *al-Fiqh al-Islami wa Adillatuhu*. In my view, the two terms often overlap and mean 'Islamic Law'. A similar conclusion is also maintained by Ahmad Hasan, a noted Pakistani scholar.

is subject to change, but as a legal source in itself, sometimes viewed on a par with the Qur'an and Sunna. If we endeavor to change *fiqh*, we must cast aside such thoughts. There is a hadith that states that if engage in *ijtihad* and the results are correct, we will receive two rewards; if we are mistaken, we will still receive one reward.

Once again, *fiqh* (*shari'a*) is not din (religion), which can not be changed by anyone. On the contrary, *fiqh* is always in an evolutionary process, and must change with the times. This point is acknowledged in a principle of *fiqh*: *al-hukmu yadurru ma'a illatihi* – so, clearly, changes in *fiqh* regulations are acceptable.

Asghar Ali Engineer, a noted Indian writer, once claimed that it was a common mistake for people to think of *fiqh* as God's word and that it could not be changed – a position supported by several conservative *ulamas*. Furthermore, he said that *fiqh* was not formulated at one time, but through a complicated evolutionary development over hundreds of years. *Fiqh* is not a static product (*jumud*), but something always conducted in a dialogue according to context.[3]

There is still hope to include principles of gender equality and justice in *fiqh*, and to enrich and reinterpret old concepts on women's rights which were no longer suitable for contemporary times and new tendencies in the sciences, both religious and general.

Fiqh has been slow in facing new developments, especially in the women's liberation movement (*tahrir al-mar'a*). Re-formulation of *fiqh* with a new perspective would provide two main benefits:

1) It would enlarge the scope of *fiqh* as an open discourse which is ready to conduct dialogue with time and context; and
2) It would open the possibility of accommodating new developments. In other fields – politics, for instance – there is now a body of *fiqh* on politics. In environmental issues, there are environmental *fiqh*. There is also *fiqh* on general elections.

---

[3] Asghar Ali Engineer, *Hak-Hak Perempuan dalam Islam*, Yogyakarta: LSPAA Prakarsa Foundation, 1994, p.9.

FIQH AL-NISA': A NEW *FIQH* WITH A GENDER PERSPECTIVE

The embryonic material for a *fiqh al-nisa'* (*fiqh* of women) has in fact existed for a long time, although it was still in a simple form, including only categorizations and classifications on women's duties and prohibitions in matters such as worship, *mu'amala*, and *ahwal shaksiyya*. However, this *fiqh* lacked a clear gender perspective and rational advocacy for women.

Developing women's *fiqh* or feminist theology – to borrow Riffat Hassan's term – is an urgent matter these days. It should free Muslim women and men from a social structure and system of teaching that hinders the development of patterns of equal and just relations.

Developing and formulating the new *fiqh*[4] with a perspective on gender equality and justice perspective, requires us to engage with the wider framework of human rights. In Islam, it has been agreed that there are several individual rights that must be guaranteed: the right to life (Al-Ma'ida [5]:32), the right to dignity (Al-Isra' [17]:70, Al-Ahzab [33]:72, Al-Baqara [2]:30-34, and Al-Tin [95]:4-6), the right to justice (Al-Ma'ida [5]: 8 and Al-Nisa' [4]:13), the right to freedom from slavery, the right to knowledge, the right to food, personal rights protecting us from slander and mockery, rights to develop our own sensibility and enjoy God's blessings, the right to leave our home in oppressive situations, and the right to live well.

It is also necessary to reevaluate the misogynistic interpretation of certain hadiths that are often used as a basis for Islamic law. These include those on human creation narrated by Abu Huraira, and those on political leadership (*imama*) narrated by Abu Bakra. It is also necessary to reevaluate the opinions of old *fiqh* scholars which have no strong basis in the Qur'an or the *mutawatir* hadiths. Cultural, ideological and political influences should also be clarified. And the new *fiqh* should also include new developments in the social sciences, including studies of the various schools of feminism, sociology, historical criticism, anthropology, language (semiotic and linguistic), and so on.

The *fiqh al-nisa'* has various agendas, depending on how we read the term. *Fiqh* fi al-nisa means '*fiqh* about women' and discusses Islamic laws

---

[4] This does not mean creating a new *fiqh* which is not based on the Qur'an and hadith, but rather upholding methodologically the old theories for formulating legal maxims (*Usul al-Fiqh*).

that relate to women. Secondly, *fiqh li al-nisa'* (*fiqh* for women) means *fiqh* that are formulated specifically for women's interests. In order to combine the two approaches above, we need a *fiqh min al-nisa'* (*fiqh* from women), formulated by women. *Fiqh al-nisa'*, with the three agendas listed above, is expected to become a paradigm for women to engage with the development of civil society – free from oppression.

A METHODOLOGICAL PROPOSAL

I do not intend to suggest a new methodological proposal here. Rather, I am seeking a synergy between the various currents of critical thought on *fiqh*. This small effort is like a grain of salt in the sea compared to the *ijtihad* of the past *ulamas*. However, this is no excuse to avoid engaging with the methodological reconstruction of *fiqh*.

This methodological proposal is very important because, as we know, the emergence of scientific methodology can not be separated from the discourses around it. We need to begin from methodology, because it is often subjective. For an illustration, we can look at the emergence of methodological criticism on the narrators of the hadiths, known as *Rijal al-Hadith* (male figures in hadith). I argue that this term should be changed, and made neutral rather than patriarchal, by not only referring to male narrators (*rijal*), but also female narrators. We find a similar lack of neutrality in *fiqh* methodology, in both literal and substantive meanings.

In Islamic literature, *fiqh* methodology is known as *Usul al-fiqh*. But, as a formal scientific discipline, *fiqh* was born before *Usul al-fiqh*. *Fiqh* was initiated by Hanafi, whereas *Usul al-Fiqh* was invented by Hanafi's student, Shafi'i.

Etymologically, *usul* originates from al-ashlu, which means 'origin' or 'principle', and *fiqh* means 'understanding'. Terminologically, *Usul al-Fiqh* refers to the principles of *fiqh* formulation. The problem here is why the form developed prior to the formulation.

In Islam, the discipline of knowledge originated from sacred sources, God's words in the Qur'an and the Sunna of the Prophet, which were recorded in hadiths. All the sciences, such as Arabic grammar (*nahwu*), Arabic literature (*balagha*), and interpretation (*tafsir*), etc. were based on these sacred sources. But they also referred to the exact sciences, although all had to verified by the Qur'an. So the formulation of knowledge was a response God's verses, both *kauniyya* and *qur'aniyya*. So, it makes sense the scientific knowledge preceded the methodology.

In this context, a new methodology is needed to understand our old *fiqh*, which have not developed for centuries. There are important reasons why our understanding of *fiqh* needs renewal: 1) As *fiqh* was developed centuries ago, the existing methodology is no longer capable of facing the challenges of our times; and 2) The development of science depends on the development of its methodologies. Development does not mean total change, but small contributions can be considered to be part of the process of development.

The following is an exploration of the development of *fiqh* methodology. Of course, it is far from perfect, but it should be respected as an effort towards improvement in the future.

DEVELOPMENTS IN CONTEMPORARY *FIQH* METHODOLOGY: REINTERPRETATION OF THE CONCEPTS OF *ZHANNIY* AND *QAT'IY*

Current theoretical inventions can not be separated from the theoretical inventions of the past. For example, Imam Shafi'i did not start from scratch when he proposed *Usul Fiqh* and related theoretical methods. Shafi'i's existence can not be separated from Hanafi and Malik before him, nor they from the *tabi'in* and the companions of the Prophet. Likewise, the *tabi'in* and the companions can not be separated from the teachings of God as revealed to the Prophet – they are all part of a causal process. The development of scientific knowledge starts simply and develops according to the times. It can progress to the highest pinnacle, or quickly disappear – we require continuous change in order to avoid such problems.

The concepts of *zhanniy* and *qat'iy* are well known in textual interpretation. They were developed by Shafi'i as a tool for interpreting the Qur'an. There are the two patterns of meaning in the Qur'an: 1) Qur'anic verses that have clear meanings and need no interpretation. These kinds of verses are called *qat'iy*; and 2) Quran'ic verses that need interpretation. These are called *zhanniy*. This division is upheld by many *ulamas* until now.

Basically, the dichotomy between *qat'iy* and *zhanniy* is only popular for interpreting the Qur'an, but they are used by both *fiqh* experts and theologians. The concepts are not used for interpreting the hadiths. See, for instance, the debates between *salaf* and *khalaf ulamas* on verses with unclear meanings (*mutashabihat*) and those with clear meanings (*muhkamat*), which have similar connotations to *qat'iy* and *zhanniy*, respectively. According to many theologians, *muhkamat* verses have definite meanings, while mustashabihat verses have indefinite meanings.

This next section will discuss the concepts *zhanniy* and *qat'iy*, as discussed by Masdar Farid Mas'udi, an Indonesian Muslim intellectual whose main concern is Islamic law. Masdar's proposal was a breakthrough in the development of *Usul al-Fiqh*, and the first of its kind in Indonesia. There has been a renewal of *fiqh* in Indonesia, but only the products of *fiqh*, rather than *fiqh* methodology. Indonesian *fiqh* experts only interpret the *fiqh*, instead of interpreting the methodology and creating new methodologies.

Predictably, when Masdar proposed the reinterpretation of the concepts of *zhanniy* and *qat'iy*, many Indonesian clerics were cynical, but did not offer alternative solutions. Masdar first used this methodology in his book, *Agama Keadilan: Risalah Zakat Pajak* (Just Religion: A Treatise on Alms and Tax). This book received both compliments and criticisms. One of the compliments came from Martin van Bruinessen, an Indonesianist who said the book was a monumental work of *fiqh* because it managed to present original thinking and a reinterpretation of alms-giving. Abdurrahman Wahid, then the chairman of the country's largest Muslim organization, Nahdlatul Ulama, said that the book was the result of an almost perfect *ijtihad*.[5] Before Masdar, Harun Nasution had also used these two concepts similarly in the field of theology, but Nasution only measured *qat'iy* and *zhanniy* verses relevant to theology.

According to Masdar, *qat'iy* is a teaching expressed in firm language (*sarih*), while *zhanniy* is a teaching expressed unclearly and ambiguously so it could be interpreted as having more than one meaning.[6] Masdar said that the characteristics of *qat'iy* verses are that they are absolute, principled,

---

[5]   See Masdar F. Mas'udi, *Agama Keadilan: Risalah Zakat Pajak*, P3M, 1991.
[6]   Masdar F. Mas'udi, *Islam dan Hak Reproduksi Perempuan: Dialog Fiqh Pemberdayaan*, Mizan 1996, p.29.

fundamental, and need no further argument from outside the verse. They are just, universal, and need no further *ijtihad*. *Zhanniy* verses are classified as the opposite of this. He said that *zhanniy* is the explanation of *qat'iy* or *muhkamat* verses.

Masdar's efforts have helped us to reinterpret many standard *fiqh*, as well as some that could not previously be reinterpreted. Some groups, however, viewed Masdar's method as very abstract, and this weakness emerged when Masdar was asked to list which specific verses in the Qur'an could be categorized as *qat'iy* and which as *zhanniy*. He was only able to give the characteristics listed above. This is clearly not sufficient.

But there are other reasons why Masdar's discussion of *qat'iy* and *zhanniy* were controversial. Firstly, Masdar's concept does not have a strong theoretical or epistemological basis in the Islamic treasury of sciences – something Masdar admitted. Classical *fiqh* books defined *qat'iy* and *zhanniy* verses in way similar to Masdar's, but it is still not clear exactly which verses they refer to. All the Qur'anic verses have the *qat'iy* vision, because, if they didn't, they would no longer be *rahmatan lil 'alamin* (useful for the universe).

Secondly, some of Masdar's theoretical constructions seem ahistorical, and could not be found in classical *fiqh* books. Masdar himself did not know whether his theory could be counted on as *Usul al-Fiqh*. He then asked Indonesian *ulamas* to find legitimacy for his theory, for instance, on the verse on the cutting off of hands (*qat'ul-yadd*). The *ulamas* of the past agreed that the verse was *qat'iy*, but Masdar said this verse was *zhanniy* since it related to an explanation of the principle of justice. Since the verse was an explanation, the punishment of hand-cutting was not required. The problem is how to establish the criteria used to categorize *zhanniy*, since the verse can be said to have clear meaning and shows justice, humanity and so on.

Historically, the punishment of cutting of hands was applied in early Islam. Fazlur Rahman, a noted Pakistani Muslim intellectual, made a similar interpretation of this verse similar, but did not use the concepts of *qat'iy* and *zhanniy*, but rather the method of contextual interpretation. Fazlur Rahman viewed that the verse was *qat'iy*, but that its contextual meaning should be adjusted according to time and space.

Husain Muhammad, an *ulama* from Cirebon, West Java, criticized Masdar's perspective and offered an alternative. He also defined *qat'iy* as a verse which has definite meaning, but questioned whether it should be implemented literally and whether its validity was timeless. He acknowledged that the cutting off of hands as a punishment could be applied in its time, but that it could be interpreted differently at other times. He maintained that *qat'iy* verses are not legally binding, a view shared by Husein Muhammad.

Both Masdar's and Husein Muhammad's concepts have their strengths and weaknesses. Masdar's reinterpretation of the terms had a strong ontological basis, but it was confusing as an operational concept. Both Masdar and Hushain wanted to return to the main purpose of *shari'a*: to benefit public interests. I also suggest that we should return to the main purpose of the *shari'a*, with strong theoretical references, and more effectiveness and flexibility, in an effort to strengthen the liberalization process towards more responsible interpretation.

THE RE-ACTUALIZATION OF ISLAMIC LAW

The re-actualization of Islamic law was the proposal made for the renewal of *fiqh* methodologies proposed by Munawwir Syadzali, a former Minister of Religious Affairs under the Soeharto administration in Indonesia. As far as I remember, his idea was as controversial as Masdar's conception of *qat'iy* and *zhanniy*. There was even a book, published by Panji Masyarakat, devoted to discussing Munawwir's proposal for the re-actualization of Islamic Law. The book, edited by Syu'bah Asa, also contained the works of several noted Muslim intellectuals, such as Nurcholish Madjid, Jalaluddin Rakhmat, and Syafruddin Prawiranegara.

As a discourse, the idea of re-actualization was very interesting because it managed to open up the previously frozen discourse on Islamic law methodology. However, Munawwir did not focus on methodological change, but on the products of methodology. Although it started with practical problems, this did not mean that it did not contribute to Islamic law methodology.

Munawwir's ideas on the re-actualization of Islamic law was triggered by the simple implementation of Islamic law, especially *Fara'id* (the sciences of inheritance) and the prioritization of sons over daughters, which has caused so much injustice in society.[7] In Indonesia, it is common for sons to be given the money for school fees etc., while daughters and women earn money for the family by working in the market and such. So it is unfair to divide inheritances according to the 2:1 division – this is what inspired Munawwir.

However, Munawwir still based his proposal on *Usul al-Fiqh* which guaranteed the reinterpretation process. He maintained that, although there were differences among *fiqh* experts and schools, they all agreed that there were two categories of Islamic law: 1) Laws that relate to pure worship; and 2) Laws that relate to *mu'amala* (social relations). Munawwir maintained that while the first category gave no space for rationality and reinterpretation, the second category gave space for rationality and interpretation in keeping with the public interest. To be clearer, Munawwir based his thinking on the concept of *maslaha* (utility).

A complete explanation of Munawwir's Islamic re-actualization can be found in *Ijtihad Kemanusiaan* (*Ijtihad for Humanity*), published by Paramadina in 1997. Here, Munawwir tries to explain the problems facing Islam (Islamic law) in relation to modern issues such as women's rights, bank interest, the position of non-Muslims, etc. The book makes it clear that Islamic law is facing problems in navigating these modern issues.

MECCA AND MEDINA OF *AL-NA'IM*

Theories on the *Makkiyya* and *Madaniyya* verses are nothing new in *tafsir* (interpretation) books. These books, both old and contemporary, include this theory in their introductions. According to conventional understanding, *Makkiyya* verses are those that were revealed to the Prophet before he moved to Medina, while *Madaniyya* verses were revealed after he moved to Medina.

Most interpretation books state that *Makkiyya* verses usually have the following characteristics: 1) They refer to all human beings (*ya ayyuhan nas*); 2) They are a firm response to the Quraish infidels; and 3) The verses are usually short.

---

[7]   Syu'bah Asa (ed), *Polemik Reaktualisasi Ajaran Islam*, Jakarta: Pustaka Panjimas, 1988, p.6.

The characteristics of *Madaniyya* verses are the converse of these. Abdullah Al-Naim offered a theory about Mecca and Medina, which he adopted from his teacher, Mahmoud Taha. According to Al-Na'im, Taha proposed an open examination on the contents of the Qur'an and hadiths which resulted in the two levels of the Islamic treasury: the Mecca and Medina periods.[8] According to Taha, the message of the Mecca verses were universal, eternal and upheld human dignity without discriminating against gender, religion, race and so on. Al-Na'im called this *isma*, or the freedom of action and choice without the threat of violence.[9]

Al-Naim proposed that the deadlock in Islamic law could be resolved using the *Makkiyya* verses, with their universal and eternal character. At the very least, Al-Na'im hoped that *Madaniyya* verses would be abrogated (*nasakh*) by *Makkiyya* verses, since the latter were more in keeping with contemporary issues like human rights and democratization. Why? According to Al-Naim, the messages of the *Makkiyya* verses were rejected in the seventh century H. because the community was not ready at that time. The more realistic messages for that time were found in the Madiniyyah verses. So the *Madaniyya* verses were applied, while the implementation of the *Makkiyya* verses was postponed. But, according to Al-Naim, it is now high time to implement the *Makkiyya* verses to make Islamic law more accommodative to modern developments.

Al-Naim gave an interesting account of women issues. He claimed that all the verses that were used to discriminate against women were *Madaniyya* verses. He said that Al-Nisa', verse 34, for instance, was a *Madaniyya* verse which was used by legal experts to demonstrate that men were the protectors and superiors of women. On their interpretation of the verse, women were disqualified from public positions.

According to Al-Na'im, still using his teacher's thesis, the evolutionary interpretive principle was reversing the process of *nasakh* on *Madaniyya* verses with *Makkiyya* verses so that the old texts can be used in the present day.

In the conclusion of his book, *Towards an Islamic Reformation* (Dekonstruksi *Shari'a*, LKis, Yogyakarta), Al-Naim wrote specifically about

---

[8]   Abdullah Ahmed al-Na'im, *Dekonstruksi Syariah*, LkiS, p.103.
[9]   *Ibid.*

sharî'a and human rights, paying serious attention to gender discrimination and religion. He noted that there were several discriminative treatments against women based in *sharî'a*, including the law that allowed men to marry four women, and divorce them whenever he wanted to, while wives could only ask for a divorce if the husbands consented to it; and, in inheritance, Muslim men get a larger portion than Muslim women.

According to Al-Naim, these were violations by *sharî'a* against human rights. He regretted the ambivalence shown in Muslim countries towards women's problems. On the one hand, many Muslim countries had contributed to the formulation of international documents on human rights, but, on the other, they could not implement it in their own countries due to the limitations created by *sharî'a* law. Egypt, for instance, contributed to the formulation of the CEDAW agreement, article 1, 1979, on the elimination of all discrimination against women, but its administration could not apply it in their own country.

It is this kind of ambivalence that makes the reconciliation between *sharî'a* and modern human rights more urgent. According to Al-Naim, such a reconciliation could be reached by replacing *Madaniyya* verses with *Makkiyya* verses in modern Islamic law.

Several groups viewed that Al-Naim had contributed a new perspective for the reform of Islamic law, although it still had weaknesses. Firstly, not all *Madaniyya* were unsuitable for facing modern challenges. Some of the verses had been proven capable of being interpreted to meet modern challenges without using Al-Naim's method. Secondly, not all *Makkiyya* verses were suitable for modern situations. Critics of Al-Naim said that some *Makkiyya* verses were not inclusive, especially those relating to Muslim and non-Muslim relations. Thirdly, Al-Naim's idea, which was adopted from his teacher Mahmoud Taha's thought, was exceptional, but difficult to implement in practice. What is the status of *Madaniyya* verses which had been cancelled (nasakh) by *Makkiyya* verses? Don't all the verses of the Qur'an have their own functions, either in the form of *rasmiy* (formal-scriptural) or *hukmiy* (formal-substantial)?

IT IS BETTER TO RETURN TO THE PURPOSE OF SHARI'A

(MAQASID AL-SHARI'A)

If we look at the proposals above – of Masdar, Husein Muhammad, Munawwir Sadjali and Al-Naim – all of them ended up with the same goal – the realization of public welfare (*maslaha*). Discussion of *fiqh* reinterpretation can not be separated from the theological aspect, which is the main purpose of *shari'a* (*maqasid al-shari'a*). The purpose of *shari'a* should become the backbone of *fiqh* formulation. But are *fiqh* we have now, especially those relating to women's rights, compatible with *maqasid al-shari'a*?

Maqasid al-shari'a was frequently discussed among classical and contemporary *fiqh* scholars. Historically and theoretically, the discussion on *maqasid al-shari'a* started during the era of Al-Juwaini (478 H) in his book, *Al-Burhan fi Usul al-Fiqh*. Here, he stated that whoever does not understand Allah's orders and prohibitions intelligently does not have the authority to rule on *shari'a*.[10]

After Al-Juwaini, theories on *maqasid al-shari'a* were developed by Al-Ghazali (505 H). According to Ismail Al-Hasani, Al-Ghazali treated *maqasid al-shari'a* on two levels: 1) *Maqasid* as a principle of welfare (*maslaha*); and 2) *Maqasid* as an indication of intended meaning (*dilalah maqsuda*).[11] According to Al-Ghazali, *maqasid* as a principle of welfare protected the meaning given by the lawmaker (*shari'*) – God. *Maqasid* as *dilalah maqsuda*, however, was to maintain the five principles that protected religion, the soul, reason, genealogy, and property. Everything that conformed to the five principles could be considered to be a form of *maslaha*, while everything that violated them could be considered to be *mafsada*.[12] In one of his commentaries, Muhammad Al-Hasani said that Al-Ghazali's statement on the five principles was the first priority in realizing *maslaha*.

Fakhr Al-Din Al-Razi and Al-'Amidi were the next generation after Al-Juwaini and Al-Ghazali to renew the concept of *maqasid*. Al-Razi had special position in *Usul al-fiqh*, having memorized two books: *Al-Mu'tamal*

---

[10] Al-Juwaini Abul Ma'ali, *al-Burhan fi Usul al-Fiqh*, Cairo: Dar Al-Inshar, 1400 H, vol. II, p.295.

[11] Muhammad Al-Hasani, *Nadhiriya al-Maqasid Inda al-Imam Ibn Asur*, pp.67-8, Al-Ma'had al-Fikr al-Islami, 1995.

[12] Al-Ghazali, *Al-Mustasfa fi 'Ulum al-Usul*, vol. I, pp.289-90.

fi Al-Usul al-Fiqh by Abu Husain Al-Bisri and Al-Mustasfa by Al-Ghazali. Al-Razi's book *al-Mahsul fi 'Ilm al-Usul al-Fiqhi* can be considered to be an encyclopedia in the discipline.

There were two important points in Al-Razi's work: 1) The reasons (*ta'lil*) behind *shari'a* laws. 2) The importance of indication (*qara'in*) in the *istidlal* or foundational arguments of *shari'a* laws, ranging from assumption (*zhann*) to certainty (*yaqin*). Al-Razi's thinking on these matters is also found in Al-'Amidi's book, *al-Ahkam fi Usul al-Ahkam*, which was a summary of Al-Bisri's *Al-Mu'tamad*, Al-Juwaini's *Al-Burhan*, and Al-Ghazali's *Al-Mustasfa*.

The theoretical framework of *maqasid al-shari'a* that was proposed by these *ulamas* and theologians was then developed by *fiqh* scholars, such as Izzu Al-Din ibn Abd Al-Salam, Al-Qarafi and Al-Tufi. In the hands of these three experts, *maqasid al-shari'a* was developed and improved.

According to Izzu Al-Din ibn Abd Al-Salam (660 H), the purpose of *shari'a* law was to uphold *maslaha* and avoid damages (*mafsada*). This stance was based on three points: 1) The adaptation of creation (*ittifaq al-khalqi*), both before and after the arrival of *shari'a*, which aimed to realize welfare (*maslaha*) and avoid damages; 2) The ways to know *maslaha* and *masfada* in the world and the hereafter was through the study of texts and the *istidlal* found within them; 3) The method of knowing *maslaha* and *mafsada* and their causes was based on emergency situations and experience.[13]

Later, Al-Qarafi (685 H), a student of Izzu Al-Din ibn Abd Al-Salam, took a progressive step with a more theoretical approach, using the concepts of principles (*Usul*) and branches (*furu'*) in *shari'a*. He maintained that *shari'a* consisted of two parts: 1) *Usul al-fiqh* as the principles of Islamic law, found through the Arabic and developed in *qiyas* and other forms of *ijtihad*; 2) The general principles of *fiqh*, which consisted of the secrets and laws of *shari'a* excluded from the body of *Usul al-Fiqh* discussed above.[14]

Al-Qarafi focused more on the principles of *fiqh* (*qaida fiqhiyya*) than the language of *fiqh*, because herein contained the secrets and laws of *shari'a*. This was an important point made by Al-Qarafi, one that was followed up by Ibn Taiymiyya, Shathibi, and Ibn Asur.

---

[13] Muhammad Al-Hasani, p.51.
[14] Shihab Al-Din Al-Qarafi, *al-Faruq*, vol. I, pp.2-3.

According to Al-Qarafi's perspective, the meaning of the secrets and the laws of *shari'a* (*asrar wa hukm al-shari'a*) was very similar to *maslahiya* (maintaining welfare and avoiding damages). For instance, wealth would cause people to give alms, while intoxication caused liquor to be forbidden.

The theoretical development was then conducted by Najm Al-Din Al-Tufi (716 H), an *ulama* of the Hambali school who was hated by many due to his sympathies towards the Shi'ite and Rafidhite groups. This prejudice meant that many did not see his intelligence. He was eventually noted as a *mujtahid* by the *ulamas* in the tenth century, although his name then vanished until the beginning of the twentieth century. Al-Tufi maintained that if the main purpose of making *shari'a* was to keep welfare and avoid damages, customs and traditions should be prioritized, even where they contradicted the texts and the consensus of *ulamas*. This can be seen in his statement: "In truth, maintaining public welfare is more important than upholding *ijma'* (consensus), so public welfare is the strongest principle of *shar'i...*"[15]

All Al-Tufi's thoughts were based on a hadith, which stated: *la dharara wala dhirara* – meaning that the formulation of *shari'a* rejected all damages. Al-Tufi differentiated between *maqasid* (aims) and *wasa'il* (means), and he maintained that *maqasid* was the purpose of *shari'a*, especially in *mu'amala*, while *wasa'il* was the means to reach the aim.

Later, *maqasid al-shari'a* was further developed by Ibn Taymiyya, Ibn Al-Qayyim and Al-Shathibi. Ibn Taimiyyah (728 H) was a pioneer in the development of the theory of *maqasid*. According to him, the creation of *shari'a* basically aimed to create welfare and perfection, and terminate or reduce damages.[16] Ibn Taimiyyah had often criticized the conceptions of *maqasid* propounded by his predecessors. He claimed that *maqasid* was not limited to *maqasid kulliyya*, but had many different forms. From Ibn Taiymiyya's point of view, both physical and spiritual worship, such as the belief in the ten angels, the Holy Book, the twenty-five prophets and so on, could all be considered to be part of *maslaha*. So, fulfilling promises, maintaining good relations, honoring the rights of slaves, neighbors, and

---

[15] Najm Al-Din Al-Tufi, *Al-Maslahah fi Tashri' Al-Islami*, p.81.
[16] Ibn Taimiyyah, *Al-Fatawa*, Dar al-Ma'arif, Rabat, vol. 20, p.48.

other Muslims, as well as honoring all the orders and prohibitions handed down by God were also included in the concept of *maslaha*.[17]

In defending the justness and usefulness of *shari'a*, Ibn Taiymiyya said that valid (*sahih*) rational analogy (*qiyas*) would not contradict valid (*sahih*) texts; *sahih qiyas* would always share the aims of *shari'a*.[18]

Ibn Taimiyyah's conception of *maqasid al-shari'a* was then developed by his close student, Ibn Qayyim (751 H), in his famous book, *I'lam al-Muwaqqi'in*. Here, he wrote that the basis and construction of *shari'a* was law and goodness for human beings in the world and the afterlife. All things which deviated from justice, mercy and *maslaha*, could not be considered to be *shari'a*.[19] Furthermore, Ibn Qayyim said *shari'a* and *maslaha* should also be in line with rationality, and that the strength of *shari'a* was centered in reason.[20]

However, Ibn Qayyim said that *ibada* (worship) contained things that could not be rationalized by human beings according to reason. If our rationality could understand it at all, it was only in a global sense.[21]

According to Ibn Qayyim, *shari'a* functioned to explain the aims and intentions of the lawmakers. As such, understanding *fiqh* should not only rely on its literal meanings, but should also take into account the implications behind the statements. So we should also understand the context of the *shari'a* texts, such as those that clarified general matters, metaphoric texts, and those that explained one text in relation to another.[22] Ibn Qayyim said: "Specific statements can sometimes change into general statements (in meaning), and general ones can likewise become specific ones, because of a certain meaning."[23]

Ibn Qayyim's perspective was similar to the Post-Structuralist way of reading texts to try and understand the driving force behind the them. Ibn Qayyim called this "An understanding that lives, and enters the heart without permission" (*al-fiqh al-hayyu al-ladzi yadkhuluhu al-qulub bi*

---

[17] Ibn Taiymiyya, vol. 32, p 234.

[18] Ibn Taiymiyya, *al-Qiyas fi Shar'i al-Islami*, Beirut, Lebanon: Dar al-Faq al-Jadida, 1980, p.50.

[19] Ibn Al-Qayyim, *I'lam al-Muwaqqi'in min Rab al-'Alamin*, Dar Al-Fikr, vol. 3, p.55.

[20] Ibn Al-Qayyim, *Miftah al-Dar al-Sa'ada wa Manshur al-Wilaya al-Ilmi wa al-Irada*, Egypt: Matba'ah Sa'adah, vol. 2, p.218.

[21] Ibn Qayyim, *I'lam al-Muwaqqi'in*, vol. II, p.88.

[22] Ibn Qayyim, p.68.

[23] "*Al-lafdh al-khas qad yantaqilu ila al-amm bi-irada, wa al-amm qad yantaqilu ila al-khusus bil-irada.*" See *I'lam al-Muwwaqi'in*, vol. I, p.218.

ghairi isti'dzan).[24] Ibn Qayyim also introduced a theory on *sadd al-dhara'i* (protecting people from bad things) and *hila* (legal engineering) to complete his contribution to *maqasid al-shari'a*.

Ibn Qayyim's step was followed by Al-Shatibi (790 H). *Fiqh* experts agree that his book, *al-Muwafaqat fi Usul al-Shari'a* was pioneering work in *Usul al-Fiqh* since he managed to put the paradigm into a perfect form.[25] 'Ajil Jasim Al-Nashmi considered the *al-Muwafaqat* equal to Shafi'i's *al-Risalah*,[26] which was already established as the leading source for making the general basis of *shari'a* principles in his *Usul al-Fiqh*. Al-Shathibi was viewed as having managed to maintain the spirit of *shari'a* with his deep attention to the theory of *maqasid al-shari'a*.

On this basis, we can conclude that *maqasid al-shari'a*, with its strong theoretical basis, makes it more possible to reinterpret *fiqh*. We may still have the problem of deciding which kind of *maqasid* should be used, although I think it is sufficient to utilize the existing theories of *maqasid* to make a proper methodological synthesis.

BASIS FOR THE DEVELOPMENT OF A NEW *FIQH*

After choosing to use *maqasid* as our methodology for developing a new *fiqh*, we must give it basis in the universal principles of the Qur'an. These principles are justice, equality, democracy, and good social relations. These four principles are very useful as the basis from which to develop a new *fiqh*.

THE PRINCIPLE OF JUSTICE

There is no doubt that the formulation of *fiqh* is inseparable from the principle of justice. The *imams* of the four law schools who developed *fiqh* were famous for their just attitudes and capacity for memorizing texts (they were known as *dhabid*). So why does the question of justice arise again?

---

[24] Ibn Qayyim, *I'lam*, vol. III, p.120.

[25] 'Ali Shami' Al-Nashar, *Manahij al-Bahth Inda Mufkir al-Islam Iktishaf al-Manhaj al-'Ilm fi al-'Alm al-Islami*, Cairo: Dar Al-Ma'arif, 1978, p.72.

[26] Ajil Jasim Al-Nashmi, "Muqaddimat fi Usul al-Fiqh," *Majalla al-Shari'a wa al-Dirasah al-Islamiyya*, Kuwait, Second Edition, 1984, p.72.

In my view, the discourses pertaining to women in the classical Islamic books had a masculine gender bias. This factor showed the injustice inherent in *fiqh*. In a short essay, Masdar F. Mas'udi listed the injustices in our *fiqh*, such as judging women as of half the worth of men, objectifying and domesticating them, and other pejorative views which are still found in our *fiqh*.[27]

A classical book written by Al-Nawawi Al-Bantani – an Indonesian *ulama* from Banten who resided in Mecca – remains the main reference in studies on women. It stated that a wife who is patient in the face of her husband's bad behavior, would be blessed by God, as He had blessed the wife of Pharaoh, A'isha.[28] This statement is contradictory to the principle of justice which should be upheld in the household. Ironically, this illustration can be found in many works of *fiqh*.

As such, what I mean by justice in *fiqh*, in this context, is that there should be a balance between the rights and obligations of men and women, proportional to their equal creation by God.

This kind of justice is in line with the teachings of God the Most Just – it is clearly stated in the Qur'an that God would never do an injustice. The Qur'an can not be used as the basis for human injustice, and injustice against women can not be viewed as God-derived. The aim of Islam is to maintain justice on earth.[29]

Equality and balance as the main principles of justice should be key in the agenda of formulating a new *fiqh* that serves gender equity, without disparities made on the basis of biological difference.

EQUALITY (MUSAWAH)

The second principle which should be upheld in developing this women's *fiqh* is equality (*musawah*), in all levels and areas of life. But many people still question how to measure the principle of equality (*musawa*). Is it possible to say women are the same as men? Aren't there biological differences to take into account?

---

[27] Masdar F Mas'udi, *op. cit.*, pp.155-63.

[28] Shaykh Nawawi Banten, *Sharh Uqud al-Lijaini fi Bayani Huquq al-Zaujani*, Semarang: Maktaba al-Alawiya, n.d., p.5.

[29] Riffat Hassan, *Women's Rights and Islam: From the ICPD to Beijing*, (unpublished draft), 1996, p.12.

Equality does not mean that men and women are biologically the same, a suggestion strongly denied by Muslim feminists. Equality means our equality in the eyes of God. Inequality between men and women occurred because of social constructions, instead of the religious teachings themselves. God said that all His believers were equal before Him. They were differentiated on the basis of their obedience. Obedience has no gender bias; we all have the same potential for obedience.

DEMOCRACY (SHURA)

Although *shura* was mentioned just once in the Qur'an, it was regularly practiced by the Prophet, especially when formulating war strategy and matters related to the public interest. In dialogues between the Prophet and his companions there were sometimes sharp differences of opinion, such as when they discussed the strategy for the Uhud war, for example.

In the modern world, the concept of *shura* is identical to democracy. Epistemologically, they have differences, but they are similar in practice. Another crucial similarity is that they both took on people's aspirations and made decisions based on the opinions of a majority. This is why Muslim intellectuals identify *shura* as democracy.

Moreover, the concept of *shura* is not only useful on the macro level of public interest and state politics, but also in private life, such as in household issues, where it was expected that people use the principle of *shura* to solve conflicts. In relation to the agenda of *fiqh* reconstruction with a gender perspective, the concept of *shura* can also be expected to give an epistemological platform for the claim that knowledge should be formed democratically and free from bias, including gender bias.

MU'ASHARA BI AL-MA'RUF

Mu'ashara bi al-ma'ruf is humane behavior towards others, particularly in the relationship between husband and wife. *Ma'ruf* doesn't just mean goodness (*khair*), but also goodness with attention to particularity and locality. Through the use of the concepts listed above, we can develop a new *fiqh* that does not take sides only with women, but is also inclusive of men.

TAZAMUNI AND *ISQATI*: INTRODUCING A NEW WAY OF READING *FIQH*

After this discussion of *maqasid al-sharia*, I will introduce a new method for understanding *fiqh*. This method has been borrowed from the philosophical school of Structuralism which was introduced by Ferdinand de Saussure. According to Saussure, there were two ways to read a text: synchronically (*tazamuniy*) and diachronically (*isqatiy*). These ways of reading have been utilized by contemporary Muslim intellectuals studying old texts. Among these Muslim intellectuals is Mohammed Arkoun.

The reading principle of *tazamuniy* means reading with an awareness of past and present realities – using the past to understand the present and learning to differentiate the two. In the context of a women's *fiqh*, *tazamuniy* took the old meanings from the past, related them to women's issues (such as marriage, divorce, etc.) so that they can be used in the present day, as in the concept of *ijbar* (forced marriage) propounded by Shafi'i, which is still used at the current time. The past and present situations are completely different however, and every era has its own epistemologies, resulting in its own meanings. This way of reading, in excess, can cause anachronism.

On the other hand, the *itqatiy* way of reading means reading with a contemporary perspective, cut away from all the old meanings. According to this perspective, the history of textual meaning is the history of cutting off the flow of decision-making. As such, it is deemed impossible to replicate the old meanings in the current meaning. But, this does not mean that the past is not relevant. The old meanings are still utilized, but as historical information about the past; they are not considered binding today. For example, if a *fiqh* from the past agreed with the practice of *ijbar*, we need to rethink it in the present day, because the context of the past may render *ijbar* inappropriate for the current context. With this method, it is hoped that a new *fiqh*, relevant to today, can be developed. In the context of *fiqh*, the itsqathi way of reading means that we read the texts of the past as historical knowledge, rather than binding documents.

Of these two ways of reading, the second, itsqathi, is the most useful, especially in the context of *fiqh*. Using *itqati* we can develop new textual meanings of *fiqh* that are relevant to the present day.

BIBLIOGRAPHY

Abdul Rasul Abdul Hassan Al-Gafar *Wanita Islam dan Gaya Hidup Modern*, Jakarta: Pustaka Hidayah, 1993

Aelen Tiermey (ed.) *Women Studies Encyclopedia, View from the Sciences*, New York: Greenwood Press, 1989

Effendi, Agus *Perempuan dalam Pandangan Tafsir Modern* (in a discussion held by Forum "Rahim", April 19, 1996, P3M, Jakarta.

Hasan, Ahmad *Pintu Ijtihad Belum Tertutup*, Bandung: Pustaka, 1984

Ajil Jasim Al-Nasymi, "Muqaddimat fi Usul al-Fiqh," *Majallah Al-Syari'ah wa Al-Dirasah Al-Islamiyyah*, Kuwait, Second Edition, 1984

Ali Syami' Al-Nasyar, *Manahij al-Bahth Inda Mufkir al-Islam Iktishaf al-Manhaj al-'Ilm fi al-'Alm al-Islami*, Cairo: Dar Al-Ma'arif 1978

Al-Juwani Abul Ma'ali, *Al-Burhan fi Ushul Al-Fiqh*, Cairo: Dar Al-Inshar, 1400 H

Al-Zuhaili, *Al-Fiqh Al-Islam wa Adillatuhu*, Damascus: Dar al-Fikr, 1983, Second Edition

Armstrong, Karen *The End of Silence, Women and Priesthood*, London: Fourth Estate, 1993

Asghar Ali Engineer *Hak-hak Perempuan Dalam Islam*, LSSPA: Yayasan Perkasa, 1994

Asghar Ali Engineer *Hak-Hak Perempuan dalam Islam*, Yogyakarta: LSPAA Prakarsa Foundation, 1994

Esposito, John *Women in Muslim Family Law*, Syracuse University Press, 1982.

Faisar Ananda Arfa "Debate on the Birth of Islamic Law," *Ulumul Qur'an*, No. 1 vol. IV, 1995

H.S.A. Alhamdani *Risalah Nikah Hukum Perkawinan*, Jakarta: Pustaka Amani, 1989, vol. III,

Hassan, Rif'at *Women's Interpretation of Islam, Women and Islam in Muslim Societies*, The Hague: Poverty and Development, 1994

Hassan, Rif'at *Women's Rights and Islam: From the ICPD to Beijing,* (unpublished draft copy), 1996

Ibn Taimiyyah *Al-Qiyas fi Syar'i Al-Islami,* Beirut, Lebanon: Dar Al-Faq Al-Jadidah, 1980

Jansen, J.J.G. *Diskursus Tafsir Al-Qur'an Modern,* Tiara Wacana, 1997

Jalal Al-Din Al-Suyuti, *Al-Dur Al-Mat'sur* Beirut: Dar Al-Fikr, 1983

Jalaluddin Al-Suyuthi *Al-Durr Al-Ma'tsur fi' Al-Tafsir Al-Ma'tsur,* Dar Al-Fikr, vol. II

Jallaludin Al-Mahali *Al-Mahalli Syarah Minhaj Thalibin al-Nawawi,* Dar al-Kutub al Arabiyah, vol. III

M. Iqbal *The Reconstruction of Religious Thought in Islam,* Lahore, 1962

Mahmud Abd al-Hamid Muhammad *Huquq al-Mar'ah,* Maktabah Madbouli: Egypt, 1990

Mas'udi, Masdar F. *"Perempuan di antara Lembaran Kitab Kuning,"* in Lies Marcoes-Natsir and J.H. Mouleman, *Wanita Indonesia dalam Kajian Teks dan Kontekstual Islam.* Jakarta: INIS, 1993

Mas'udi, Masdar F. *Islam dan Hak Reproduksi Perempuan: Dialog Fiqh Pemberdayaan,* Bandung: Mizan: 1996

Munawar Ahmad Anees, *Islam dan Masa Depan Biologis Umat Manusia,* Bandung: Mizan 1991

Roded, Ruth *Kembang Peradaban: Citra Wanita di Mata Para Penulis Biografi Muslim,* Bandung: Mizan: 1995

Schacht, Joseph *Introduction to Islamic Law,* (Indonesian edition), Jakarta: Department of Religion, 1985

Syu'bah Asa (ed.) *Polemik Reaktualisasi Ajaran Islam,* Jakarta: Pustaka Panjimas, 1988

van Bruinessen, Martin *"Kitab Kuning dan Perempuan, Perempuan dan Kitab Kuning"* in Lies Marcoes-Natsir and J.H. Moeleman, *Wanita Indonesia and Kajian Tekstual and Kontekstual Islam,* Jakarta: INIS, 1993

Watt, Montgomery *Muhammad at Medina,* Oxford University Press, 1972

Watt, Montgomery *The Majesty That was Islam,* Edinburgh University Press, 1961

INDEX

Printed in the United States
221915BV00002B/8/A